T0303041

PRAISE FOR

## MEDICAL MALPRACTICE LITIGATION

"This is an important contribution to the study of medical malpractice reform efforts with recommendations for the future. It is based upon peer-reviewed articles and underlying datasets that are made available for those who wish to review. Despite the academic bonafides and data-driven analysis, it is easy to read. The reader may or may not agree with the conclusions, but as the authors quote Edward Deming, 'In God we trust, everyone else bring data.' They challenge those who disagree to bring the data. For the serious student of medical malpractice reform, this is the book to begin with."

—Sen. Bill Cassidy, MD, (R-LA)

"This book offers a careful and comprehensive assessment of more than a decade's worth of leading empirical research about the medical malpractice system in Texas and across the United States. It is a must-read for anyone interested in a better understanding of the costs and benefits of the medical liability system and efforts to reform it."

—Seth A. Seabury, associate professor, Keck School of Medicine and Leonard D. Schaeffer Center for Health Policy and Economics, University of Southern California

"The authors—and their pathbreaking work—reflect the best of empirical legal scholarship and supply scholars, policymakers, and citizens with essential information on and insights into how the medical malpractice system actually works. Efforts at 'reforming' medical malpractice that lack a secure empirical foundation—like the one provided in this book—are doomed to failure."

—Michael Heise, William G. McRoberts Professor in the Empirical Study of Law and coeditor of the *Journal of Empirical Legal Studies*, Cornell Law School

"An invaluable resource that presents a thorough, compelling, and data-driven analysis of the reality of the medical malpractice system."

—Maxwell J. Mehlman, Arthur E. Petersilge
Professor of Law and codirector of the Law-Medicine Center,
Case Western Reserve University School of Law

"This book is a must-read for anyone interested in the so-called medical malpractice crisis. The authors totally debunk the myth that tort lawsuits are to blame for high malpractice insurance premiums, doctor shortages, and increased health care costs. They find—based on meticulous empirical studies—that tort reforms like damage caps are the wrong treatment for a misdiagnosed disease. They conclude with some cogent suggestions for improving the tort system's handling of medical malpractice cases."

—Paul F. Rothstein, Carmack Waterhouse Professor of Law,
Georgetown University Law Center

"Whenever I give a talk about why U.S. health care costs are high and rising, I am inevitably asked if malpractice reform is the answer. It is great to have a thorough treatment that shows that, based on evidence so far, meaningful changes in our spending and health outcomes will not come from changing malpractice damage caps or similar glib fixes. Changes could improve the quality of care, but making the case for them requires attention to the facts and framing in this book."

—Mark V. Pauly, Bendheim Professor,
Department of Health Care Management, Wharton School,
University of Pennsylvania

"Anyone interested in medical malpractice must read and understand this book before making public pronouncements. The authors show that the facts support none of the favorite, facile arguments about medical malpractice and its crises. Further, the favorite remedies for the problems, particularly damages caps, do not solve the underlying problems. Instead, one must look elsewhere for useful ideas."

—Matthew L. Spitzer, Howard and Elizabeth Chapman Professor and director, Northwestern University Center on Law, Business, and Economics, Northwestern University Pritzker School of Law

"The medical malpractice system is slow, expensive, contentious, and largely ineffective, but that doesn't make every proposed reform worthwhile. In *Medical Malpractice Litigation*, the authors make a convincing case for the failure of damage caps, with powerful data, sharp writing, and cogent explanations. Instead, they propose 'seven sensible reforms' that would truly benefit patients, doctors, and pretty much everyone else (including most lawyers)."

—Steven Lubet, Edna B. and Ednyfed H. Williams Memorial Professor and director, Fred Bartlit Center for Trial Advocacy, Northwestern University Pritzker School of Law

"George Stigler once joked, 'The plural of anecdote is data.' Anecdotes (rather than a systematic evaluation of the evidence) drive too much public policy in civil litigation and medical malpractice—whether it is the McDonald's coffee case or the psychic who sues after losing her powers. We are lucky to have Black, Hyman, Paik, Sage, and Silver, whose careful work over many years has brought systematic evidence to this vital area of public policy."

—Eric Helland, William F. Podlich Professor of Economics and George R. Roberts Fellow, Claremont McKenna College

"Medical malpractice litigation has a terrible reputation—as a scourge that bankrupts doctors and leaves people without health care providers. The esteemed authors of *Medical Malpractice Litigation* have provided an exceedingly useful antidote to these claims in the form of 15 years of invaluable research about medical malpractice litigation in Texas, tort reform efforts, and their effects. They prove, based on their careful analysis, that many claims made by proponents of damages caps and other limitations on the right to sue are simply false. The book shows readers not only what is wrong with the current system but how it can be improved. It is an essential read for those engaged, in any form, in the design and implementation of our medical malpractice system."

—Joanna C. Schwartz, professor of law, UCLA School of Law

"For any serious student of medical malpractice, this volume is quite simply a must-read."

—Max M. Schanzenbach, Seigle Family Professor of Law, Northwestern University Pritzker School of Law

"It's been said that the contemporary medical malpractice landscape is the 'law's Vietnam—an unpleasant quagmire of unending skirmishes and full-scale engagements' with, I would add, raised voices and pointed fingers, all while the casualties mount. To this dark battlefield, *Medical Malpractice Litigation* brings, if not a lasting peace, then at least a powerful light. Compelling and eminently readable, this book shows us what's truly happening in our clinics and courtrooms. It details the many reforms that have been tried and failed. And finally, it maps a humane and sensible path forward."

—Nora Freeman Engstrom, professor of law and Deane F. Johnson Faculty Scholar, Stanford Law School

"A clearly laid out vision of the problems and promise of the American medical malpractice system, starting with the way any medical problem must be addressed: figuring out the right diagnosis. Synthesizing decades of their own and others' research on medical liability, the authors unravel what we know and don't know about our medical malpractice system, why neither patients nor doctors are being rightly served, and what economics can teach us about the path forward."

—Anupam B. Jena, MD, Ruth L. Newhouse Associate Professor
of Health Care Policy, Harvard Medical School

"Is tort reform the panacea for the ills in our health care system, or is it the wrong tree to bark up? This book compiles objective, uncontroversial, apolitical facts and offers sensible solutions. A must-read for anyone interested in evidence-based policy reforms in medical malpractice."

—Ge Bai, associate professor of accounting,
Johns Hopkins Carey Business School

"Anyone who would like to know how the American malpractice liability system *really* works could not do better than to read this book. Over the years, its authors have consistently produced some of the most illuminating empirical research on that system and on the effects that tort reforms have had. This book lucidly synthesizes that research."

—Michael J. Saks, Regents Professor, Sandra Day O'Connor
College of Law, Arizona State University

"Read this carefully researched book to find out that most of the loudest voices on both sides of malpractice reform have been consistently wrong if not mendacious. Then keep reading for a master class in policy evaluation. The book shows how much we can learn by making sure that open-minded researchers have the resources and data they need to produce rigorous answers to big legal questions. The authors conclude with sensible reform ideas rooted in evidence and driven by the goal of a fair, sensible system of medical liability."

—Scott Burris, professor of law and director, Center for Public
Health Law Research, Beasley School of Law, Temple University

"Conventional tort reform, such as flat damage caps, has been promoted by special interest groups as a means to improve patient access to care by attracting and retaining physicians and curbing health care cost inflation by reducing 'defensive medicine.' Using data from Texas and from the U.S. as a whole, the authors present in-depth empirical evidence that such statutory changes have achieved neither objective. Damage caps as implemented by many states have had unintended consequences such as disproportionately reducing compensation for injuries incurred by elderly persons. The book is well written and is free of technical jargon and thus is highly accessible to public policy makers and the interested public at large."

—Frank A. Sloan, J. Alexander McMahon Distinguished
Professor Emeritus of Health Policy and Management and professor
emeritus of economics, Duke University


"Written by the team that has done the most extensive work testing the empirical claims behind medical malpractice reform legislation, *Medical Malpractice Litigation* is a must-read for anyone willing to be persuaded by the evidence. The verdict is in: damage caps benefit doctors at the expense of injured patients, without cutting the costs of health care or improving access to health care."

—Tom Baker, William Maul Measey Professor of Law,
University of Pennsylvania Carey Law School, author of
*The Medical Malpractice Myth*


"This book provides a comprehensive analysis of medical malpractice litigation that recognizes the complex interrelationships between physicians, patients, insurers, attorneys, regulators, and taxpayers. The authors have succeeded, not only in providing an authoritative review of the limitations of tort reform for addressing medical malpractice liability problems but also in covering a range of topics essential to understanding these limitations from various stakeholders' perspectives. The book brings together the authors' extensive knowledge of litigation trends and is a must-read for anyone who wants a better understanding of the need for medical malpractice reform."

—Patricia Born, Payne H. and Charlotte Hodges
Midyette Eminent Scholar in Risk Management and
Insurance, College of Business, Florida State University

"The lifeblood of first-rate legal scholarship is data. That is most particularly true with respect to the medical malpractice system—a setting where far too much fake news and far too many half-baked views have been propounded and embraced. *Medical Malpractice Litigation* is that rare volume that delivers the data. Its wide-ranging analysis takes readers inside the medical malpractice system, most particularly in Texas, both before and after tort reform. It demonstrates the real-world consequences of partisan "reform" designed to curtail medical malpractice claiming. The findings are hard to dispute—more uncompensated suffering for victims (especially the elderly) and enrichment for health care providers through a system increasingly costly to operate and incapable of promoting genuine safety improvement. *Medical Malpractice Litigation* points a way forward. Perhaps its evidence will be heeded in the new political era arguably dawning."

—Stephan Landsman, emeritus professor of law,
Robert A. Clifford Professor of Tort Law and Social Policy,
DePaul University College of Law

"*Medical Malpractice Litigation* offers policymakers, practitioners, and academics a singular contribution to the debate over the appropriate role of tort claims in compensating for physician-related injury and, correspondingly, in creating incentives for more careful professional conduct. For more than a decade, this team of leading authorities in the field has published illuminating data and analysis on every aspect of claims, compensation, and costs in the area of medical practice. Here, their work is pulled together in a volume that is bound to be highly influential in continuing evidence-based reflection on this critical field of public health."

—Robert L. Rabin, JD, PhD, A. Calder Mackay
Professor of Law, Stanford Law School

"*Medical Malpractice Litigation* provides a hard-headed, empirical analysis of medical malpractice reform. The authors' diagnosis of the problem finds some of the simpler solutions wanting and instead leads them to a more constructive prescription for reforming the medical malpractice system. Their compelling analysis cuts through the dueling ideologies, interests, and talking points that too often drown out rational consideration of this topic."

—Jason Furman, professor, Harvard University,
and former chairman of the Council of Economic Advisers

"Today, there are all-too-many claims, positive and negative, about the effects of medical malpractice litigation on patient safety and social welfare. But few people have bothered to assemble and analyze the wealth of evidence on this problem. This knowledge gap has been bridged in large measure by a team of first-rate authors who show just how difficult it is for any reform movement to achieve its stated goals. *Medical Malpractice Litigation* tells a cautionary tale about the consequences of utopian reform proposals, with implications across other disciplines."

—Richard A. Epstein, Laurence A. Tisch Professor of Law,
New York University School of Law

"The inner workings of the medical malpractice litigation system and its relationship to important markets, including physician labor and medical malpractice insurance, have been misrepresented in reform circles for decades. The authors use recently uncovered data sources to reveal a number of unintuitive findings, debunking several myths that have played an outsized role in reform efforts. This book is a must-read for anyone interested in understanding the problems with the medical malpractice litigation system and how to solve them."

—Kathryn Zeiler, professor of law, Nancy Barton Scholar,
Boston University School of Law

"Drawing on an unusually rich trove of data, the authors have refuted more politically convenient myths in one book than most academics do in a lifetime. Their meticulous research not only shows that malpractice reform in the United States has rested on a tangled set of misplaced assumptions, false statements of fact, and self-serving anecdotes; it also demonstrates that malpractice reform has done little or nothing to curb health care spending, reduce defensive medicine, or improve quality of care. The book should be required reading for any policymaker who may be tempted to think that malpractice reform will magically cure what ails the American health care system. The authors have the data to prove that it won't."

—Nicholas Bagley, professor of law,
University of Michigan Law School

"*Medical Malpractice Litigation* shines a bright, data-driven light on the controversial topic of medical malpractice litigation. Tort reform debates about medical malpractice are full of often-untested claims about frivolous lawsuits that drive good doctors out of markets, reduce health care access, and dramatically increase insurance premiums. The authors test these assertions and more by rigorously analyzing the best datasets available on medical malpractice claims and case outcomes. The results make a convincing case that tort reformers have misdiagnosed the problems with the medical malpractice system and consequently have applied the wrong treatments. The authors draw on their combined medical, legal, and empirical expertise to propose a variety of innovative solutions.

They also stress the importance of continual testing and analysis so that tort reform promotes justice rather than undermines it.

*Medical Malpractice Litigation* is a superb contribution to our understanding of how the medical malpractice litigation system works. It is sure to be immensely valuable as a guide to future tort reform efforts."

—Valerie P. Hans, Charles F. Rechlin Professor of Law,
Cornell Law School

# MEDICAL MALPRACTICE LITIGATION

# MEDICAL MALPRACTICE LITIGATION

*How It Works*

---

*Why Tort Reform Hasn't Helped*

BERNARD S. BLACK | DAVID A. HYMAN

MYUNGHO PAIK | WILLIAM M. SAGE

CHARLES SILVER

Print ISBN: 978-1-948647-79-3
eBook ISBN: 978-1-948647-80-9


Cover design: Lindy Martin, Faceout Studio
Imagery: Stocksy

Library of Congress Cataloging-in-Publication Data

Black, Bernard S., 1953- author. | Hyman, David A., author. | Paik,
    Myungho, author. | Sage, William M., author. | Silver, Charles,
    1957- author.
    Medical malpractice litigation : how it works, why tort reform
    hasn't helped / Bernard S. Black, David A. Hyman, Myungho Paik,
    William M. Sage, Charles M. Silver.
            pages    cm
    Washington, D.C. : Cato Institute, 2021.
    Includes bibliographical references and index.
    ISBN 9781948647793 (hardcover) | ISBN 9781948647809 (ebook)
    1. MESH: Malpractice--legislation & jurisprudence.  2. Liability, Legal
    3. Legislation, Medical.  4. Physicians--supply & distribution.  5. Health
    Care Reform.  6. Texas.

    K4365   2021
    344.04/11--dc23                             2020054406

Printed in the United States of America.

CATO INSTITUTE
1000 Massachusetts Avenue NW
Washington, DC 20001
www.cato.org

# CONTENTS

# TERMS AND ABBREVIATIONS

| TERM | MEANING | CHAPTER DEFINED OR FIRST USED |
|------|---------|-------------------------------|
| ADR | Alternative dispute resolution | 6 |
| adjusted allowed verdict | Allowed verdict plus reported or imputed pre- and post-judgment interest | 2 |
| adjusted verdict | Trial verdict (by jury or judge) plus reported or imputed pre- and post-judgment interest | 2 |
| adult nonelderly | Plaintiff age at date of injury reported as 19–64 years | 2 |
| ALAE | allocated loss adjustment expenses | 6 |
| allowed verdict | Portion of jury award that defendant is liable for, after damages caps and judicial oversight | 2 |

| TERM | MEANING | CHAPTER DEFINED OR FIRST USED |
|---|---|---|
| AMA | American Medical Association | 2 |
| baby | Plaintiff age at date of injury reported as 0 or 1 month | 2 |
| CBO | Congressional Budget Office | 6 |
| child | Plaintiff age at date of injury reported as 2 months through 18 years | 2 |
| compensatory damages | Sum of economic plus non-economic damages | 2 |
| CRP | Communication and resolution program | 15 |
| damage cap | Cap on non-economic or total damages | 1 |
| death cap | Texas cap on compensatory damages in wrongful death cases (see Chapter 3 for details) | 2 |
| DiD | difference-in-differences research design | 9 |
| dollars | 2010 dollars (unless specified otherwise) | 2 |
| DPC physicians | Active, nonfederal, direct patient care physicians | 10 |

| TERM | MEANING | CHAPTER DEFINED OR FIRST USED |
|---|---|---|
| duration | Length of time a case is open, measured as days from suit to closing unless otherwise specified | 3 |
| elderly | Plaintiff age at date of injury reported as 65 years or more | 1 |
| haircut | Fraction of adjusted verdict that is unpaid | 4 |
| HSA | Hospital Service Area, a single county or cluster of contiguous counties that is relatively self-contained with respect to hospital care | 9 |
| JNOV | Judgment notwithstanding the jury verdict (rendered by the judge) | 2 |
| Large paid claim | Payout greater than $25,000 (1988$) for Texas, and greater than $50,000 (2010$) for National Practitioner Data Bank | 2 |
| limits | Policy limits on a primary medical malpractice insurance policy | 4 |
| *ln*( ) | Natural logarithm of whatever variable is in the parentheses | 4 |

| TERM | MEANING | CHAPTER DEFINED OR FIRST USED |
|------|---------|-------------------------------|
| medical malpractice dataset | Dataset of large paid medical malpractice claims, closed from 1988 to 2010, involving payout of at least $25,000 in 1988 dollars ($46,000 in 2008 dollars), included in the Texas Closed Claim Database | 2 |
| MLM | *Medical Liability Monitor* | 5 |
| MPLA | Medical Professional Liability Association | 15 |
| new-cap states | The nine states, including Texas, that adopted non-economic caps during 2002–2005 | 1 |
| no-cap states | The 20 states that did not have caps on non-economic or total damages during 1999–2010 | 1 |
| non-econ | Non-economic | 1 |
| non-econ cap | Cap on non-economic damages | 1 |
| NPDB | National Practitioner Data Bank | 2 |
| ob-gyn | Obstetrics and gynecology | 1 |
| old-cap states | The 22 states that had damages caps in place during 1999–2010 | 1 |
| PIAA | Physician Insurers Association of America | 15 |

| TERM | MEANING | CHAPTER DEFINED OR FIRST USED |
|------|---------|-------------------------------|
| PTL | Payment-to-limit ratio | 5 |
| punitives cap | Texas cap on punitive damages (see Chapter 2 for details) | 2 |
| remittitur | Judicial order reducing an excessive jury verdict | 2 |
| settled cases | Cases that are settled prior to a verdict, including cases in which a trial was begun but not completed | 1 |
| TCCD | Texas Closed Claim Database, maintained during 1988–2010 by the Texas Department of Insurance | 1 |
| TDI | Texas Department of Insurance | 1 |
| TDSHS | Texas Department of State Health Services | 2 |
| TMB | Texas Medical Board | 2 |
| TMLT | Texas Medical Liability Trust | 3 |
| VSL | Value of a statistical life, which measures willingness to pay for risk reduction | 8 |
| winsorization | A method for reducing the influence of outlier observations by assigning values to them that are more reflective of the rest of the dataset | 2 |

# FOREWORD

Health reform has been a passion of mine for decades. Health policy issues routinely came before me when I was in the U.S. House of Representatives from 1979 to 1987 and the U.S. Senate from 1987 to 2005. I became even more enmeshed in health reform when I became Senate minority leader in 1995 and Senate majority leader in 2001. When I left the Senate in 2005, I remained active in health policy, writing two books on the subject and working with a broad array of leaders and organizations in the health care area.

Though Congress tends to focus on the cost of the major federal health spending programs, I became interested early on in health care quality—particularly the problem of medical errors. Recent studies have put the annual death toll from preventable medical errors in the United States at 250,000 or even 440,000. These estimates may well be conservative. Some experts assert that less than 10 percent of medical errors are ever reported, let alone acted on. Even the lower figure of 250,000 deaths per year suggests medical errors are the third leading cause of death in the United States, after heart disease and cancer.

That death toll is the equivalent of two fully loaded Boeing 787 airplanes crashing every *single day*. One can only imagine the scandal were that to occur. As I write this foreword, the Federal Aviation Administration (FAA) has grounded all Boeing 737 Max aircraft for almost

MEDICAL MALPRACTICE LITIGATION

two years because two crashes of those aircrafts within a five-month period killed a total of 346 people. There is little doubt those tragedies will spur major reforms at both Boeing and the FAA. Those tragedies garnered far more attention and outrage than preventable medical errors, whose death toll year after year is three orders of magnitude greater.

Health care is not aviation. The combination of limited transparency and a diverse and diffuse regulatory framework means there are no easy solutions to improving health care quality. That is why I have long supported and advocated for the rights of victims of medical error. Injuries and deaths resulting from medical errors have extraordinary health and emotional consequences. But they have financial consequences as well. The death or serious injury of a family's primary breadwinner usually has a catastrophic economic impact and can even lead to bankruptcy—burdening both the family and health care providers whose bills don't get paid.

Throughout my 26 years in Congress, health care providers advocated for state and federal legislators to cap providers' financial liability in medical malpractice cases. The results are plain to see. More than 30 states currently cap either non-economic or total damages. Since 2002, the U.S. House of Representatives has passed legislation on five separate occasions that would have imposed a nationwide cap of $250,000 on non-economic damages. Each time, the legislation has failed.

Providers argue that limiting physicians' exposure to liability will improve access to care, asserting that such protections would attract physicians to areas with physician shortages, reduce the cost of running a physician practice, and make it more appealing for physicians to treat high-risk patients. I was on the receiving end of many such briefings.

On the other side, trial lawyers are equally insistent that limiting physician liability would not reduce health care costs or improve access. They predict there would be many more injured patients once caps on damages reduced or eliminated the liability risk for negligent treatment.

Every member of Congress, regardless of party or political philosophy, wants to find meaningful ways to reduce health costs, improve access, and ensure high quality. The challenge is always to find out what the real facts are before making our best judgments—a challenge that seems to become more difficult and complex with each passing year. With the rise of social media, truth seems to have become optional in many debates.

The national debate on medical malpractice reform may have gone into hibernation, but I fully expect it to return once physicians' malpractice insurance premiums spike again. When that happens, peer-reviewed empirical studies like those in this book will be invaluable to policymakers and others as they seek objective, reliable, and accessible information about the real effects of medical malpractice reform. This book collects years of expert academic research into what we know, what we don't know, and what we know that just isn't so about the medical malpractice liability system. Better still, funding for this research came not from the typical stakeholders but from multiple academic institutions.

The authors present research suggesting that while the medical malpractice liability system is unlikely to be the cause of those premium spikes, it isn't doing nearly enough to make health care safer or better. And the usual reforms that some health care providers seek may not be doing much to help patients or taxpayers. Where states have enacted those reforms, they mostly seem to benefit health care providers and liability insurers. For those interested in the details, the authors exhaustively document their findings and show their work. They offer creative suggestions for improving the medical malpractice system that can benefit everyone involved.

I commend the authors for this enormous contribution to our understanding of medical malpractice liability reform. I wish we in Congress had had access to this book when debating medical malpractice policy during the last medical malpractice crisis. Fortunately, it will be available to guide policymakers through future crises.

*Tom Daschle*
*Former U.S. Senate minority leader*

## CHAPTER 1

# WHY THIS BOOK MATTERS

Mistakes happen. When mistakes happen in medicine, the results can be deadly.

Courts have responded to the problem of medical mistakes by allowing patients to sue health care providers for medical malpractice. If a jury determines that carelessness on the part of a doctor or other health care provider caused injury to a patient, the jury can award damages—an amount of money, set by the jury, that the provider or the provider's insurer must pay the patient. Providers do not face liability for all mistakes. Our system imposes liability only for negligent mistakes—that is, mistakes that fall below the customary standard of care that physicians and hospitals are expected to provide.

In theory, the medical malpractice liability system promotes two goals. The first is justice. Forcing negligent providers to compensate their victims—to make their victims "whole"—makes providers bear the cost of their mistakes and protects victims from having to bear those costs. The second is deterrence. Forcing providers to bear the cost of their own negligent mistakes will lead providers to devote more resources to preventing mistakes. Most providers purchase medical malpractice insurance to protect themselves from liability. Insurers may seek to reduce their exposure by researching how to provide safer, higher-quality medical care and encouraging providers to adopt those practices.

Insurers may also charge higher premiums or refuse to cover physicians with worse-than-expected claim rates. "Deterrence" is another way of saying that imposing liability on providers can improve the quality of medical care, thereby reducing the risk of medical injury.

In practice, the medical malpractice liability system often fails to live up to the theory. While there is evidence that the system does improve the quality of care, it could do a much better job.[1] The system is slow and costly. It undercompensates some plaintiffs, especially the most severely harmed, while overcompensating others. Court decisions have both false positives (a jury finds negligence where none exists) and false negatives (a jury does not find negligence, when it in fact exists).

In this book, we examine some of the limitations of the medical malpractice liability system. We also examine the effect of tort reforms—legal reforms, promoted by physicians and insurers and adopted by many states—that limit medical malpractice liability in various ways. We assess the evidence for whether these reforms provide a cure for the limitations of the medical malpractice system that is worse than the disease—whether these reforms can frustrate the system's ability to deliver justice and higher-quality care. Our story begins with three medical malpractice "crises."

## A TALE OF THREE CRISES

Over the past 40 years, the United States experienced three major medical malpractice crises, each marked by a dramatic increase in the cost of malpractice liability insurance. The first crisis hit in the mid-1970s, the second happened in the early 1980s, and the third occurred around 1999–2005.

Each crisis fostered a vigorous debate about the causes of the premium spikes and considerable disagreement as to what, if anything, should be done about them. Physicians and plaintiffs' lawyers were the primary adversaries in this debate, but the dispute quickly became politicized. Liability insurers and Republicans sided with physicians. Consumer groups and Democrats sided with plaintiffs' lawyers.

Physicians and their supporters insisted that the premium spikes were attributable to problems with the legal system, including rising claim rates driven by frivolous lawsuits; rising payout per claim fostered by runaway juries; and plaintiffs' ability to find experts who would propound junk medical science to gullible jurors. Using these arguments, physicians and their supporters proposed a variety of tort reforms, including damage caps, screening panels composed of physicians or other medical experts, higher standards of proof, and limits on contingent fees and on expert testimony—all targeting different aspects of the medical malpractice litigation process. They portrayed these reforms as crucial, lest rising malpractice premiums drive physicians away from practicing medicine; away from accepting sicker, higher-risk patients; and away from high-malpractice-risk states toward lower-risk ones.

On the other side, plaintiffs' lawyers and their allies blamed different causes for the premium spikes. Their favorite target was insurance companies. They claimed that malpractice insurers were gouging their physician clients and that insurers contributed to premium spikes by underreserving during "soft markets." To the extent that plaintiffs' lawyers conceded that their activity had anything to do with malpractice premiums, they portrayed their clients as innocent victims of "bad doctors." Plaintiffs' lawyers argued that the proposed reforms would not prevent future premium spikes but would make it difficult or impossible for injured patients to obtain compensation. They argued that the solution to medical malpractice crises was to get rid of bad doctors and use antitrust laws to keep medical malpractice insurers from colluding with one another to raise prices.

These debates also involved larger issues of health policy. Physicians claimed that malpractice suits both drove physicians away, thus reducing patients' access to care, and increased health care costs by causing physicians to engage in "defensive medicine." Defensive medicine means that physicians conduct extra tests and procedures that have little or no value to patients—or that even have negative value—but that reduce the risk of a later malpractice claim. Physicians argued that adopting damage caps and other restrictions on lawsuits would attract more physicians to the cap-adopting states and reduce incentives to engage in defensive medicine, thereby reducing health care spending.

In response, plaintiffs' lawyers argued that the evidence indicating that defensive medicine was responsible for a large fraction of health care spending was weak—and often based on self-serving statements by physicians. Plaintiffs' lawyers also claimed that damage caps would not save money but would instead simply transfer the costs of medical injuries from providers to patients. Since most damage caps apply to noneconomic damages, the burden would fall disproportionately on patients who are less likely to be employed and thus have lower economic damages (e.g., infants, elderly patients, and women).

Physicians' second argument was that premium spikes and malpractice suits reduced access to care—particularly from physicians practicing high-risk specialties, such as obstetrics and gynecology (ob-gyn) and neurosurgery, and from physicians practicing in rural areas. Figure 1.1 shows how this contention was typically framed.

Plaintiffs' lawyers argued in response that many factors influence physicians' decisions concerning location and choice of specialty and that liability insurance premiums were a minor factor in those decisions.

## Figure 1.1

### The conventional wisdom about medical malpractice (according to physicians)

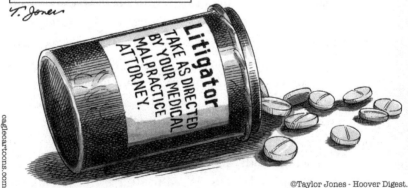

WARNING: Overuse of this medication may result in a sharp decline in available physicians in your community, an immediate transfer of wealth from you to your lawyer, and an uncontrollable urge to chase ambulances.

©Taylor Jones - Hoover Digest.

*Source:* Medical malpractice attorneys by Taylor Jones, *Hoover Digest.*

They also argued that the evidence of a connection between more lawsuits and less access to medical care was weak.[2]

Malpractice crises brought these disputes to a boil. But even when premiums are low, physicians complain that most malpractice claims are frivolous and that the litigation system is stressful, slow, expensive, and prone to error. Physicians have used the high frequency with which claims close without payment (between 75 percent and 80 percent) as evidence that most lawsuits are indeed frivolous. They argue that the defense costs associated with frivolous claims drive up the cost of malpractice coverage. They have also cast doubt on jurors' ability to decide complex malpractice cases correctly. In physicians' views, the cases with no payout were rightly decided, and many of those with a payout were wrongly decided, with juries prone to award huge amounts to patients who may have suffered harm, but not because of bad care.

In response, plaintiffs' lawyers blame physicians and insurers for many of the problems with the malpractice liability system. They argue that the system is slow and expensive because physicians refuse to admit medical errors to patients and because medical malpractice insurers often litigate to the hilt even when negligence is clear. They also argue that the liability system is more often stingy than generous. Patients with valid claims are regularly sent home empty-handed, and those with severe injuries are routinely undercompensated. In the view of plaintiffs' lawyers, the high rate at which medical malpractice claims close without payment reflects the difficulty in obtaining compensation even for strong cases, rather than the merits of the underlying claims.

Plaintiffs' lawyers also argue that frivolous cases are uncommon. Because they are paid on contingency, plaintiffs' lawyers assert that they cannot afford to bring weak cases and in fact reject most people who approach them seeking representation. Finally, plaintiffs' lawyers observe that courts are the only public way to hold bad doctors accountable for the injuries they inflict. Their basic position is that the medical malpractice system may be imperfect, but it is better than the alternatives.

Many state legislatures have responded to physicians' pleas for relief from frivolous suits with a variety of reforms. Some states took action during the first medical malpractice crisis (i.e., during the mid-1970s);

others waited until the second crisis (i.e., during the 1980s) or the third crisis (i.e., 1999–2005) to do something about the problem. A few states enacted reforms during all three of the crises—while others largely did nothing. The most popular reforms, embraced by more than 30 states— including 9 during the most recent crisis—have been caps on damages.[3] Most of the cap-adopting states limit non-economic damages, which are primarily intended to compensate for pain and suffering. A few limit total damages—both economic and non-economic. A fair number also limit punitive damages, but these caps are far less important in practice because punitive damages are rarely awarded and even more rarely paid. Caps vary in severity, with non-economic (non-econ) damage caps ranging from $250,000 in a number of states, including California, Idaho, Kansas, Montana, and Texas, to $1 million for death cases in Florida. Total damage caps range from $500,000 in Louisiana to $1.95 million in Virginia. Some caps are indexed for inflation, but most are not, and thus these caps become stricter over time.

The intense political debate has been marked by a shortage of evidence—as well as by a predilection for all those involved to misstate and overstate the evidence that appears to support them and to ignore contrary evidence. What effect did these reforms have? Did they make malpractice insurance cheaper by reducing the number of claims and the size of payouts? Did they improve access to health care by attracting physicians to states that adopted reforms? Did they make medical services cheaper by reducing defensive medicine? Both sides have strong opinions about these matters, but their positions are mostly talking points— often based on anecdotes rather than data.

In this book, we adopt the perspective of the late Senator Daniel Patrick Moynihan that "everyone is entitled to his own opinion, but not his own facts."[4] We have done our best to provide factual answers to these and other questions about the performance of the medical malpractice system, based on more than a decade of research. Our core findings, which we synthesize here, are based on work published in major peer-reviewed journals. These are listed in a separate section of the bibliography.

Part One focuses on Texas prior to its adoption in 2003 of a package of tort reforms—including a strict cap on non-economic damages in 2003.

Part Two focuses on Texas during the post-reform period, to evaluate the impact of tort reform. Part Three evaluates nationwide malpractice trends and examines whether the Texas findings in Part Two generalize to the other eight states that enacted damage caps at around the same time. To cut to the chase, our Texas findings indeed generalize to the other states. Part Four synthesizes our findings and explores the policy implications.

Why do we devote so much effort to studying Texas? First, Texas is where the best data are—or at least were through 2012. Detailed claim-level information is crucial for analyzing many of the issues involved in assessing the effects of tort reform. Texas and Florida are the only two states that make this information publicly available. As we explain in Chapter 2, from 1988 to 2015, commercial liability insurers were required to file reports with the Texas Department of Insurance (TDI) for all claims with payments that exceeded $10,000. TDI made this information available to the public, although only through 2012. Texas's database is better than Florida's for the range of issues we study. For the large claims (with payouts that exceed $25,000 [1988$]) that account for 99 percent of the dollars paid to claimants, the Texas Closed Claim Database (TCCD) includes, among other things, information on claimant age, the date of injury, the dates the claim was initiated and closed, the amount paid to resolve each claim, the cost of defending each claim, the size of the applicable primary insurance policy, and whether or not the case was tried or settled. For tried cases that closed with payments, the TCCD also contains detailed information about jury verdicts and post-judgment proceedings. These rich data let us paint a detailed picture of Texas's medical malpractice liability system in action.

A second reason to focus on Texas is that Texas adopted strict reforms in 2003, in the middle of the period for which we have data. This allows us to study Texas both before and after these reforms, and thus assess what differences the reforms made—or didn't make. For the first decade or so covered by our dataset, Texas had a pro-plaintiff reputation, including a state constitutional right to tort damages that was guarded by a Democratic legislature and judiciary. All three branches of the state's government became solidly Republican toward the close of the 20th century. This turnover led to greater receptiveness to tort reform and, in 2003, to an amendment to Texas's constitution authorizing the legislature to enact a damages cap. The Texas cap on non-economic damages, also adopted in 2003, ranges from $250,000 to $750,000, depending on the number and type of defendants.

Texas's size also justifies a detailed examination of its medical malpractice system. Texas is the second-largest state in the United States by population, after California, and is growing fast. If Texas were a country, it would be the 45th largest by population and the 10th largest by gross domestic product.

Finally, Texas's medical malpractice insurance crisis and the effects of the resulting damages cap have already attracted considerable attention. In 2002, the American Tort Reform Association named four Texas counties as "judicial hellholes" where plaintiff-friendly juries denied defendants a fair shake. The same year, the head of the American Medical Association claimed that Texas was one of 12 states where the medical malpractice crisis had reached a "critical stage."[5] And in the national debate over tort reform, Texas's 2003 reforms have replaced California's mid-1970s reforms as the model to which reform proponents argue that other states should aspire.

So what do we find? Part One (Chapters 3–6), "Misdiagnosing the Problem: Texas's Medical Malpractice Liability System in Action," examines Texas's medical malpractice liability system during the pre-reform period (1988–2003).

In Chapter 3, "The Texas Medical Malpractice Insurance Crisis: Smoke without Much Fire," we show that while Texas indeed experienced a crisis in medical malpractice *insurance*, it did not experience an underlying crisis in medical malpractice *liability* that might explain the insurance crisis. Instead, changes in the medical malpractice system (the number of paid claims and the payout per claim) can explain only a fraction of the premium spikes that hit Texas during 1999–2003. There is no evidence of a spike in the number of claims, in the payout per claim, or in jury verdicts that might account for the premium spikes. We also find that smaller paid claims are increasingly being squeezed out of the medical malpractice system—they are simply uneconomic for plaintiffs' lawyers to bring, even when the merits are strong.

In Chapter 4, "Haircuts: Jury Verdicts and Post-verdict Payouts," we show that patients who win at trial routinely fail to collect the portion of the jury awards that exceeds their doctors' insurance policy limits. The runaway jury verdicts that are featured in news reports and blamed by partisans for driving up insurance costs are routinely limited by defendants' policy limits and other post-trial factors. These "haircuts," the difference between what the jury awards and the plaintiff collects, become more likely and more severe as verdict size increases. These dynamics make it implausible that occasional, very large jury awards can drive premium spikes.

In Chapter 5, "Impact of Policy Limits in Cases against Physicians," we show that although doctors routinely claim that malpractice lawsuits threaten them with ruinous personal liability, patients almost never recover compensation from doctors directly. Insurers provide all but a tiny fraction of the amounts that patients receive. Policy limits effectively cap payouts in both tried and settled cases.

In Chapter 6, "Defense Costs," we show that defense costs rose steadily and roughly doubled in real dollars over the period we study, even though real payouts were flat and hourly rates for personal injury defense lawyers were flat. However, defense costs are only a modest share of indemnity payouts and rose predictably over time. These rising defense costs, if matched on the plaintiff side, could explain why smaller claims are being squeezed out of the medical malpractice system. We also show that the tort system is an expensive way to transfer resources from defendants to plaintiffs. We estimate that it costs $1.33 in overhead to deliver $1 to negligently injured plaintiffs.

As noted above, we titled Part One "Misdiagnosing the Problem: Texas's Medical Malpractice Liability System in Action." Texas adopted a damages cap because a majority of voters and a majority of legislators believed that the medical malpractice system was responsible for the premium spikes that hit Texas starting a few years earlier. We find no evidence to support that belief. Of course, the findings in Part One do not indicate that the medical malpractice system is operating perfectly. Far from it; not least because no matter how severe their injuries or how strong the evidence of negligence, plaintiffs can rarely recover more than the defendants' policy limits, even for economic damages. Physicians increasingly realize this, and many maintain quite low limits—sometimes only $100,000–$200,000.

Moreover, as we point out in Part Four, the medical malpractice system is slow, expensive (which is why small claims are being squeezed out), stressful to both sides, contentious, prone to error in both directions (i.e., payment for weak claims and nonpayment for strong claims), and perceived by everyone involved as inhumane. But Part One makes it clear that whatever problems the medical malpractice system has, the best evidence is that the premium spikes that generated the Texas reforms were *not* attributable to factors within the legal system. Texas voters reacted to the smoke of rising premiums by wrongly assuming that the cause was a fire of rising claims and payouts. There was no fire.

Part Two (Chapters 7–10), "Mistreating the Problem: The Impact of Tort Reform in Texas," examines the effect of tort reform on the medical malpractice liability system and the broader health care system.

In Chapter 7, "The Impact of Capping Damages," we analyze the actual effect of Texas's cap on non-economic damages. We find that the damages cap substantially reduced both claim frequency and payout per claim. In combination, we find a 75 percent reduction in aggregate payouts to plaintiffs. The reduction reflects the combined effect of both a dramatic decline in the number of paid claims and a large drop in payout per claim that is concentrated in the larger claims that were most affected by the cap.

Chapter 8, "Medical Malpractice Claiming by Elderly Patients," examines whether the Texas non-economic damages cap had a disparate effect on elderly patients. During the pre-reform period, elderly plaintiffs were "catching up" with the nonelderly population on two important indicators—the rate of paid claims and payout per paid claim. This convergence stopped, and indeed reversed, after the 2003 reforms, which disproportionately reduced payouts per claim for elderly claimants.

Chapter 9, "Defensive Medicine? Impact on Health Care Spending," examines whether tort reform can "bend the cost curve" by weakening or eliminating physicians' incentives to practice defensive medicine. Texas's 2003 reforms dramatically reduced physicians' medical malpractice risk.

Yet health care spending did not decline. Indeed, we find some evidence that Medicare spending actually increased in the post-reform period relative to states without damage caps.

A core argument by the proponents of the Texas reforms was their claim that rising insurance premiums and fear of litigation were driving doctors out of Texas. After the reforms were adopted, physicians and legislators argued that the reforms had succeeded in attracting thousands of doctors to Texas. In Chapter 10, "Impact on Physician Supply in Texas," we examine these claims and find that both are false. Physician supply was not measurably stunted prior to the 2003 reforms—and did not measurably increase thereafter. Instead, Texas's physician supply grew slowly and steadily throughout both the pre- and post-reform periods—indeed, overall physician supply grew a bit faster prior to reform. Whether we study all direct patient care physicians, physicians who practice in high-risk specialties, or rural physicians, the picture is the same. Tort reform had no measurable impact on Texas's physician supply.

To summarize, Texas's damage cap dramatically reduced the number of medical malpractice cases and total payouts to plaintiffs, with an especially strong effect on elderly plaintiffs. But Texas's tort reform package had no discernible, favorable impact on broader measures of health system performance. Health care spending growth did not slow, and physician supply did not increase. We titled Part Two "Mistreating the Problem: The Impact of Tort Reform in Texas" because while reform strongly benefited providers, the evidence that it had significant benefits for the broader health care system is simply not there.

As noted above, for any single-state study, a natural question is whether the results are generalizable. Texas is a large, diverse state, but still, it is only one state. Is there something unique about "Lone Star Justice"? In Part Three (composed of Chapters 11–13), "Mistreating the Problem: A National Perspective on the Impact of Medical Malpractice Reform," we expand our horizons and study Texas together with the eight other states that adopted caps on non-economic damages around the same time. There are some questions we can't answer because we don't have the detailed claim-level data for other states that we have for Texas. But we can answer the core big picture questions: Do caps reduce medical malpractice litigation? Do caps reduce health care spending? Do caps increase physician supply?

We find that the conclusions from our close study of Texas do generalize to the other eight "new-cap" states. Damage caps indeed reduce both the number of claims and payout per claim. But caps don't reduce health care spending or attract more physicians to the new-cap states. Except, perhaps, plastic surgeons—but this is scarcely the effect on physician movement that reform proponents claim.

Chapter 11, "The Receding Tide of Medical Malpractice Litigation," provides two main results. First, we confirm that damage caps reduce both claim rates and payout per claim, and thus sharply reduce medical malpractice payouts per physician. Thus caps ought to sharply reduce medical malpractice insurance premiums. Second, we find that nationwide claim rates for smaller claims have been trending downward since 1992—as far back as we can measure—and claim rates for all claims, including larger claims, have been dropping steeply since 2001. These drops are nationwide, across all 50 states, including states without damage caps ("no-cap" states). Payout per physician has been dropping as well, along with larger paid claims, and by 2012, it was roughly half of its level in 1992.

Second, we show that caps on non-economic damages (non-econ caps) substantially reduce both claim rates and payout per claim in the new-cap states, even relative to the national decline in claim rates. Thus, some (but not all) of the post-reform drops in claim rates that we observe in Texas (see Chapter 7) and in the other new-cap states were partly attributable to an underlying nationwide trend and partly to cap adoption. However, the drops in payout per claim that we observe in Texas, and in the other new-cap states, are directly attributable to adoption of non-econ caps. In that narrow sense, damage caps do the job that physicians hoped they would—claim rates drop, payout per claim drops, and payout per physician drops sharply. And with a lag, medical malpractice insurance premiums drop as well.[6]

Chapter 12, "Defensive Medicine in the New-Cap States," reexamines the issue of defensive medicine—this time using nationwide data and studying all nine new-cap states. We compare Medicare spending in the 9 new-cap states to spending in the 20 no-cap states, as well as

22 states that adopted caps early on, during the 1970s and 1980s ("old-cap" states). We find that damage caps have no statistically significant impact on Medicare Part A spending, which is how Medicare pays for most in-hospital care, but predict roughly 4 percent *higher* Medicare Part B spending—Part B is how Medicare pays for physician services and outpatient treatment. Further work is needed to understand the clinical decisions that underlie our finding that Medicare Part B spending increases. But no matter how we slice the data, we find no evidence that tort reform *lowers* health care spending.

Chapter 13, "Does Tort Reform Attract Physicians to the New-Cap States?," examines whether tort reform is a useful strategy for attracting physicians. At a national level, this is a zero-sum game; the aggregate national supply of physicians is determined by national decisions. But we can still study whether cap adoption attracts physicians to the new-cap states at the expense of other states. We compare growth in physician supply in new-cap states—for all patient care physicians, for physicians in high-malpractice-risk specialties, and for rural physicians—to growth in no-cap and old-cap states. We find no evidence that cap adoption attracts more physicians in any of these categories.

Part Four is titled "If Damage Caps Aren't the Answer, What Is?" It is a truism in medicine that the wrong diagnosis will not lead to the correct treatment—and that the wrong treatment will not cure the patient's illness. Part One makes it clear that the debate over tort reform has been based on a *misdiagnosis* of the problem. Parts Two and Three show that damage caps *mistreat* the underlying problem. In addition, they neither reduce health care spending nor attract physicians. But Parts One through Three do not answer the question of where we should go from here.

Accordingly, Part Four, which is composed of Chapter 14, "Synthesis: Lessons and Pathologies"; Chapter 15, "Reform Strategies: Toward a Better Medical Malpractice System"; and Chapter 16, "Three Concluding Points," pulls together our findings and offers some thoughts on how to make the medical malpractice system work better for everyone involved. Part Four shows that the medical malpractice system responds in predictable ways to changes in the rate and severity of medical injury.

Factors that determine the frequency and severity of injuries change slowly, so we should expect medical malpractice liability outcomes to change slowly as well.

This has two important implications. First, large premium spikes are unlikely to be the result of factors within the medical malpractice system. Over the long run, insurance premiums should reflect total liability costs. But in the short run, premiums can vary greatly without accompanying changes in the operation of the medical malpractice liability system. For example, premiums can rise steeply even when claim frequency or payout per claim holds steady or declines.

Second, although plaintiffs' lawyers often seek to blame high medical malpractice insurance premiums on greedy insurance companies, that dog won't hunt. At least in the medium term, the medical malpractice insurance market is reasonably competitive in many states. In others, it is dominated by physician cooperatives. In neither instance is it plausible that insurers conspired to manufacture an insurance crisis by massively overcharging their physician customers relative to the costs and risk that are being transferred.

Third, even dramatic changes to the medical malpractice system, in the form of strict damage caps, have little or no impact on health care spending and physician supply. Indeed, damage caps might even cause health care spending to *rise*, by removing the brakes on doctors' willingness to perform medical treatments that expose patients to serious risks of bad outcomes. Medical malpractice reform is, therefore, a misguided remedy for a misdiagnosed problem. It is not a solution to the larger ills that plague our high-cost, middling-quality health care system.

Medicine routinely involves matters of life and death—with high stakes for getting the correct diagnosis and selecting the right treatment. The same approach should apply to medical malpractice reform. We need to take action, but we need to take the right action. Part Four provides some suggestions on what to do. We believe our suggested approach will provide a far better prognosis than the dominant "damage caps or bust" approach that has prevailed to date.

Finally, to paraphrase Oliver Wendell Holmes, a page of data is worth a volume of logic.[7] For centuries, physicians used bloodletting to treat a host of ills. The theory for this treatment changed and became more sophisticated over time. Originally, patients were bled to release demons and bad energy. Later, bleeding was used because it was thought to restore the body's balance of fluids and reduce inflammation. The technology evolved as well—from leeches and pointed sticks to finely crafted lancets and specially designed blades called fleams. Everyone believed in bloodletting—but eventually it fell out of fashion once it became clear that bloodletting failed to accomplish the desired objectives.

In our view, conventional tort reforms are akin to bloodletting—good for the physicians' pocketbooks but not based on solid research and not so good for the patient or for society. It is time to apply data to the questions we ask in this book: How does medical malpractice litigation actually work? And what effects does tort reform actually have? It will then be time to move beyond the failed set of conventional tort reforms and find something better, just as bloodletting was eventually replaced by better treatments. The standard medical malpractice reforms—especially damage caps—need to be similarly scrutinized and then replaced as well.

---

The individual chapters of this book started out as separately published academic articles. This is an important strength; our principal results have been peer reviewed and published in top journals. Yet this book is much more than a compilation of prior articles. We have completely rewritten each, dropping the dry statistical details so we can focus on presenting our main conclusions in a straightforward fashion. We use figures and graphs rather than the regression tables from our academic articles. And we have updated each chapter to reflect new developments and the availability of more years of data. Of course, for the interested reader, the full treatment is available in the original articles, all of which are included in a separate list of references.

The work presented in this book and in the earlier articles was funded through the generosity of the academic institutions with which we are affiliated. We did not receive external funding from any source, other than our respective universities. The authors have diverse political affiliations too. One would self-identify as a liberal Democrat; one as a liberal-leaning libertarian; two as more conservative libertarians; and one is Korean with no U.S.-specific political leanings. If we have a common bias, it is toward the view that markets tend to work—even markets as flawed as those for medical malpractice insurance or health care. The results we present in this book tend to gore Republican oxen more than Democratic ones. But we did not know or prejudge the outcomes when we started. Indeed, we have other research that questions Democratic articles of faith.[8]

Four of us are law professors, and the fifth is an economics professor. We thus have reason to appreciate both the strengths and the weaknesses of the legal system—as a means to assign fault, when appropriate, following a bad medical outcome and as a means to compensate injured patients or their families.

The articles on which this book is based were published over more than a decade—between 2005 and 2017. They have been repeatedly cited by other researchers. To be sure, some researchers may have different takes on the explanations or implications of our findings; they may think that Texas is unique, or they may believe that more research is needed to establish certain points. We welcome the opportunity to continue discussing those issues. Still, our sense of the literature is that our core findings—damage caps reduce medical malpractice claims and payouts; they do not reduce overall health care spending (although they may affect spending in discrete areas); and they have at most a modest effect in attracting physicians to cap-adopting states—are widely accepted. The research that underlies this book has contributed to strengthening that consensus view.

Given the importance of basing reform on solid evidence, we are proud—we hope justifiably so—to have produced a comprehensive account of the operation of the medical malpractice liability system, both in Texas and in the United States as a whole.

## CHAPTER 2

# OUR DATA SOURCES AND LIMITATIONS

This chapter describes the medical malpractice and other datasets we rely on. It also contains an overview of the principal Texas damage caps and provides some details on our statistical methods. Readers who want more details on our datasets and methods should consult our published articles.

## THE TEXAS CLOSED MEDICAL MALPRACTICE CLAIMS DATASET

Chapters 3–10 of this book focus on Texas, a large and diverse state, second only to California in population and third, after California and New York, in health care spending. Texas is also one of only two states (Florida being the other) that maintained a publicly available dataset containing paid medical malpractice claims over an extended period of time. We rely on the Texas Closed Claim Database (TCCD), which was maintained by the Texas Department of Insurance (TDI) and covered 1988–2012. The TCCD contained individual reports of closed paid personal injury claims covered by five lines of commercial insurance: mono-line general liability, commercial auto liability, commercial multiperil, medical professional liability, and other professional liability insurance. From 1990 on, TDI audited the TCCD for completeness and accuracy, a feature not shared by either the Florida dataset or the

National Practitioner Data Bank (NPDB), which contains information on paid medical malpractice claims against physicians in all states. Data in the TCCD are at the county level; patients, physicians, and hospitals are not identified.

Unfortunately, the TCCD has been terminated and its data are no longer publicly available. Unless otherwise indicated, all figures and tables in Chapters 3–10 are based on our calculations using the TCCD.

As will emerge in later chapters, the TCCD contains a wealth of information about closed paid claims. Its richness lets us study many aspects of the medical malpractice liability system about which little is otherwise known, and which academic researchers are otherwise unable to study. We know of no other comparable dataset.

The TCCD's richness derives mainly from its Long Form reports, which contain detailed information about closed claims. From 1988 through August 2009, TDI required insurers to file Long Form reports for claims that closed with payouts by all defendants of more than $25,000 (nominal). In September 2009, TDI raised the Long Form threshold to $75,000 (nominal).

From 1988 through August 2009, TDI also required insurers to file Short Form reports for claims that closed with payouts by all defendants of more than $10,000 (nominal), but that fell below the Long Form threshold. The Short Form threshold was raised to $25,000 (nominal) in September 2009. The Short Form reports are less detailed than the Long Forms. TDI also published aggregate annual reports on all closed claims, including zero and small payout claims, by line of insurance.

The chapters in Part One of this book examine the performance of the medical malpractice liability system before Texas adopted major restrictions on medical malpractice lawsuits in 2003. Because of the lag between claim filing and closing, these reforms have only a modest effect on claims closed through 2005, but they have an increasing effect thereafter. Accordingly, in Part One, we study claims closed from 1988 to 2005. In Part Two, we use data through 2010 (except as otherwise specified) and study how the 2003 reforms affected the medical malpractice liability system, health care spending, and the number of physicians practicing in Texas.

We focus in this book on Long Form claims to take advantage of the additional information reported by insurers. All amounts in this book are in 2010 dollars, unless explicitly stated otherwise. Our "medical malpractice dataset" contains all Long Form claims in the TCCD with the following characteristics:

- Payout by all defendants of at least $25,000 in 1988 dollars (roughly $46,000 in 2010 dollars).[9] Although claims meeting this threshold are only 66 percent of all paid medical malpractice claims in the TCCD, they account for 99 percent of the dollars paid out on all medical malpractice claims.
- Additionally, the claim meets at least two of the following three criteria:
    - It was paid under medical professional liability insurance.
    - It was against a physician, hospital, or nursing home.
    - It involved injuries caused by "complications or misadventures of medical or surgical care."
- We exclude claims against dentists or dental surgeons even if they meet the two-of-three rule.

As mentioned, TDI raised the reporting threshold for Long Form claims to $75,000 as of September 1, 2009. This means that a few claims with payouts between $25,000 and $75,000 (nominal), which would have been reported on Long Forms in prior years, were reported instead on Short Forms: 11 claims in 2009 and 43 claims in 2010. We include these Short Form claims in our medical malpractice dataset.[10]

Initially, TDI did not audit individual claim reports. After discovering that some insurers were not filing reports for all claims, in 1990, it began to reconcile the payouts shown on individual reports against aggregate payout data that insurers also had to report. TDI also reviewed individual claim reports for internal consistency. When we study time trends (for example, large paid claims with payouts that exceed $25,000 [1988$] per year), we exclude 1988 and 1989 because of underreporting. We include these years when assessing per claim amounts because we have no reason to believe that the underreporting introduced any biases.

When we study all claims (i.e., not just large paid claims), we rely on TDI's aggregate annual reports by line of insurance. These reports are available from 1995 on.

Some claim reports are "duplicates"—that is, they reflect two or more payouts by different defendants stemming from the same underlying injury. TDI identifies duplicates in the TCCD, but it does an imperfect job and does not link particular original claims to the corresponding duplicate claims. We supplemented TDI's efforts by hand-reviewing all medical malpractice claim reports. We match original to duplicate reports, identify some apparent duplicate reports that TDI missed (including cases where claims involving different defendants closed in different years, which TDI does not seek to identify), and remove some TDI-identified duplicates without a true match in the dataset. When duplicate reports exist, we generally treat the last-filed report as the primary report because it should capture all prior payouts, including payouts by defendants who did not file claim reports, such as self-insured hospitals.

Table 2.1 provides summary information for the resulting medical malpractice dataset. For 1988–2005, our dataset includes 17,106 claim reports (including duplicate reports), involving 15,065 non-duplicate *cases* with total payouts of $8.8 billion. Unless stated otherwise, we study only nonduplicate cases. The 1988–2005 dataset includes 350 jury cases with plaintiff verdicts involving adjusted verdicts (defined below) of $905 million and payouts of $461 million.[11] This is an average of 837 large paid claims and 19 trials with payouts per year. As Table 2.1 shows, the annual flow of claims drops sharply in the post-reform period to an average of 506 large paid claims and 11 trials with payouts.

In some chapters, we compare results for medical malpractice cases to those for four other lines of commercially insured personal injury claims, also covered in the TCCD: auto, general commercial, commercial multiperil, and other professional liability. Table 2.1 provides summary statistics for these claims.

Table 2.2 shows the distribution of pre-damage-cap cases by payout range. Cases with small payouts (< $100,000) represent 19.9 percent of cases but only 2.4 percent of payout dollars. Conversely, cases with

## Table 2.1

Summary information for medical malpractice dataset, large paid claims

| Type of case | 1988–2005 | 2006–2010 | 1988–2010 |
|---|---|---|---|
| Large paid claim reports | 17,106 | 2,817 | 19,923 |
| Nonduplicate large paid cases | 15,065 | 2,529 | 17,594 |
| Non–nursing home cases | 13,951 | 2,490 | 16,441 |
| Elderly cases | 2,231 | 556 | 2,787 |
| Adult nonelderly cases | 8,876 | 1,531 | 10,407 |
| Nonduplicate cases/year | 837 | 506 | 765 |
| Total payouts | $8,800M | $895M | $9,695M |
| Jury trials with plaintiff verdicts | 350 | 57 | 407 |
| Jury trials with plaintiff verdicts/year | 19 | 11 | 18 |
| Total adjusted jury verdicts | $905M | $221M | $1,126M |
| Total payouts in jury verdict cases | $461M | $69M | $530M |
| Mean (median) damages award | $1,986k ($589k) | $3,065k ($649k) | $2,137k ($592k) |
| Mean (median) adjusted verdict | $2,587k ($790k) | $3,876k ($756k) | $2,767k ($778k) |
| Mean (median) payout | $1,317k ($483k) | $1,206k ($458k) | $1,302k ($480k) |
| **Other large, nonduplicate personal injury claims** | | | |
| Auto claims | 99,046 | 26,651 | 125,697 |
| General commercial claims | 33,350 | 5,304 | 38,654 |
| Commercial multiperil claims | 23,671 | 3,959 | 27,630 |
| Other professional liability claims | 1,444 | 260 | 1,704 |
| **Total other large paid claims** | **157,511** | **36,174** | **193,685** |

*Note:* Millions are abbreviated as M, and thousands are abbreviated as k. Monetary amounts are in 2010 dollars.

*Source:* Texas Closed Claim Database.

payouts of $1 million or more are only 13.3 percent of cases, but they represent 58.8 percent of payout dollars.

In the remainder of this section, we provide details on some limitations of the TCCD data and how we handle them. This is relatively technical material that can be skipped by those so inclined.

*Claims closed soon after the non-economic cap.* The data for 1988–2005 include only three tried cases that were subject to the cap on non-economic

## Table 2.2

Large paid claims by payout range, 1988–2005

| Payout range | Claims | | Payout | |
|---|---|---|---|---|
| | **Number** | **Percentage of total** | **Amount** | **Percentage of total** |
| $25,000–$100,000 | 2,996 | 19.9 | $209 million | 2.4 |
| $100,000–$500,000 | 7,898 | 52.4 | $1,895 million | 21.5 |
| $500,000–$1 million | 2,172 | 14.4 | $1,514 million | 17.2 |
| $1 million–$2.5 million | 1,416 | 9.4 | $2,089 million | 23.7 |
| $2.5 million+ | 583 | 3.9 | $3,093 million | 35.1 |
| **Total** | **15,065** | **100** | **$8,800 million** | **100** |

*Note:* Monetary amounts are in 2010 dollars.
*Source:* Texas Closed Claim Database.

(non-econ) damages that Texas adopted in 2003 ("non-econ cap"). By "subject to the cap," we simply mean that the cases were filed after September 1, 2003. However, in none of these tried cases did awarded non-econ damages exceed the cap. We treat all tried cases during this period as if they were pre-cap cases. The 1988–2005 data include a larger number of settled claims that were subject to the non-econ cap—2 closed in 2003; 56 closed in 2004; and 164 closed in 2005—altogether 8 percent of the large paid claims that closed in these three years and 1.5 percent of all claims that settled in these years. Because the TCCD does not contain reliable figures on the breakdown of damages in settled cases, we cannot determine how often the non-econ cap would have limited damages in these 222 cases. Including these cases has a small effect on our overall results for settled cases. Excluding them would bias the sample by differentially excluding quick-to-close claims in these years. We judged that the bias from leaving them in the data was likely smaller than from removing them.

*Adjusted verdict and allowed verdict.* For each jury verdict, we compute an "adjusted verdict," that is, the amount the plaintiff was entitled to receive based on the jury award alone, before taking into account damage caps or a decision by the judge to reduce the damages award (a practice known as "remittitur"). The adjusted verdict equals reported damages plus pre- and post-judgment interest calculated as provided for by Texas law. We allocate interest to each type of damages (economic, non-economic, and punitive) to determine adjusted damages within each type. We also compute *allowed* economic, non-economic, and punitive damages and an "allowed verdict" (the sum of these three components), computed after the effect of damage caps and any remittitur.

*Plaintiff age.* The Long Form requires insurers to report a plaintiff's age in years, and in months when age is less than one year. However, the Long Form does not indicate whether claims are related to childbirth. We treat claims with plaintiff age at date of injury reported as 0 or 1 month as "perinatal" claims, principally involving childbirth. We designate claims with plaintiff age from 2 months through 18 years as "child"; claims with plaintiff age 19–64 as "adult nonelderly"; and claims with plaintiff age 65 or older as "elderly" claims.

## TCCD LIMITATIONS

No dataset is perfect, and the TCCD is no exception. The principal limitations are the following:

*Data only for Texas.* The TCCD is limited to Texas. We can't be sure of the extent to which Texas is representative of other states. That said, Texas is a large and diverse state that may be reasonably representative of the United States as a whole. Moreover, in Part Three, we extend our Texas-specific results to include eight other "new-cap" states that adopted damage caps during the third wave of medical malpractice reforms over 2002–2005. As Part Three indicates, we find consistent results across the new-cap states.

*Dataset covers only insured claims.* The TCCD includes only "insured" claims. We lack claims against "pure" self-insured health care providers, which don't rely on wholly owned captive insurers. Most physicians carry malpractice insurance, but some hospitals do not. For example, we lack data on claims against the University of Texas hospital system and University of Texas–employed physicians. Overall, our dataset likely captures most cases in which physicians made payments. It also contains

many but not all cases in which the sole payers were hospitals and other
institutional providers.

*Dataset covers only large paid claims.* The most important limitation of
the TCCD is that the individual claim reports cover only claims with
payouts above the reporting threshold. We have no claim-level data
on claims that closed without payouts or with small payouts below the
threshold for the Short Form. This means that we have data mainly on
voluntary settlements and on trials that were won by plaintiffs—each
with payouts that exceed the reporting threshold. Trials won by defendants appear in the dataset only when a payment in excess of the reporting threshold was made even though the plaintiff lost, perhaps pursuant
to a pretrial "high-low" agreement. In a high-low agreement, the parties
agree that whatever the jury decides, the plaintiff will receive at least the
"low," but no more than the "high."[12] We do have limited information
about zero payout and small payout claims from TDI's annual aggregate
reports.

*Dataset covers only claims actually made.* It has long been known that
the vast majority of medical injuries do not lead to medical malpractice
claims.[13] We have data only on medical injuries that do result in medical
malpractice claims, and thus can assess the impact of the medical malpractice system and tort reform only on the subset of patients who bring
claims.

*Some data fields we wish we had.* The Long Form includes many
details on claims, but it omits some information we wish it included.
We lack data on injury severity, the patient's gender, and the defendant's
specialty and identity. Thus we cannot track the number of payments
made by, or, more accurately, on behalf of a single provider. The dataset
does not include insurer or defendant identities. We know policy limits
for the primary policy covering the insured defendant but not limits
for any additional coverage under another policy, nor limits for other
defendants.

*The 2009 change in reporting thresholds.* For claims closed on or after
September 1, 2009, the thresholds for Long Form reporting increased
from $25,000 to $75,000 (nominal), and the threshold for Short Form
reporting rose from $10,000 to $25,000. This change means that

11 medical malpractice claims from 2009 and 43 from 2010 are reported on the Short Form that would have been reported on the Long Form in previous years. These reports therefore do not include plaintiff age. This change affects our comparison of claim rates for elderly patients to adult nonelderly patients in Chapter 8. We use claim frequency for the first eight months of 2009 to assign these claims to the three relevant age categories: baby and child, adult nonelderly, and elderly.

## TEXAS'S DAMAGE CAPS

Texas has several damage caps: a cap on damages in death cases ("death cap"); a cap on punitive damages ("punitives cap"); and, since September 1, 2003, a non-econ cap. Judges can also reduce jury awards of damages that they consider excessive (remittitur) or reverse the jury entirely (called "judgment [for the defendant] notwithstanding the verdict," often abbreviated as JNOV). In practice, remittitur and JNOV are uncommon. In Chapter 7, where we study the non-econ cap, we use the term "other caps" to refer to the combined effect of the death cap, the punitives cap, remittitur, and JNOV. We use "all caps" to refer to "other caps" plus the non-econ cap.

*Remittitur and JNOV.* Judges reduced 16 jury awards in our dataset through remittitur and reversed one case through JNOV. The remittitur cases involved primarily non-econ damages. We assumed that the remittitur applied first to non-econ damages, and then to economic damages, except for one case in which the remitted amount exactly matched the economic damages award. For tried cases, the 16 remittiturs, taken together, trivially reduced the adjusted allowed verdict attributable to economic damages by $35,000 and reduced the adjusted allowed verdict attributable to non-econ damages from $496 million to $481 million.

*Death cap.* Texas has a cap on the sum of compensatory (economic and non-econ) damages plus pre-judgment interest in medical malpractice cases resulting in death (a death cap) of $1.8 million in 2010 dollars. This cap was set at $500,000 in 1977 but has increased since then because it is indexed for inflation. The death cap does not apply to medical expenses that the patient incurred before dying, but we lack data on the breakdown between medical expenses and other economic damages, so we assumed that the death cap applied to all compensatory damages. We treat the death cap as reducing otherwise-allowed non-econ damages first, and reducing economic damages second. It applied on a per defendant basis until 2003, but we generally treat it as a single amount, regardless of the number of defendants.[14] With these assumptions, the death cap affects 28 cases and reduces the adjusted allowed verdict attributable to economic damages from $359 million to $356 million and the adjusted allowed verdict attributable to non-economic damages from $481 million to $423 million. Both amounts are after taking into account the effects of remittitur and JNOV.

*Punitives cap.* Texas law caps punitive damages and provides that these damages are available only if the claimant proves by clear and convincing evidence that the harm with respect to which the claimant seeks recovery of exemplary damages results from (a) fraud, (b) malice, or (c) gross negligence. The punitives cap was tightened in 1995 to equal the greater of (a) $200,000 or (b) [(2 × economic damages) + (the lesser of awarded non-economic damages or $750,000)]. Amounts are in nominal dollars.[15]

Three tried cases in our sample involve very large punitive damage awards (from $13 million to $76 million, before interest), most of which exceeded the punitives cap and none of which were paid. We winsorize these awards at the level of the next-largest punitive award ($4.9 million). That is, we treat the three very large awards as if the award was $4.9 million in each case; this is done to limit the effect of these very large but clearly anomalous awards on our statistical analysis. This reduces the total adjusted verdict in our 350 jury cases from $1.2 billion to $905 million. After this winsorization, the punitives cap reduced the adjusted allowed verdict attributable to punitive damages from $50 million to $39 million.

*Non-econ cap.* In 2003, Texas capped non-economic damages at $250,000 for medical malpractice cases against one or more physicians and other individual health care providers. An additional $250,000 is available against a hospital or other health care institution, with a maximum of $500,000 for all health care institutions. Thus, the total cap ranges from

$250,000 to $750,000, depending on the number and type of defendants who are found liable. These amounts are not adjusted for inflation.

Other components of the 2003 reforms include making the death cap apply per claim rather than per defendant, higher evidentiary standards for cases involving emergency room care, a requirement that plaintiffs file an expert report within 120 days of suit with regard to each defendant's negligence (by a practicing physician, if the defendant is a physician), and a 10-year statute of repose (a statute of repose completely bars any claim, whether harm was knowable or not; a principal effect is to bar claims for harm during childbirth brought by the child once he or she becomes an adult).

*Public hospitals cap.* Texas law caps total damage awards against public hospitals at $250,000 (nominal, not adjusted for inflation) for each defendant and $500,000 for each occurrence. We cannot identify which claims involve public hospitals, so we ignore the effects of this cap on verdicts and payouts.

*Appellate review of contested issues.* Prior to appellate review, it is not always clear how a cap should be applied. For example, the Texas Supreme Court decided in 2002 that the death cap applied to the sum of compensatory damages plus pre-judgment interest, rather than compensatory damages alone. Similarly, when the death cap was enacted in 1977, it applied to all medical malpractice cases and not just death cases. The Texas Supreme Court struck down the general cap in 1988 but held in 1990 that this cap was valid for death cases. We assume that appellate interpretations were in effect during the entire period the statute was effective, regardless of when the appellate case was decided. Thus we treat the death cap as applying to death cases closed in 1988 and afterward, and we use the 2002 Texas Supreme Court interpretation for all such cases.

## STUDYING THE IMPACT OF TEXAS'S 2003 REFORMS

The second part of this book studies the impact of Texas's 2003 reforms—principally a cap on non-economic damages that applies to all cases filed after September 1, 2003. There is an important complication in assessing the impact of the 2003 reforms, which we return to in subsequent chapters. For each closed claim with a lawsuit filed, we know whether the cap applies.[16] Some claims close quickly, while others take longer—so the claims that close in a post-reform year are a mix of pre- and post-reform claims.[17] Stated differently, the 2003 reforms either apply or do not apply to any given claim, but the overall effects of reform phase in over time when viewed across all claims closed in each year. In Chapter 8, we address this issue as part of our analysis of the effect of Texas's 2003 tort reforms.

## OTHER DATA SOURCES

We summarize our data sources in this section. For additional details, see the original articles on which this book is based, which are listed in a separate section in the list of references.

Unless otherwise specified, we adjust all dollar amounts to 2010 dollars, using the national Consumer Price Index for All Urban Consumers as the inflation index.[18] In Chapter 3, we adjust medical malpractice claim rates alternatively for growth in population and for growth in the number of physicians. We rely on Census Bureau data for population counts, including age, ethnic and racial subcategories, and percentage in poverty.[19] We obtain a number of control variables from the publicly available Area Health Resources Files dataset: median household income; percentage disabled (percentage of Medicare enrollees receiving Social Security Disability Insurance); and managed care penetration (Medicare Advantage enrollees/all Medicare-eligible persons).[20] We obtain data on United States health care spending from the Centers for Medicare and Medicaid Services.[21] We obtain county-level per capita personal income from the Regional Economic Accounts compiled by the Bureau of Economic Analysis,[22] and percentage unemployed from the Local Area Unemployment Statistics compiled by the Bureau of Labor Statistics.[23] We assign urban versus rural status to counties using the U.S. Department of Agriculture's 1–9 classification.[24] We extrapolate or interpolate when data are missing in a particular source for a particular year or years.

For Chapter 6 on defense costs, we obtain information on defense counsel hourly rates from the Texas State Bar.[25]

For Chapter 8 on medical malpractice claims by elderly plaintiffs, we use three measures of the intensity of health care system use by different age groups: share of health care spending, hospital inpatient days, and hospital discharges. We obtain data on discharges and inpatient days by patient age for the "South" U.S. census region (which includes Texas) from the National Hospital Discharge Survey.[26]

For Chapters 9 and 12 on defensive medicine, we obtain county-level Medicare spending for 1998–2011 from the Centers for Medicare and Medicaid Services. This source provides annual amounts for total Medicare spending, Part A (hospital) spending, and Part B (physician-directed) spending, but not spending within subcategories of Part B.[27]

For Chapters 10 and 13 on physician supply, we obtain national data on the number of active, nonfederal, patient care physicians from annual surveys by the American Medical Association.[28] For Chapter 10, we obtain Texas-specific data on active, nonfederal physicians from the Texas Medical Board and the Texas Department of State Health Services.[29] For Chapter 13, we also use data from the American Community Survey, which provides counts of total active and inactive physicians but not counts by specialty.[30]

For Chapter 11 on the receding medical malpractice tide, we obtain data on closed paid medical malpractice claims from the NPDB Public Use Data File. This dataset includes 259,941 paid claims against physicians closed from 1992 to 2012, including 197,979 "large" claims (payout > $50,000). We convert all payouts to 2010 dollars.[31]

For state adoptions of damage caps and other medical malpractice reforms, we rely on Avraham's (2014) Database of State Tort Law Reforms, version 5.1.[32]

# Misdiagnosing the Problem: Texas's Medical Malpractice Liability System in Action

## CHAPTER 3

# THE TEXAS MEDICAL MALPRACTICE INSURANCE CRISIS: SMOKE WITHOUT MUCH FIRE

## OVERVIEW

Beginning in 1999, Texas experienced a medical malpractice insurance crisis. In response to spikes in medical malpractice premiums, Texas enacted a non-economic (non-econ) cap and other tort reforms in 2003. Was there a crisis in medical malpractice *litigation* that explains the insurance crisis? This chapter provides evidence on time trends in claim frequency, payout per claim, defense costs, and total insurer costs over 1988–2005. The data present a picture of stability in most respects and moderate change in others. Adjusted for the number of physicians, the number of large paid claims (over $25,000 in 1988 dollars) was gradually declining over 1990–2004, before beginning a much steeper slide in 2005, attributable largely to the 2003 tort reforms. Controlling for inflation, payout per large paid claim was roughly flat over 1988–2004. Defense costs rose gradually but were a small portion of total cost and cannot explain the insurance crisis.

There was a mild rise in payouts around the time of the insurance crisis, but the magnitude was far too small to explain the crisis. At least in Texas, the malpractice insurance crisis appears to have largely reflected insurance market dynamics rather than changes in medical malpractice claim outcomes.

## INTRODUCTION

In the past 40 years, the United States experienced three major medical malpractice insurance crises, one each in the 1970s, the 1980s, and the 2000s. Each crisis prompted an outcry from politically influential physicians, who demanded protection from lawsuits. Legislators responded by restricting medical malpractice cases, and sometimes personal injury lawsuits of other types, in ways designed to limit claim rates and payouts. Common restrictions included caps on non-economic damages, punitive damages, and sometimes total damages; limits on contingent fees; denial of recovery of some types of damages (mostly medical costs) that were already covered by health insurance or another source; limits on joint and several liability; and requirements for experts to testify about the quality of medical care.

Texas restricted lawsuits during the first wave in the 1970s. However, in 1988, the state's supreme court ruled that the core of the reforms, a $500,000 cap on total damages in medical malpractice cases (indexed for inflation), was unconstitutional as applied to nondeath cases. However, as detailed in Chapter 2, this cap survives as applied to wrongful death cases.

Texas again faced rapidly rising premiums starting in 1999. As Figure 3.1 shows, premiums for the Texas Medical Liability Trust (TMLT), the state's largest carrier, shot up 136 percent, net of inflation, from 1999 to 2003. The average increase for all medical malpractice insurers, weighted by the number of physicians each covered, was 110 percent. These rising premiums were part of a broader national trend toward higher premiums.

Texas physicians responded to this insurance crisis by convincing the legislature to adopt a package of tort reforms and persuading Texas voters to amend the state constitution to permit the legislative reforms. We study the impact of these reforms in Chapters 7–10. In this chapter, we ask whether the smoke of the malpractice insurance crisis reflected an underlying fire in the medical malpractice liability system. Our bottom line is simple: there was no fire. Measured in a variety of ways, before and during the insurance crisis, the performance of the liability system was stable.

The theory supporting the belief that the smoke in the medical malpractice insurance market must be derived from a tort system fire

# Figure 3.1

## Changes in medical malpractice insurance premiums by Texas carrier

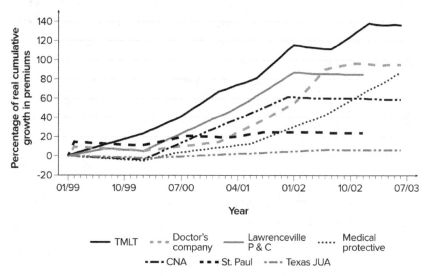

*Notes:* Percentage changes in real physician medical malpractice insurance rates for principal Texas carriers, relative to Jan. 1, 1999, based on rate filings with TDI. CNA = CNA Financial Corporation; JUA = Joint Underwriting Association; P & C = property and casualty; TDI = Texas Department of Insurance; TMLT = Texas Medical Liability Trust.

*Source:* For nominal rates, Texas Department of Insurance, "Medical Malpractice Insurance: Overview and Discussion," April 22, 2003, chart 1.

is straightforward. In reasonably competitive markets, which Texas and most other states seem to be,[33] premiums for medical malpractice coverage should reflect insurers' expected costs, which are driven principally by predicted payouts on liability claims and the expenses of defending those claims, but will also respond to expected investment income and administrative costs. Premium spikes, such as Texas observed at the end of the last decade, should therefore reflect dramatic changes in these inputs—starting with payouts. Because past and present claims provide information about likely future costs, by studying them, one should be able to identify the trends or tendencies upon which future payout spikes are based. For example, one might discover skyrocketing jury verdicts, outsize punitive damage awards, an increase in the frequency of frivolous lawsuits, a rising number of claims, or other pathologies about which tort reform groups have long complained.

There are, however, other views of the causes of insurance crises. One is that competition among carriers can cause insurance prices to spike without corresponding changes in liability costs.[34] On this view, insurers attempt to gain market share during "soft" insurance markets— characterized by expanding capacity, declining prices, and falling insurer profits—by undercutting each other's prices. Because insurers are regulated, and prices are supposed to reflect future costs, insurers who want to compete aggressively on price have an incentive to lower their loss estimates and thus underreserve. This strategy cannot be sustained indefinitely. When actual losses exceed insurers' optimistic estimates, thus depleting reported reserves, insurers have to raise prices, perhaps quickly, leading to a "hard" market. Higher prices produce high profits and enhanced reserves. At some point, price competition strengthens, and the hard market ends. Under this "insurance cycle" theory, medical malpractice insurance premiums in Texas would likely have moderated to some extent even without the 2003 tort reforms.

A related theory contends that the entire property-casualty insurance industry is subject to occasional shocks, such as disasters and other causes of large losses.[35] These losses create the need for new equity, which insurers can satisfy in the short run only by raising prices. Medical malpractice insurers limit their risks and expand their capacity to write coverage by ceding some of their risk to other insurers, called "reinsurers." Shocks that affect the price of reinsurance will drive up prices for many types of insurance, thus helping to generate a hard market. Over time, insurers and reinsurers replenish their capital, and prices revert toward long-term equilibrium levels.

The fundamental question is simple: To what extent do short-run changes in the price of liability insurance reflect underlying changes in the liability system, rather than other factors, such as insurance market cycles? There is broad agreement that liability costs drive insurance prices over the long term. But how long it takes for the long term to arrive, and the extent to which changes in liability costs drive short-term changes in insurance costs are disputed.[36]

In this chapter, we provide evidence on the link between liability system outcomes and liability insurance prices by studying the operation of the medical malpractice liability system in Texas from 1988 to 2005.

We find that claim frequency and payments were generally stable over this period. They fluctuated but with no apparent time trend. Jury verdicts, which we study in Chapter 4, also showed no strong time trend. Defense costs, which we address in Chapter 6, rose steadily over our time period but were a small portion of total cost, and a predictable one.

This evidence suggests that short-term fluctuations in medical malpractice insurance rates, even large ones, are unreliable gauges of the performance of the tort system. This should not be surprising. Legal reform aside, the main drivers of medical malpractice liability costs (including injury frequency and severity, health care costs, wages, and legal fees) are likely to change slowly and predictably. Thus, sizable short-term fluctuations in medical malpractice insurance rates are likely to reflect dynamics external to the liability system.

To assess the extent to which the smoke from medical malpractice insurance rates reflects an underlying fire in medical malpractice claim rates or litigation outcomes, it is useful to look separately at claim rates, then at payout per claim, and then at total payouts, which reflect a combination of claim rates and payout per claim.

## TIME TRENDS IN MEDICAL MALPRACTICE CLAIM RATES

Figure 3.2 shows the annual number of large paid medical malpractice claims, by closing year, from 1990 to 2005. The top line of Figure 3.2 shows the total number of paid claims, which is generally rising through 2003. However, this is not a sensible measure of changes in claim rates, if only because one should expect the volume of paid claims to rise as consumption of medical services increases. At a minimum, one should adjust for growth in the Texas population. We make this adjustment in the middle line. With it, the number of closed paid large claims is basically flat through 2000, and then it begins to fall.

During this period, the number of physicians grew faster than the population, both in Texas and nationwide. This likely led to greater use of health care services and more opportunities for patient-physician encounters that generate malpractice claims. Thus, controlling for growth in the number of physicians is likely a better adjustment than controlling for population. Adjusting for the number of physicians also

## Figure 3.2

Number of large paid claims in Texas per year by closing year

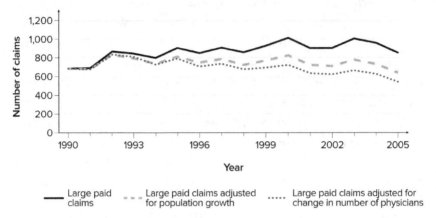

_Notes:_ Number of large paid medical malpractice claims per year from 1990 to 2005, unadjusted (top line) and adjusted for population growth (middle line) or for growth in the number of physicians (bottom line). Large paid claims = claims with payout that exceeds $25,000 (1988$).

_Source:_ Based on authors' calculations using the Texas Closed Claim Database.

makes sense if we are interested in the exposure faced by each physician, which is what should drive medical malpractice insurance premiums. That adjustment is shown in the bottom line of Figure 3.2. With it, the number of large paid claims peaks in 1992 and steadily declines after that. By 2002, large paid claims per physician are 25 percent below their 1992 level. Regression analysis confirms the visual impression that claim rates adjusted for population were roughly flat over our time period and that claim rates per physician fell.[37] Simply stated, there is no evidence of an increase in large paid claims. Adjusting for growth in the number of physicians, the opposite is true.

Insurers see claims as they come in as well as when they close. We discuss claim duration in more detail below, but on average, about two years separates an injury from the filing of a claim, and it takes another two years to resolve most claims. The spike in premiums could reflect a spike in incoming claims. Figure 3.3 explores this possibility. It parallels the analysis in Figure 3.2 but is presented in terms of the year in which claims were opened rather than when they were closed. To ensure time consistency, we limit Figure 3.3 to claims closed by the end of the seventh year after the reporting year, and we extend our data through 2010. The per year number of newly opened claims actually

# Figure 3.3

## Number of large paid claims in Texas per year by opening year

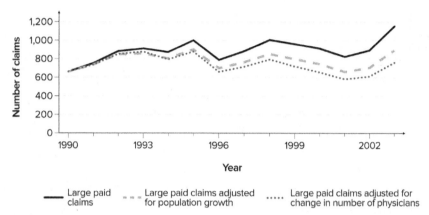

 Large paid          Large paid claims adjusted          Large paid claims adjusted for
claims               for population growth                change in number of physicians

*Notes:* Number of large paid medical malpractice claims per year from 1990 to 2003, by year claim was reported to insurer, unadjusted (top line) and adjusted for population growth (middle line) or for growth in the number of physicians (bottom line). Sample is limited to claims closed by end of year $t + 7$, where $t$ is opening year. Large paid claims = claims with payout that exceeds $25,000 (1988$).

*Source:* Based on authors' calculations using the Texas Closed Claim Database.

declined over 1998–2001, then trended modestly upward in 2002 and 2003. The premium spike thus began when the number of new claims per physician per year was well below the levels reported for 1992–1995, and falling.

Figures 3.2 and 3.3 are limited to large paid claims. But most medical malpractice claims close with little or no payout. In theory, there could have been a rise in claims that later closed with small payouts or no payouts, but that may have worried insurers as they arrived and may also have contributed to higher defense costs. We address this possibility in Figure 3.4. We rely here on a separate Texas Department of Insurance (TDI) annual reports, available from 1995 on, that encompass all closed claims covered by medical professional liability insurance, including duplicate claims (claim reports for different defendants when a plaintiff sues more than one defendant). This is a broader measure of "medical malpractice" claims than we otherwise use.

The bottom line in Figure 3.4 shows the total number of closed claims (both paid and unpaid) from 1995 to 2005.[38] Putting aside the spike in 2003, which likely reflects an effort by plaintiffs' lawyers to file new cases before the effective date of the 2003 reforms, there is a general upward trend in total claims, consistent with the rise in large paid claims shown in

# Figure 3.4

## Total claims and total claims per 100 physicians, Texas

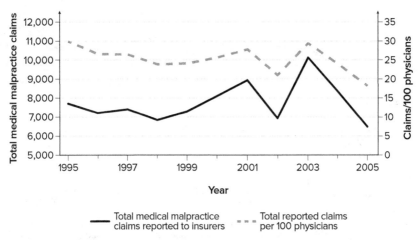

*Note:* Total (paid and unpaid) medical malpractice claims reported to insurers, and total claims per 100 physicians, including duplicate claims, from 1995 to 2005, using dataset of all claims reported under Medical Professional Liability Insurance, including unpaid claims.

*Source:* Based on authors' calculations using the Texas Closed Claim Database.

Figures 3.2 and 3.3. But the trend reverses and is slightly downward in the top line, which shows claims per 100 physicians. This too is consistent with the trends for large paid claims. In short, no matter how we slice the data, there is no rise in claims per physician, let alone a rise sufficient to spark a doubling in medical malpractice insurance premiums.

The medical malpractice insurance crisis of the early 2000s was not limited to Texas. Yet national evidence on claim rates tells a similar story. In Chapter 11, we study paid claims by physicians in all 50 states. We find no precrisis trend toward higher claim rates in states without caps on non–econ or total damages over 1992–2003.

## TIME TRENDS IN PAYOUT PER CLAIM

What about payout per claim? In theory, payout growth could have more than offset the decline in the number of large paid claims per physician. Rising payouts could have led to higher insurance premiums. In fact, payout per claim was reasonably stable as well.

# Figure 3.5

## Mean and median payout per large paid claim, Texas

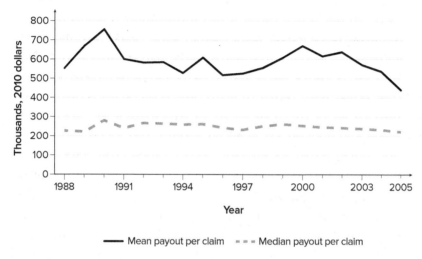

*Note:* Mean and median payout (in thousands of 2010 dollars) per large paid medical malpractice claim in Texas during 1988–2005.

*Source:* Based on authors' calculations using the Texas Closed Claim Database.

Figure 3.5 shows mean and median payout per large paid claim from 1988 to 2005. The median payouts are highly stable. There is more fluctuation in the mean but no overall trend. The mean payout per claim peaked at $755,000 in 1990, fell in the first half of the 1990s to a low of $518,000 in 1996, then rose to $669,000 in 2000, before falling again. Regression analysis confirms that there is no trend toward rising payout per claim.[39] There is no change in litigation that might account for the insurance crisis to be found here either.

Real payout per claim was stable even though health care costs, which account for a significant fraction of damages in medical malpractice and other personal injury litigation,[40] rose much faster than general consumer inflation over our sample period. One might have expected payout per claim to rise for this reason alone. In fact, no increase occurred, meaning that payouts failed to keep up with rising medical costs.

Could jury awards have been rising, which might have predicted rising future settlement payouts? No. As we discuss in Chapter 4, awards were rising slowly, and post-verdict payouts were flat.

Note that we would have found a rise in mean and median payout per claim had we considered *all* paid claims, rather than only large paid claims. The cause of this seemingly inconsistent result is the gradual disappearance of claims with small payouts. From 1995 to 2005, the number of closed paid medical malpractice claims with payouts below the "large" claim threshold fell by 38 percent, compared to a 4 percent fall in large paid claims over this period. Because the rate of small claims fell faster than the rate of large claims, this would cause median and mean payouts to increase. Thus, examining mean and median payouts for all claims is misleading. Doing so suggests that indemnity costs are rising when, in fact, as best we can tell, payouts for the same types of claims were roughly steady.

A likely explanation for the drop in small paid claims is that plaintiffs' lawyers increasingly found it impracticable to litigate claims with less severe injuries and smaller damages.[41] Because the declining frequency of small paid claims is a nationwide phenomenon,[42] a reasonable inference is that medical malpractice claims have become more expensive to pursue or less profitable in many jurisdictions and that plaintiffs' lawyers have responded to the new litigation environment by altering their client intake practices.

The changing composition of the medical malpractice caseload thus makes it perilous to accept publicly quoted statistics about rising medical malpractice payouts. When the nature of claims changes over time, an increase (or decrease) in the average payout is not meaningful unless one also addresses changes in case mix.

## TIME TRENDS IN TOTAL PAYOUTS AND INSURER COST

Since the number of large paid claims per physician was declining and payout per large paid claim was roughly stable, we would expect total payout per physician to also be stable or declining. And so it was. Figure 3.6 shows total payout per year on all large paid claims (top line). The middle line shows total payout adjusted for population growth. The bottom line adjusts for growth in the number of physicians.

Over the 1990–2004 period, there is no discernible significant trend in total payout adjusted for population growth, and there is a decline

## Figure 3.6

### Total medical malpractice payouts, Texas

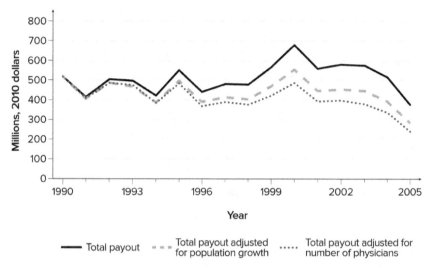

Total payout —— 　Total payout adjusted = = = 　Total payout adjusted for ·····
for population growth　　number of physicians

*Note:* Total payout (in 2010 millions of dollars) for large paid medical malpractice claims over 1990–2005, adjusted for population growth (middle line) and number of physicians (bottom line).
*Source:* Based on authors' calculations using the Texas Closed Claim Database.

in total payout per physician. Regression analysis confirms these visual impressions. The falloff in 2005 likely reflects the initial impact of the 2003 tort reforms, a subject we return to in Chapter 7. To be sure, if we focus on the period immediately before the medical malpractice insurance crisis, there is an upward trend from 1998 to 2000 (a two-year rise in total payout per physician of 29 percent). But total payout per physician in 2000 was lower than in 1990—similar to the levels in 1992, 1993, and 1995—and fell again in 2001. Yet the spike in insurance prices continued into 2003.

We discuss defense costs, which also influence insurance premiums, in Chapter 6. We note here that defense costs rose steadily during our sample period but were a modest proportion of overall insurer spending. If we add defense costs for large paid claims to total payouts on these claims, we arrive at Figure 3.7. Here, too, there is no statistically significant trend in total cost adjusted for population, but there is a statistically significant decline in total cost per physician. Including a reasonable

## Figure 3.7

Total insurer cost for large paid claims, Texas

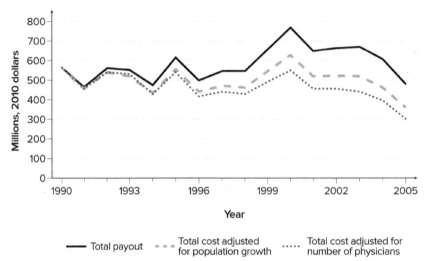

*Note:* Total payout plus defense cost (in millions of 2010 dollars) for large paid medical malpractice claims, 1990–2005, adjusted for population growth (middle line) and number of physicians (bottom line).

*Source:* Based on authors' calculations using the Texas Closed Claim Database.

estimate of the defense costs we can't directly measure (for claims closed with zero or small payment) does not affect that conclusion.

## DISCUSSION: WHY THE CRISIS?

Over 1999–2003, Texas physicians experienced a medical malpractice insurance crisis. They attributed it to a medical malpractice liability crisis and used their political clout to convince the state legislature and voters to change Texas law. In fact, no litigation crisis existed. Measured per person, total medical malpractice payouts were roughly flat over 1990–2004. Measured per physician—an appropriate measure if one is concerned with the financial impact of medical malpractice liability on physicians—total payouts declined, driven by a decline in the rate of large paid claims. In Chapter 4, we find no evidence of dramatic changes in jury awards during 1988–2005. In Chapter 6, we find that defense costs rose steadily, but gradual growth in defense spending is not the stuff from which an insurance crisis is made.

Payout per physician did rise by around 30 percent from 1998 to 2000 after being flat from 1996 to 1998. Insurers may have raised prices to reflect this actual rise. But the trend in payout per physician reversed in 2001—yet insurance premiums continued to rise. Moreover, a rise that brought payout per physician back to only about the same level as in four of the six years from 1990 to 1995 could hardly be the main driver for a larger, longer-lived crisis in medical malpractice insurance, with rates more than doubling over four years.

Nor would one expect medical malpractice insurers to assume that short-term fluctuations reflect long-term trends. Instead, they should understand the liability system well enough to know that the drivers of liability costs are likely to change slowly. The biggest drivers of malpractice claims are the rate of medical mistakes and the severity of resulting injuries. These drivers depend on the volume and mix of medical services patients receive, patients' characteristics, and technological developments, all of which change slowly. Although medical errors occur far more often than they should, there is no obvious reason why the error rate or the claim rate should spike for an entire state. Drivers of claiming behavior, such as patients' attitudes, access to counsel, wages, physicians' insurance limits, and the existence of first-party health insurance coverage, also matter but also are unlikely to experience sudden shifts. Nor, as we have seen, was there any evidence of a spike in claim rates.

Claim values should also be reasonably stable. Juries tend to be parsimonious and, according to one study, they have if anything become stingier over time.[43] As we discuss in Chapter 5, policy limits cap recoveries in most cases. Thus, outlier jury verdicts have little effect on payouts. Health spending rises faster than general inflation, but it does not spike. Defense costs rose faster than inflation during our study period, but they too do not spike. Moreover, insurers ought to be good Bayesians. When new information arrives, it should affect insurers' prior beliefs, but through an updating process that takes history into account. They should expect reasonable stability, which has been the case in the past, and not assume that a one- or two-year trend—whether up or down—will continue indefinitely when a longer look at the past shows similar fluctuations.

What caused the medical malpractice insurance crisis? We can only speculate. We do know that many insurance markets, including medical malpractice, tend to cycle from soft markets, in which insurance is underpriced, to hard markets, where it is overpriced.[44] And the medical malpractice insurance crisis was not limited to Texas. As of 2004, the American Medical Association listed 21 states, including Texas, as having medical malpractice insurance crises.[45] Insurance prices also rose rapidly around this time for many other coverage lines, not just medical malpractice.[46] Thus, to explain the Texas medical malpractice insurance crisis, one should look for causes within the insurance industry, rather than causes specific to medical malpractice or to Texas.

One obvious candidate is the returns that insurers earn by investing the "float" (i.e., the funds that insurers hold from the time that policyholders pay premiums until the later time that claims are paid).[47] Insurer returns were low in the late 1990s and early 2000s.[48] Reinsurance prices also matter. If reinsurance prices change rapidly, primary insurers have to raise their prices quickly as well. Put simply, the cost of primary coverage depends in part on the cost of reinsurance. Prices for medical malpractice reinsurance rose by 50 to 100 percent early in the 2001–2005 hard market.[49] The increase is thought to have had several causes, only one of which was medical malpractice losses. Catastrophes that depleted reinsurers' capital, including the terrorist attacks of September 11, 2001, and Tropical Storm Allison, also in 2001, were another. A third was underreserving during the prior soft market, which led to "adverse development" (rising expected payouts on older policies) in property casualty markets during this period in general, not only for medical malpractice policies.

A fourth explanation involves the long-tail nature of medical malpractice insurance.[50] When the lag between receipt of claims and payout can extend forward many years, small changes in loss expectations or expected investment returns can exert significant upward or downward pressure on prices. Medical liability insurance also faces other risks, ranging from changes in medical technology to changes in public expectations, which accentuate the uncertainty of actuarial estimates. Still, changes in technology and expectations are also likely to be gradual, and thus should not lead to large price spikes.

A fifth consideration is that many medical malpractice insurers are undiversified, single-line companies sponsored by state and local medical societies. In Texas, the Texas Medical Liability Trust has more than a 50 percent market share in covering physicians. Member-owned insurers may feel pressure to keep premiums low by estimating future losses on the low side. Then, to compensate for past underpricing, they must charge more when their reserves are depleted. To the extent that other insurers follow their lead, the result may be industry-wide premium swings.

A sixth, Texas-specific source of underpricing could have been the limited tort reforms that Texas adopted in 1995. As part of those reforms, the legislature instructed TDI to estimate insurers' savings and required rate rollbacks designed to pass these savings on to policyholders. The TDI-imposed rollbacks expired in 2000. If the rollbacks overstated actual savings, a correction would have been inevitable.

The Texas medical malpractice insurance rate spike during 1999–2003 could then have reflected a combination of factors, including insurers catching up for past underpricing; insurers overestimating future losses by relying heavily on then-recent loss experiences from 1998 to 2000; TDI overestimating the impact of the 1995 reforms; low investment returns; and unrelated reinsurer losses, leading to high reinsurance rates.

Is the combination of rapidly rising premiums and the absence of an underlying medical malpractice liability crisis unique to the 2000s? We cannot answer that question with our dataset, but the likely answer is no. For the prior medical malpractice insurance crisis, during the mid-1980s, the Texas State Board of Insurance in 1987 found no strong time trend in payouts from 1983 to 1986.[51]

In a tolerably competitive medical malpractice insurance market, which Texas appears to have, insurance premiums should reflect insurers' costs over the long run. But in the short- and medium-term swings, even large ones, can be mostly disconnected from true changes in expected medical malpractice liability. One needs to understand what is happening to claim outcomes before deciding on policy responses to those premium swings. Otherwise, the reforms may bear little relationship to the problem they seek to remedy. In Texas, the political driver for the 2003 reforms was a presumed crisis in medical malpractice liability. That crisis never existed.

## CHAPTER 4

# HAIRCUTS: JURY VERDICTS AND POST-VERDICT PAYOUTS

## OVERVIEW

In this chapter, we study the difference between jury verdicts and actual payouts following a plaintiff verdict, during the period prior to Texas's adoption of a cap on non-economic damages. We find that most plaintiffs receive "haircuts" relative to jury awards. Seventy-four percent of plaintiffs received a payout less than the "adjusted verdict" (jury verdict plus pre- and post-judgment interest), 20 percent received the adjusted verdict (within ±2 percent), and 6 percent received more than the adjusted verdict. Overall, plaintiffs received a mean (median) per case haircut of 29 percent (19 percent) relative to the adjusted verdict. The aggregate haircut for the sum of all payouts relative to the sum of adjusted verdicts was 49 percent. The larger the verdict, the more likely and the larger the haircut. Insurance policy limits are the most important factor explaining haircuts. Damage caps are also important, but defendants often paid substantially less than the "adjusted allowed verdict" after these caps. Punitive damage awards are often unpaid. Even in tried cases, out-of-pocket payments by physicians are uncommon, rarely large, and usually not related to punitive damage awards. Most cases settle, presumably in the shadow of the outcome after trial. But that outcome is the post-verdict payout, not the jury award.

## INTRODUCTION

Although the vast majority of paid cases result from a settlement rather than a trial, juries and jury verdicts occupy center stage in the political debate over tort reform and in academic analyses of the tort system. In the political arena, critics claim that juries are out of control, and that they are prone to dispense unjustified blockbuster verdicts, especially against defendants with deep pockets. These critics argue that this "lawsuit lottery" encourages defendants to settle nonmeritorious cases and imposes a "tort tax" on the economy. Conversely, defenders argue that juries generally make reasonable decisions on liability and that blockbuster verdicts are both rare and often reduced by judicial oversight.

Legal scholars also assume that most cases are resolved in the shadow of jury awards. An extensive literature models parties' settlement decisions as actions taken in light of predicted trial outcomes. As one set of scholars noted, "jury trial verdicts form the basis of what we think we know about tort litigation."[52] However, focusing on jury verdicts can be misleading if post-verdict payouts differ significantly from jury awards. Downward departures can result from settlement dynamics, influenced by insurance policy limits, statutory damage caps, and judicial oversight. Upward departures can also result from settlement dynamics.

We study here Texas medical malpractice cases with plaintiff jury verdicts, decided before Texas adopted a cap on non-economic (non-econ) damages in 2003. We consider the effects of the non-econ cap in Chapter 7. We find that most jury awards, especially larger ones, receive a substantial haircut before they are paid. In particular we note the following:

- Of the 350 plaintiff verdict cases in our dataset, 258 cases (74 percent) had payments less than their "adjusted verdicts" (jury award plus pre- and post-judgment interest), 71 cases (20 percent) had payments roughly equal to their adjusted verdicts (within ±2 percent), and 21 cases (6 percent) had payments greater than 102 percent of their adjusted verdicts.
- Across all 350 cases, plaintiffs received total adjusted verdicts of $905 million but payouts of only $461 million, for an aggregate haircut (total payouts/total of adjusted verdicts) of 49 percent.

- The larger the adjusted verdict, the more likely and the larger the "haircut" (the percentage difference between the payout and the adjusted verdict). For cases with adjusted verdicts less than $100,000, 19 percent of plaintiffs received haircuts, with a mean per case haircut (for cases with haircuts) of 4 percent. For cases with adjusted verdicts greater than $2.5 million, 95 percent of plaintiffs received haircuts, with a mean per case haircut of 55 percent.

- Policy limits are by far the most important factor in explaining haircuts. Caps on punitive damages and on damages in death cases and judicial oversight also matter, but they explain a much smaller fraction of the aggregate haircut. However, haircuts were common even when "adjusted allowed verdicts" (the adjusted verdict, after applying caps or judicial reductions in the award) were within policy limits.

- In cases tried to plaintiff verdicts, out-of-pocket payments by physicians were rare, usually small, and unrelated to punitive damage awards. Physicians made out-of-pocket payments in only 12 cases; in only one did the physician pay punitive damages.

- In the 21 "verdict bonus" cases, where the plaintiff received more than 102 percent of the adjusted verdict, the bonuses were small—a total of $3 million and a mean (median) of $132,000 ($54,000).

## LITERATURE REVIEW

The empirical literature on payouts following jury verdicts is modest. Table 4.1 summarizes the prior studies. All have important weaknesses. Two studies date from the early 1980s; the more recent studies have small datasets; three studies cover only larger verdicts; and two (including the only one that includes smaller verdicts) rely on verdicts reported by plaintiffs' lawyers to a trade source, the *Jury Verdict Reporter*. This is likely to lead to bias toward larger reported verdicts. None has a comprehensive source for post-verdict payouts.

## Table 4.1

Summary of past research on jury verdicts and post-verdict payouts

| Author | Minimum verdict size | Case type | No. of verdicts (source) | No. of known payouts | Source for payouts |
|---|---|---|---|---|---|
| Vidmar, MacKillop, and Lee (2006) | $1 million (nominal) | Medical malpractice | 50 (hand collected) | 54 | Florida public medical malpractice data |
| Vidmar (2002) | $500,000 (nominal) | Medical malpractice | 202 (hand collected) | 22 | Pennsylvania patient compensation fund |
| Broder (1986) | $1 million (nominal) | Various | 472 (*Jury Verdict Reporter*) | 198 | Surveys |
| Shanley and Peterson (1983) | No minimum | Various | 747 (*Jury Verdict Reporter*) | 456 | Surveys |

*Sources:* Ivy E. Broder, "Characteristics of Million Dollar Awards: Jury Verdicts and Final Disbursements," *Justice System Journal* 11, no. 3 (1986): 349–59, 382–87; Michael G. Shanley and Mark A. Peterson, *Comparative Justice: Civil Jury Verdicts in San Francisco and Cook Counties, 1959–1980*, No. R-3006-ICJ (RAND Corporation, 1983); Neil Vidmar, "Juries and Jury Verdicts in Medical Malpractice Cases: Implications for Tort Reform in Pennsylvania," unpublished report, 2002; Neil Vidmar, Kara MacKillop, and Paul Lee, "Million Dollar Medical Malpractice Cases in Florida: Post-verdict and Pre-suit Settlements," *Vanderbilt Law Review* 59, no. 4 (2006): 1343–81.

## OUR DATASET

The dataset we use for this chapter includes details on jury awards, including the amounts of economic, non-economic, and punitive damages, and also post-verdict payouts, for 350 cases with pro-plaintiff jury verdicts over 1988–2005. Some claim reports include pre-judgment interest. For those that do not, we estimate pre-judgment interest based on Texas statutory rules. We also estimate post-judgment interest for all claims based on statutory rules. The sum of award plus pre-judgment interest plus post-judgment interest is the "adjusted verdict." This is the amount to which a plaintiff is entitled, before applying damage caps and any judicial reduction of the award.

We have information on insurance policy limits for the primary policy for the "reporting" defendant, but not for other defendants or for any additional insurance coverage the defendant may have under another policy. See Chapter 5 for details. Thus we can estimate the impact of policy limits only for reporting defendants and only in cases with payout by only one insurer.

During our study period, Texas law capped the sum of damages plus pre-judgment interest in wrongful death cases. It also separately capped punitive damages. Of the 84 death cases in our sample, 28 involved adjusted verdicts that exceeded the death cap. Punitive damages were awarded in 28 jury verdict cases; 10 of these awards exceeded the punitive cap. Three involved very large awards (from $13 million to $76 million, before interest). Most of these awards exceeded the punitives cap, and none of the above-cap amounts were paid. As noted previously, we winsorize these awards at the level of the next-largest punitive award, $4.9 million. That is, we treat the three very large awards as if the award was $4.9 million. The non-econ cap applies to suits filed after September 1, 2003. Only three jury verdict cases in our dataset were filed after this date. In all three, the non-econ award was below the non-econ cap, so this cap does not affect our analysis.

In counting the number of cases with haircuts, verdict bonuses (payout greater than adjusted verdict), or neither, we treat cases with payouts within plus or minus 2 percent of their adjusted verdicts as zero-haircut cases. So, a case with a haircut is a case where payout is less than 0.98 × adjusted verdict, and a case with a verdict bonus is a case where payout is greater than 1.02 × adjusted verdict. In analyzing the factors that explain haircut size, we typically exclude the verdict bonus cases and focus on the 329 jury verdicts with either a haircut or zero haircut. Chapter 2 provides summary statistics for the jury verdict cases in our dataset.

## BASIC FINDINGS ON PLAINTIFF JURY VERDICTS

*Time trends.* Although there was considerable year-by-year fluctuation in mean and median adjusted verdicts, we did not find a time trend. Figure 4.1 shows mean (top line) and median (bottom line) adjusted verdicts for all plaintiff verdict cases, as well as the mean adjusted verdict excluding the 19 cases with real adjusted verdicts over $10 million (middle line). Excluding these cases substantially dampens year-to-year

# Figure 4.1

## Mean and median adjusted verdicts over time, Texas

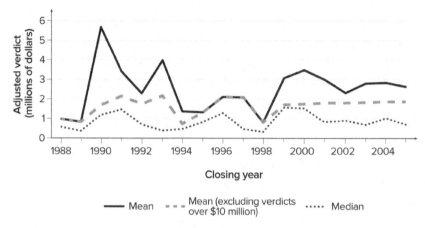

*Notes:* Annual mean (all cases), mean excluding 19 verdicts over $10 million, and median adjusted verdicts for 350 large (payout > $25,000 [1988$]) paid medical malpractice cases with plaintiff jury verdicts over 1988–2005. Adjusted verdict is trial verdict (by jury or judge) plus reported or imputed pre- and post-judgment interest.

*Source:* Based on authors' calculations using the Texas Closed Claim Database.

fluctuation in the mean and narrows the spread between the mean and median. The large difference between mean and median adjusted verdicts is consistent with other studies of medical malpractice trials.[53] Regression analysis confirms the visual impression from Figure 4.1—there was no statistically significant trend in either mean or median verdicts.

*Economic, non-econ, and punitive awards.* Juries award separate amounts for economic damages, non-econ damages, and punitive damages. Each case may include one damage type, two types, or all three types. Table 4.2 summarizes the mean, median, and frequency for each damage award type, total damages, interest, and adjusted verdict. In regression analysis, we find no discernible evidence of time trends in awards, broken down by type of damages. This is consistent with the lack of evidence of a discernible time trend in overall adjusted verdicts.

About 83 percent of cases include an award of economic damages, 84 percent include non-econ damages; 68 percent (237 cases) include both. Punitive damages are far less common—they are awarded in only 8 percent of cases. These data for Texas are consistent with prior research,

# Table 4.2

## Breakdown of adjusted verdicts, Texas

| Damages | Damages | | | | Interest | Adjusted verdict |
|---|---|---|---|---|---|---|
| | Economic | Non-econ | Punitive | Total | | |
| Mean | $793 | $1,069 | $124 | $1,986 | $601 | $2,587 |
| Median | $92 | $338 | $0 | $589 | $148 | $790 |
| Total | $277,593 | $374,291 | $43,304 | $695,188 | $210,238 | $905,425 |
| No. of cases (percentage of cases) | 292 (83.4%) | 295 (84.3%) | 28 (8%) | 350 (100%) | 350 (100%) | 350 (100%) |

*Notes:* Mean, median, and total damage awards, separated by type of damages, pre- and post-judgment interest, and adjusted verdict, for 350 large (payout > $25,000 [1988$]) paid medical malpractice cases with plaintiff jury verdicts over 1988–2005. Adjusted verdict is trial verdict (by jury or judge) plus reported or imputed pre- and post-judgment interest.

*Source:* Based on authors' calculations using the Texas Closed Claim Database.

finding that punitive damages are awarded in about 5 percent of medical malpractice cases, similar to other tort trials.[54] Punitive-damage awards against nursing homes are reasonably common (7 of 23, or 30 percent), but such awards are less common against physicians (13 of 252, or 5 percent). On average, non-econ damages are larger than economic damages. In regressions, we find a strong positive correlation between economic and non-econ damages when both are awarded, and between punitive damages and compensatory (economic + non-econ) damages.

## POST-VERDICT HAIRCUTS

### Summary Statistics

We turn now to the core of this chapter—the considerable gap between adjusted verdicts and payouts and its causes. Post-verdict haircuts are common and often large. Adjusted verdicts for our 350 plaintiff verdict cases totaled $905 million, while payouts totaled $461 million, for an aggregate dollar haircut of 49 percent. In single-payer cases, percentage haircuts were similar in cases with physicians as defendants and cases with (often deeper-pocketed) institutional defendants—hospitals or nursing homes.

### Haircuts and Verdict Size

Haircuts are typically small for smaller verdicts but substantial for larger ones. Figure 4.2 provides a scatter plot of the natural logarithm (abbreviated as *ln*) of adjusted verdict versus *ln*(payout). In this book, we take logarithms of amounts, such as verdicts and payouts, that would otherwise show a strong skew, driven by a small number of large values. Taking logarithms also allows regression coefficients to be interpreted as approximate percentage changes. The figure includes a 45-degree line indicating payout equals adjusted verdict, plus a regression line for *ln*(payout) as dependent variable, with *ln*(adjusted verdict), year, and a constant term as independent variables.

For small verdicts, payout and adjusted verdict are similar. However, as adjusted verdict increases, so does the expected haircut, and fewer cases are paid in full. Smaller adjusted verdicts are often paid in full. But as the adjusted verdict increases, so does the predicted haircut. For an adjusted verdict of $1 million, the predicted payout is $607,000, and thus a haircut of $393,000, or around 39 percent. For an adjusted verdict of $10 million, the expected payout is $3.5 million, and thus a haircut of $6.5 million, or 65 percent. On average, a 1 percent increase in adjusted verdict predicts only a 0.76 percent increase in payout.

In regression analysis, we examined the impact of policy limits in single-payer cases. Policy limits have no statistically significant impact on payouts below the policy limits, but they are an important constraint on above-limits payouts.

Table 4.3 provides details on the relationships among verdict size, probability of haircut, and expected haircut size. The larger the adjusted verdict, the more likely and larger the haircut.

Figure 4.3 shows the distribution of payouts, as a fraction of the adjusted verdict, for four different adjusted verdict ranges. The bottom two charts show results for adjusted verdicts of $1 million–$5 million and greater than $5 million. In both, payouts equal to or greater than adjusted verdicts are rare. There is a large spread of payouts at various fractions of the adjusted verdict, including small fractions of the adjusted verdict. For cases with adjusted verdicts over $5 million, 59 percent of the plaintiffs received half of the adjusted verdict or less.

## Figure 4.2

### Adjusted verdicts versus payouts, Texas

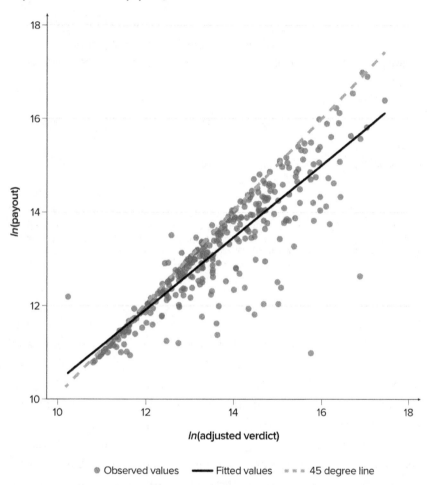

*Notes:* Scatterplot of *ln*(payout) versus *ln*(adjusted verdict) for 350 large (payout > $25,000 [1988$]) paid medical malpractice cases with plaintiff jury verdicts over 1988–2005. Dashed line is 45-degree line at which payout = adjusted verdict. Solid fitted line is from regression of *ln*(payout) versus *ln*(adjusted verdict), year, and constant term. The fitted line assumes a mean value for the year variable. The slope of the fitted line (i.e., the regression coefficient of *ln*[adjusted verdict]) is 0.76 (*t* = 28.1). Adjusted verdict is trial verdict (by jury or judge) plus reported or imputed pre- and post-judgment interest.

*Source:* Based on authors' calculations using the Texas Closed Claim Database.

## Table 4.3

Probability and size of haircut by size of adjusted verdict, Texas

| Adjusted verdict | Number of cases in range | Probability of haircut (percent) | Mean per case haircut (percent) | Aggregate haircut for all cases in range (percent) |
|---|---|---|---|---|
| $25,000–$200,000 | 65 | 42% | 6.8% | 4.4% |
| $200,000–$500,000 | 66 | 64% | 17% | 12% |
| $500,000–$1 million | 69 | 78% | 28% | 28% |
| $1 million–$2.5 million | 63 | 83% | 32% | 33% |
| $2.5 million–$5 million | 41 | 95% | 48% | 48% |
| >$5 million | 46 | 96% | 56% | 56% |
| **Total** | **350** | **74%** | **29%** | **49%** |

*Notes:* Number of cases, percentage with a haircut, per case mean of the haircut, and aggregate haircut for different ranges of adjusted verdicts, for 350 large (payout > $25,000 [1988$]) paid medical malpractice cases with plaintiff jury verdicts over 1988–2005. Monetary amounts are in 2010 dollars.

*Source:* Based on authors' calculations using the Texas Closed Claim Database.

### Time Trends

In regression analyses, we find evidence that the per case haircut increased substantially over the time period of our study, particularly in multipayer cases. A principal reason appears to be the decline in real policy limits that we discuss in Chapter 5. In a regression that controls for policy limits, the coefficient on a time trend variable shrinks and becomes statistically insignificant. Another possible reason, suggested to us by Texas medical malpractice lawyers, may be the trend, during our sample period, for Texas appellate courts to become more pro-defendant. This could increase the salience of a defendant's threat to appeal and thus produce larger haircuts in post-verdict settlements, including below-limits haircuts.

## REASONS FOR HAIRCUTS

We now turn to quantifying the factors that cause haircuts during the period before Texas adopted a non-econ cap. These factors include policy limits, statutory caps on damages, judicial oversight, and other

# Figure 4.3

## Percentage of adjusted verdicts paid by verdict size, Texas

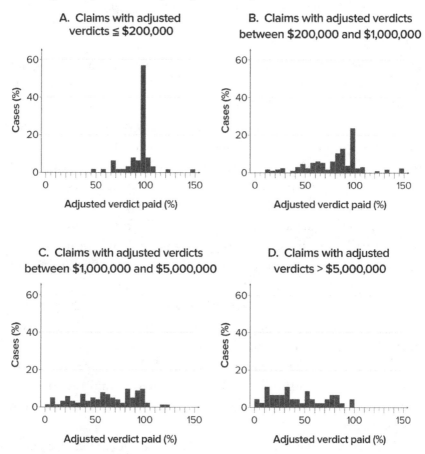

*Notes:* Distribution of percentage of adjusted verdict paid by adjusted verdict size, for 350 large paid medical malpractice cases with plaintiff jury verdicts over 1988–2005. Panel A is for cases with adjusted verdict of $200,000 or less; Panel B is for cases with adjusted verdict between $200,000 and $1 million; Panel C is for cases with adjusted verdict between $1 million and $5 million; and Panel D is for cases with adjusted verdict greater than $5 million. The rightmost bar in Panel A and Panel B shows all cases with payout greater than or equal to 150 percent of the adjusted verdict. Adjusted verdict is trial verdict (by jury or judge) plus reported or imputed pre- and post-judgment interest.

*Source:* Based on authors' calculations using the Texas Closed Claim Database.

settlement-related factors. Of these, policy limits are by far the most important. We will see in Chapter 7 that the cap on non-economic damages is also important in cases that are subject to it.

### Judicial Oversight

Judges exercise ex-post oversight over jury decisions. They may grant motions for directed verdicts, remittitur, or judgment notwithstanding the verdict (JNOV). They may also reverse jury verdicts on appeal. Legal scholars have emphasized the importance of this oversight in constraining jury discretion, especially the potential for judges to reduce or reverse very large verdicts. Our dataset lets us quantify the effect of remittitur and say a little bit about JNOV and appellate reversal.

*Remittitur.* Remittitur, which involves the judge reducing the jury verdict, is an infrequent source of haircuts. Judges reduced jury verdicts in 16 of the 350 verdicts in our sample (4.6 percent). Remittitur is concentrated in cases in which economic damages are a small proportion of total damages. The mean (median) remittitur was $995,000 ($198,000); the mean (median) per case remittitur was 26 percent (20 percent). Overall, remittitur reduced adjusted verdicts by $16 million (3.6 percent of the aggregate haircut across all cases). However, the practical importance of remittitur was likely far smaller, since the payouts in most cases with remittiturs were less than the postremittitur amounts. Thus, much of the remitted amounts might not have been collected in any event.

*JNOV.* Our dataset includes one JNOV case following a plaintiff jury verdict; we do not treat this as a plaintiff verdict case. There may have been other JNOV cases that are not in our dataset because the defendants paid less than $25,000 (nominal).

*Appellate reversal.* Our dataset includes two appellate reversals of a plaintiff verdict (one of which had already been reduced by remittitur). In these two cases, the total adjusted verdicts were $21.4 million, and defendants paid $6.9 million of this amount, for an aggregate haircut of 68 percent. Thus, appellate reversal is potentially responsible for up to $14.5 million (3.2 percent) of the aggregate haircut, depending on how much of these awards would otherwise have been paid.

Even if appellate reversal is infrequent, the risk of reversal could affect post-verdict settlements. Defendants' ability to delay payment through appeal, while imposing legal costs on plaintiffs, could also contribute to haircuts even when the risk of reversal is small.

*Summary of judicial oversight.* To summarize, the direct effect of judicial oversight can explain only about 7 percent of the aggregate dollar haircut. Despite the attention that researchers have devoted to judicial oversight of tort verdicts, the practical importance of that oversight in medical malpractice cases is limited.

### Death Cap and Punitives Cap

*Death cap.* Texas capped the sum of compensatory damages and pre-judgment interest in wrongful death cases at $1.8 million in 2010 dollars. (The cap is adjusted for inflation.) Our dataset includes 84 wrongful death cases. We can only estimate the impact of this cap because it does not apply to medical expenses, and our dataset does not break out these expenses. We assumed that none of the economic damages in wrongful death cases were for medical expenses; this will overestimate the cap's effect. The death cap reduced the adjusted verdict in 28 of the 84 wrongful death cases, by a total of $60.3 million (34 percent). Thus, this cap can explain roughly 13 percent of the aggregate haircut. However, in 8 of the 28 cases in which the cap applied (representing $18.5 million of the reduction in potential payout), the payout was less than 90 percent of the adjusted allowed verdict. Thus, some of the above-cap adjusted verdict might not have been collected in any case.

*Punitives cap.* Texas had a statutory cap on punitive damages during our sample period. After we winsorize three cases with very large, unpaid punitive damage awards to the level of the next-largest award ($4.9 million), total punitive damage awards were $137 million in 28 cases. The more generous pre-1995 punitives cap applied to 17 cases, and the stricter post-1995 cap applied to the other 11 cases. The punitives cap reduced the adjusted verdict attributable to punitive damages in 10 of the 28 cases, by a total of $10.5 million (7.7 percent).[55] Thus, the cap can explain roughly 2 percent of the aggregate haircut. The actual effect of the punitives cap is likely smaller than this because plaintiffs often collected less than the adjusted allowed verdict. Thus, some or most of the punitive damages that exceeded the punitives cap would likely not have been collected in any event.

To summarize, the death and punitives caps taken together reduced allowed adjusted verdicts by $71 million (roughly 16 percent of the aggregate haircut). However, as we discuss below, in some of the cases to which these caps apply, policy limits and other factors would likely have prevented plaintiffs from fully collecting the pre-cap adjusted verdict, which would reduce the real-world impact of these caps on payouts.

### Policy Limits

Plaintiffs in medical malpractice cases often settle at policy limits.[56] To quantify the influence of policy limits on observed haircuts and actual payouts, we limit our analysis to "single-payer" cases (one paying defendant, and payment only from that defendant's primary insurance policy). These are the only cases for which we have full information about policy limits.[57] Of the 247 single-payer cases with pro-plaintiff jury verdicts, 93 (38 percent) have adjusted verdicts greater than the policy limits (adjusted verdict > limits). Of these 93 cases, 80 are against physicians.

Figure 4.4 displays the relationship between policy limits and haircuts for these 247 single-payer cases.[58] We break the observations into below-limits and above-limits cases, and we provide separate best-fit lines for each group, from a regression of per case haircut against *ln*(adjusted verdict/limits), year, and a constant term. Figure 4.4 shows a gradual increase in expected percentage haircut as the adjusted verdict approaches the policy limits, and a much steeper increase once the adjusted verdict exceeds the policy limits. Plaintiffs simply have a hard time collecting amounts that exceed policy limits. In the aggregate, plaintiffs collect, on average, 87 percent of the adjusted verdict to the extent that the adjusted verdict is below limits but only 15 percent of the aggregate above-limits amounts.

Figure 4.5 provides a different perspective on the collectibility of adjusted verdicts in above-limits cases, focusing on payouts instead of haircuts. It shows, for the 93 above-limits, single-payer cases, a histogram of the frequency of different payout to limits ratios. As Figure 4.5 reflects, 29 percent (27/93) of above-limits single-payer cases had payouts between

## Figure 4.4

### Effect of policy limits on haircuts, Texas

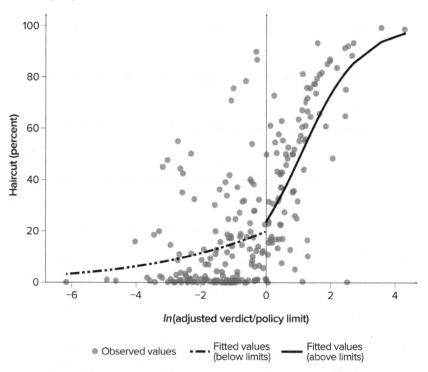

*Notes:* Figure shows per case percentage haircut (the percentage of the adjusted verdict that is not paid) versus *In*(adj. verdict/policy limits), plus best-fit lines from separate below-limits and above-limits regressions for 247 large (payout > $25,000 [1988$]) paid, single payer medical malpractice cases with plaintiff jury verdicts and zero or positive haircuts over 1988–2005. Adjusted verdict is trial verdict (by jury or judge) plus reported or imputed pre- and post-judgment interest.

*Source:* Based on authors' calculations using the Texas Closed Claim Database.

95 and 105 percent of policy limits. A majority of the above-limits cases (48/93, or 52 percent) resulted in payouts at or below policy limits.

Here are two examples of single-payer cases that settled at policy limits abstracted from the Texas Closed Claim Database (TCCD). These cases illustrate the powerful effect that policy limits can have on payouts.

- Case 7200012 (injury 1980; trial 1989). Brain damage to 55-year-old. Adjusted verdict of $24.8 million in 2010 dollars; settled for the physician's policy limit of $334,000 in 2010 dollars ($200,000 limit in nominal dollars).

# Figure 4.5

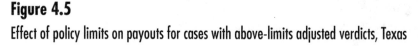

Effect of policy limits on payouts for cases with above-limits adjusted verdicts, Texas

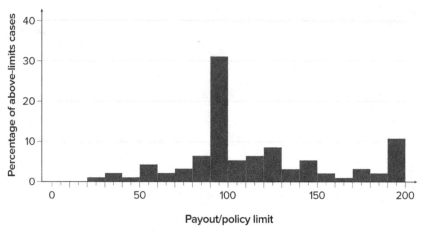

*Notes:* Percentage of cases in the indicated payout/limit ratio ranges for 93 large (payout > $25,000 [1988$]), paid, single-payer medical malpractice cases with adjusted plaintiff jury verdicts greater than policy limits over 1988–2005. Last bar includes all above-limits cases with payout of twice policy limits or more. Adjusted verdict is trial verdict (by jury or judge) plus reported or imputed pre- and post-judgment interest.

*Source:* Based on authors' calculations using the Texas Closed Claim Database.

- Case 18800505 (injury 1989; trial 1993). Injury to a 44-year-
  old. Adjusted verdict of $2.2 million in 2010 dollars; settled
  for the physician's policy limit of $147,000 in 2010 dollars
  ($100,000 limit in nominal dollars).

Cases like these make it clear that policy limits strongly affect payouts in above-limits cases. But how should we allocate "credit" for haircuts when there is more than one reason why payout is less than the adjusted verdict? For example, if both a damages cap and policy limits would each separately reduce the payout, which should be applied first? And how does applying one factor first affect the reduction attributable to the second? To answer these questions, we constructed two estimates. In the first, we use a "caps-first" approach in which we first estimate the effect of damage caps, and then the additional effect of policy limits. In the second, we first estimate the effect of policy limits, and then the additional effect of damage caps. Table 4.4 summarizes the results of this analysis. Note that Table 4.4

## Table 4.4

Factors explaining haircuts: Caps first versus limits first, Texas

| Source of haircut | Caps first | Limits first |
|---|---|---|
| Policy limits (for the limits-first approach) | — | 87.7% |
| Judicial oversight | 2.5% | 0.2% |
| Death and punitive caps | 9.2% | 0.6% |
| Policy limits (for the caps-first approach) | 76.2% | — |
| Other factors below limits | 12.1% | 11.5% |
| **Total** | **100%** | **100%** |

*Note:* Proportion of aggregate dollar haircut explainable by the indicated factors, using the caps-first approach (which ascribes haircuts to judicial oversight, the death and punitive damages caps, policy limits, and other factors below limits, in that order) and the limits-first approach (which ascribes haircuts to policy limits, judicial oversight, caps, and other factors below limits, in that order), for 247 large (> $25,000 [1988$]) paid, single-payer medical malpractice cases with plaintiff jury verdicts over 1988–2005.

*Source:* Based on authors' calculations using the Texas Closed Claim Database.

also shows the order in which each factor explaining haircuts is applied. That explains why "policy limits" appears twice. In the "limits-first" estimate, it is the first factor that is applied, while in the "caps-first" estimate, it comes after judicial oversight and the death and punitive caps.

The caps-first approach provides a lower bound on the impact of policy limits. Even so, we estimate that policy limits explain 76 percent of the aggregate dollar haircut in single-payer cases. The death and punitive caps explain another 9 percent, and judicial oversight explains 3 percent; the remainder has other causes.[59] The limits-first approach provides an upper bound on the effect of policy limits. Under this approach, policy limits explain 88 percent of the aggregate dollar haircut. Judicial oversight and the death and punitive caps fade in importance, with caps explaining 1 percent and judicial oversight explaining a small fraction of 1 percent of the aggregate haircut. Judicial oversight and damage caps become unimportant because they apply mostly in cases where the adjusted verdicts exceed policy limits. Two cautions: first, we will see in Chapter 7 that the non-econ cap has a more substantial effect on payouts than the death cap and the punitive damages cap. Second, these caps and judicial oversight likely play a larger role in explaining haircuts in

multipayer cases.[60] Providers' beliefs that judges will reduce large verdicts could also affect the collectibility of verdicts by inducing them to
purchase smaller insurance policies than they would otherwise carry.

### Other Factors Affecting Haircuts

We have explored the effect on haircuts of the factors we can quantify—
judicial oversight, damage caps, and policy limits. As Table 4.4 indicates,
12 percent of the aggregate dollar haircut in single-payer cases remains
unexplained using the caps-first approach, with most of this amount
coming from below-limits cases. These haircuts could have a variety of
explanations. Some plaintiffs may accept haircuts to receive faster payments or avoid the costs and risks of appeal. For example, a plaintiff
might waive pre-judgment interest, post-judgment interest, or both,
presumably because the extra effort and delay needed to collect interest
are thought not to be worthwhile.

Some below-limits haircuts could be explained by so-called high-
low agreements entered into prior to trial. In a high-low agreement, the
parties agree in advance to both an upper limit ("high") and a lower limit
("low") on the amount the defendant will pay the plaintiff. If the previously agreed-on high amount is less than the jury award, the plaintiff
will receive the high amount, but no more. And, even if the jury returns
a verdict for the defense, the plaintiff will still receive the low amount.

Defendants may sometimes bargain for a modestly below-limits payment in cases where limits are an effective cap by threatening to appeal
or otherwise delay payment. The plaintiff may prefer a below-limits payment today to an at-limits payment in the future. Such a negotiation
dynamic could help explain the pattern we observe in Figure 4.4, where
haircuts in below-limits cases tend to increase as the adjusted verdict
approaches policy limits.

## INSURER VERSUS DEFENDANT PAYMENTS ABOVE LIMITS

Who pays when a payout exceeds policy limits? How often does the
insurer pay, versus how often does the defendant make an out-of-pocket
payment? Table 4.5 addresses this question. As Table 4.5 reflects, insurer

## Table 4.5

Above-limits payments in single-payer cases, Texas

| Case type | | Insurer pays above limits | | Defendant pays out of pocket | |
|---|---|---|---|---|---|
| | | No. of cases | Amount | No. of cases | Amount |
| All | Total | | $29 million | | $3.3 million |
| | Mean (median) | 39 | $745,000 ($400,000) | 10 | $328,000 ($216,000) |
| Physician only | Total | | $19.3 million | | $1.1 million |
| | Mean (median) | 32 | $603,000 ($304,000) | 8 | $144,000 ($156,000) |

*Note:* Above-limits payments by insurers and defendants for 247 large (payout > $25,000 [1988$]) paid, single-payer medical malpractice cases with plaintiff jury verdicts over 1988–2005.

*Source:* Based on authors' calculations using the Texas Closed Claim Database.

payments above limits in all single-payer cases totaled $29 million, while out-of-pocket payments by all defendants totaled only $3.3 million. Thus, insurers paid 90 percent of the sum of above-limits and out-of-pocket payments. We discuss elsewhere the "duty to settle" dynamics that likely explain why insurers sometimes make payments above policy limits.[61]

Of the above-limits portions of the adjusted verdicts in these cases, 85 percent go unpaid, 13 percent are paid by insurers, and only 2 percent are paid by defendants. One might expect plaintiffs to collect above-limits payments more readily from institutional defendants than from physicians, but we find that insurers are the primary above-limits payers, regardless of defendant type.

### VERDICT BONUSES AND CASES WITH DEFENSE VERDICTS

Payment exceeded 102 percent of the adjusted verdict in 21 of the 350 plaintiff verdict cases (6 percent). In these verdict bonus cases, the adjusted verdicts were usually small and the bonuses were modest relative to the adjusted verdict. The mean (median) adjusted verdict in the 21 verdict bonus cases was $632,000 ($352,000) compared to an overall sample mean (median) of $2.587 million ($790,000). The mean (median) verdict bonus was $132,000 ($54,000). High-low agreements could explain some of the bonus cases—because as noted previously, the plaintiff will receive the agreed-on low amount even if this amount exceeds the jury award.

There are also 46 cases in our dataset with defense verdicts, with a mean (median) payout of $406,000 ($271,000). Many of these payouts occur very rapidly after defense verdicts, sometimes on the day of the verdict. Medical malpractice lawyers advised us that many of these quick payouts likely reflect high-low agreements. Other payouts following defense verdicts, especially those where the plaintiff appeals and the case is settled some years after trial, likely reflect settlement in the shadow of the risk of appellate reversal. Some, especially those with smaller payouts, could reflect a defense conclusion that it will be cheaper to settle than to defend the appeal.

## DISCUSSION

Texas is a useful setting for assessing jury verdicts and post-verdict payouts. It is the second-largest state by population, is often thought to be a pro-plaintiff state, and had only moderate damage caps in place during the period we studied. Texas was also declared to be in a "malpractice crisis" by the American Medical Association in 2002, and four counties in Texas were designated "judicial hellholes" by the American Tort Reform Association in the same year.[62] If there were a short list of states where one might expect to find runaway juries and soaring verdicts, Texas would be on it.

We find instead that verdicts were stable, physician out-of-pocket payments were rare, most of these payments were modest in size, and a large gap separated adjusted verdicts from payouts. Haircuts were common in cases involving all types of defendants. The larger the adjusted verdict, the more probable and larger the haircut. Haircuts increased sharply when the adjusted verdict is above policy limits. For our sample as a whole, juries awarded about twice as much as plaintiffs ultimately received.

Payments above policy limits were uncommon and came primarily from insurers. There were a few enormous verdicts, but these were generally settled for much smaller sums. Yet when Texas enacted a non-econ cap and other medical malpractice reforms in 2003, jury verdicts were central to the public debate, while payouts were not. In our view, this meant that much of the Texas debate over tort reform was based on an incomplete and potentially misleading factual foundation.

### The Sources of Post-verdict Haircuts

Legal scholars have emphasized the importance of judicial oversight (remittitur, JNOV, and appellate reversal) in controlling jury decision-making. We find, in contrast, that judicial oversight is a minor factor in explaining haircuts. To be sure, the threat of appellate reversal could account for some observed haircuts. The impact of JNOV rulings and appellate reversals may also be muted in our findings because cases in which defendants pay less than $25,000 do not make it into our dataset.

The same conclusion is true, though less dramatically, for the death and punitive damages caps that Texas had in place during this period. We do not study in this chapter the cap on non-econ damages that Texas adopted in the fall of 2003. That cap, as we discuss in Chapter 7, had a substantial impact on payouts. Still, caps of any sort will reduce recoveries only to the extent that the above-cap amounts would otherwise have been collected. Our results suggest that limits on collectibility—especially policy limits—substantially mute the real-world impact of damage caps.

### The Central Role of Policy Limits

We find that policy limits effectively cap recovery in many cases, but our data do not directly provide evidence on why they do so. Baker reports that plaintiffs' lawyers have a strong norm of not pursuing defendants' personal assets, but it is unclear where this norm came from or why it is durable.[63] Press reports suggest that some physicians employ asset-protection strategies, which could both encourage physicians to purchase policies with low limits and discourage plaintiffs from seeking to collect above limits. We asked a number of Texas medical malpractice plaintiffs' lawyers whether and when they try to collect above limits from physicians or other defendants. All agreed that they would not pursue a case against a physician if the physician's policy limits were insufficient to justify bringing the claim. Absent unusual circumstances, they treated policy limits as a hard cap on recovery. The prospect of obtaining an out-of-pocket payment was sufficiently remote that none of the lawyers routinely investigated defendant physicians' wealth.

Low policy limits thus may serve as a form of defendant self-help—a de facto cap, which is usually (though not always) effective in limiting recovery and which, if low enough, will discourage some suits altogether. Low limits can also discourage plaintiffs' lawyers from taking cases to trial, because the potential recovery may not justify the cost of the trial in dollars and lawyer time.

Policy limits may also provide a focal point for negotiating a high-low agreement. Because policy limits often cap recoveries, they provide an obvious upper bound for the high in a high-low agreement. Plaintiffs might well agree on a high somewhat below policy limits in exchange for an assured low, even if they lose at trial.

### Physician Out-of-Pocket Payments

Physicians are reported to be greatly concerned about the risk of personal financial loss, even bankruptcy, if they suffer an adverse jury verdict that exceeds their policy limits. Yet, as we show in Chapter 5, many physicians buy policies with limits that are moderate relative to likely damages, even when larger policies are readily available. The ratio of mean (median) policy limits to mean (median) adjusted verdict for single-payer cases against physicians in our dataset was only 0.9 (1.8). Low limits can also discourage suits from being brought and, if brought, from going to trial.

Physicians who buy low-limits policies are gambling that if they are hit with an above-limits verdict, they will not suffer material financial hardship. Our evidence suggests that this gamble is a sensible one. An out-of-pocket payment due to a large jury award requires a combination of events: (a) a malpractice case must be filed; (b) it must go to trial; (c) the jury must find for the plaintiff; (d) the verdict must be above limits; and, finally, (e) the physician must thereafter make an out-of-pocket payment. Even if the first four factors are present, physicians *still* face limited risk. Of the 121 cases with an above-limits jury verdict against a physician, only 11 led to an out-of-pocket payment, with a mean (median) payment of $126,000 ($103,000).[64] The risk of an out-of-pocket payment for cases settled without a trial is also quite small, as we discuss in Chapter 5.

These facts suggest that there can be reasons for states to require minimum policy limits for physicians. A number of states (but not Texas) have financial responsibility laws that specify a minimum level of malpractice insurance that physicians must purchase. In other areas where defendants often cannot pay damages out of pocket, including auto accidents and home construction, states often mandate minimum insurance levels. Without such rules, to the extent that physicians can carry low limits and yet avoid paying out of pocket, the medical malpractice liability system will provide neither compensation nor effective deterrence. Alternatively, physicians could be required to disclose to their patients how much medical malpractice insurance they carry, or state legislators could enact a patient compensation fund.

### Damage Caps

There has been great controversy over caps on damages in medical malpractice cases, especially caps on non-econ and punitive damages. Texas adopted a $250,000 non-econ cap (not adjusted for inflation) in 2003, near the end of our sample period. Texas also capped punitive damages throughout our sample period and tightened its punitives cap in 1995.

However, caps will reduce recoveries only to the extent that the above-cap amounts would otherwise have been collected. The de facto caps created by policy limits will thus mute the impact of damage caps on payouts. In our dataset, Texas's death and punitives caps explain a moderate fraction of the aggregate dollar haircut in single-payer cases using a caps-first approach but a much smaller fraction using a limits-first approach. Moreover, as we describe in Chapter 5, mean and median physician policy limits fell substantially over our sample period, which implies that policy limits became an increasingly strict constraint on recoveries.

### Bargaining in the Shadow of Posttrial Payout

Like other civil claims, most medical malpractice claims are resolved without trials. It is commonly believed that parties "bargain in the shadow of the law"—that is, in the shadow of the expected trial outcome. The conventional wisdom—and a standard assumption in the theoretical literature modeling tort outcomes—is that the present value of a settlement should reflect the present value of the expected outcome at trial.[65] Tort reformers accordingly assert that large verdicts, even if infrequent, increase the "bargaining floor" for future claims.

We find, however, that jury verdicts routinely exceed the amounts ultimately paid to resolve cases. Insurers and plaintiffs' lawyers are repeat players and surely understand this dynamic. They should therefore base pretrial settlements on expected post-trial payouts, rather than expected verdicts. Blockbuster verdicts should affect settlements only to the extent that these verdicts are collectible—which, our data show, they often are not. That is, we would expect cases to settle in the shadow of *what the plaintiff can expect to collect if the case is tried*. This is often a smaller amount—sometimes much smaller—than the expected jury award.

Although tort reform advocates focus on damage caps, and legal scholars focus on judicial oversight, most of the action in post-verdict payouts lies elsewhere. At least in single-payer cases, policy limits are the source of most of the haircut dollars. The parties surely bargain in the shadow of the jury, but juries cannot force payouts in excess of policy limits.

A principal conclusion from our research is that studying jury verdicts without taking into account post-verdict haircuts gives a misleading picture of the performance of the tort system. So does studying damage caps and judicial oversight without attending to policy limits and other sources of haircuts. The tort reform debate has thus been based on incomplete information. Proposed reforms should take into account the gap between payouts and verdicts. The academic literature on how jury verdicts affect claiming and settlement decisions also needs to take post-verdict haircuts into account.

CHAPTER 5

# IMPACT OF POLICY LIMITS IN CASES AGAINST PHYSICIANS

## OVERVIEW

How do policy limits affect payouts in cases involving physicians, including settled cases? How much medical malpractice insurance coverage do physicians buy—and are there any trends in the policy limits they choose? How often do physicians make out-of-pocket payments? For settled cases, much as we find in Chapter 4 for jury verdicts, policy limits often act as a cap on recovery; we find a pronounced spike in the number of cases resolved with a payment at exact limits. Out-of-pocket payments are rare, even for physicians who carry policies with quite low limits. Many physicians carry much less insurance than the $1 million coverage per claim that is conventionally assumed. Finally, real policy limits declined steadily over our sample period.

## INTRODUCTION

In Chapter 4, we examined the strong impact of policy limits on post-verdict payouts in tried cases involving all types of defendants—physicians, hospitals, and nursing homes—during the period prior to Texas's adoption of a cap on non-economic damages. But about 97 percent of the paid claims in our dataset are in cases that are settled prior to a verdict. And tort reform campaigns focus primarily on the plight of physicians, who almost always have medical malpractice insurance.[66] So in this chapter, we turn to the impact of policy limits on medical malpractice litigation involving physicians in both tried and settled cases. More specifically, we examine how much coverage physicians buy and whether there are any time trends in the amounts purchased. We also explore how policy limits affect the amount of compensation that patients receive and how often physicians make out-of-pocket payments, in both tried and settled cases. We continue to focus on cases closed during 1988–2005, and thus on cases that were not subject to the cap on non-economic damages that Texas adopted in late 2003.

Our dataset contains 12,383 large (payout > $25,000 [1988$]) paid medical malpractice claims against physicians that closed from 1988 to 2005. This includes "duplicates"—cases where two ore more physicians paid damages to the same plaintiff and filed separate claim reports. Research on this dataset generates the following findings.

- Although it is widely believed that most physicians purchase medical malpractice policies with per occurrence limits of $1 million and annual aggregate limits of $3 million, we find that many Texas physicians with paid claims had much less coverage. Perinatal claims involving children ages 0–1 months at date of injury tended to be large, but the doctors who faced these claims ("perinatal physicians") had *lower* policy limits than other physicians with paid claims.

- Nominal policy size was stable or gently rising, but inflation greatly reduced the real amount of insurance available to satisfy medical malpractice claims over the period. Physicians also appear to have responded to the malpractice crisis that hit Texas at the turn of the century by purchasing policies with lower limits in 2002 and 2003.

- Payouts rarely exceed the amount of medical malpractice insurance available to cover claims: 98.5 percent of claims were resolved with payments at or below primary malpractice policy limits. A sharp spike in payments at or near policy limits underscores the importance of policy size: 16 percent of claims were resolved with payments within

95 to 100 percent of limits. We call these "at-limits" pay-outs below. Most of these claims involved payments exactly equal to limits, which we call "at exact limits." The spike in at-limits payouts rises as policy limits fall and is exceptionally large for perinatal physicians, reflecting a combination of large claims and lower policy limits.

- As in Chapter 4 (which is limited to tried cases), we find that physicians rarely used personal assets to resolve malpractice claims. Physicians made out-of-pocket payments in only 77 cases (0.6 percent). And, most of these payments were relatively small—only 19 payments exceeded $250,000. Physicians with smaller policies, under $250,000, paid out of pocket more often than others, but even for these physicians, the probability of an out-of-pocket payment was only 1.2 percent.[67]

- Because policy limits effectively cap most recoveries in both tried and settled cases, the trend toward smaller real policies may affect both claim rates and payments to claimants. Per claim payments on all claims were stable over our study period, but per claim payments on perinatal claims rose. We lack sufficient data to estimate what payments would have been if real policy limits had been stable.

Finally, a caution. We often say that policy limits cap patients' recoveries. By this we mean that patients rarely recover more than the amount of insurance that is available to satisfy claims. But it might be equally correct to say that insurance facilitates recoveries up to the policy limits. Without insurance, patients injured by physicians' negligence might recover little or nothing at all. Because our dataset contains only insured claims, we do not know how patients who sue uninsured doctors fare. That said, we believe that insurance increases injured patients' recoveries enormously. In conversations, plaintiffs' lawyers emphasized the difficulty of collecting judgments against physicians' personal assets and told us that they often refuse to pursue claims when policy limits are low. Other scholarship also links the rise of personal injury litigation to the existence and spread of liability insurance.[68]

# DATA AND DATA LIMITATIONS

In this chapter we study only claims against physicians. The 12,383 paid claims in our principal dataset come from 10,940 nonduplicate cases. The total payout for each physician is the sum of the deductible payment, the primary carrier's payment, the excess carrier's payment, and the physician's payment above policy limits.

### Data on Medical Malpractice Policies

Most medical malpractice policies contain both per occurrence limits and aggregate annual limits. The Texas Closed Claim Database (TCCD) includes the per occurrence limit for 9,947 claims. Some policies instead have a combined single limit (2,436 claims). We obtained results similar to those reported below when we limited our analyses to claims with reported per occurrence limits.

Some medical malpractice insurance policies are "claims-made," meaning that they cover claims that are asserted during the policy period. Other policies are "occurrence" based. They cover harms associated with services rendered during the policy period, no matter when the claim is made. Our principal dataset includes 7,777 claims-made and 4,606 occurrence policies.

We study time trends in policy limits for paid claims, using the policy years that cover the claims. For claims-made policies, this is the year a claim was reported. For occurrence policies, this is the injury year. Taking into account the lag between injury or claim opening and claim closing, we have reasonably complete data on policies by purchase year for 1986–2003—a total of 11,602 policies.

### Data Limitations

We discussed general data limitations in Chapter 2. We discuss here some additional limitations that are specific to medical malpractice insurance policies. First, our data come from paid medical malpractice claims. Physicians with paid claims may not be representative of all Texas physicians. Second, we lack data on physician specialty. Thus, perinatal claims aside, we can say little about how limits vary by specialty. Third, in some cases, nominal policy limits may have been eroded by payments on prior claims under the same policy, in the same policy year, leading to a remaining limit that was lower than the nominal limit reported by the insurer. We do not have data on which policies experienced such erosion and thus had effective limits lower than the reported limits, but this should be relatively rare for the common policy pattern in which, if per claim limits are $X, per year limits are $3X, which means only providers with more than four paid claims in a given year would experience erosion. Fourth, we do not know the policy limits for "excess" policies, which provided coverage if the primary policy limits were exhausted. Thus, when studying how limits affect payments, we exclude 179 claims with payments by excess carriers. Fifth, we do not examine claims against hospitals, nursing homes, or other institutional defendants. Policy limits may influence such claims differently than they do in cases involving physicians.

## WHAT POLICY LIMITS DO PHYSICIANS CHOOSE?

The conventional wisdom is that most doctors buy medical malpractice policies with $1 million limits. For Texas physicians with paid claims, the data do not support this belief. We examined nominal limits for policies covering 1986–2003—the years for which we have reasonably complete data on the policies carried by doctors who incurred paid claims. For the full 1986–2003 time period, the median nominal policy limit was $500,000. Only 34 percent of the policies had nominal limits of $1 million. Another 6 percent had limits above $1 million. By contrast, 33 percent had nominal limits of $200,000 or less. Given the widely held belief that policies with $1 million per occurrence limits are standard, the latter finding is surprising.

Figure 5.1 shows the percentage of Texas medical malpractice insurance policies with the most common nominal per occurrence limits—$100,000 or $200,000; $500,000; and $1 million. Eighty-nine percent of policies fell into one of these categories.

Policies with nominal limits of $100,000 or $200,000 showed no discernible time trend until 2002, when their frequency increased sharply. The fraction of policies with $500,000 limits rose and then fell over time, while the fraction of $1 million policies fell, rose, and

## Figure 5.1

Texas physician nominal policy limit by purchase year

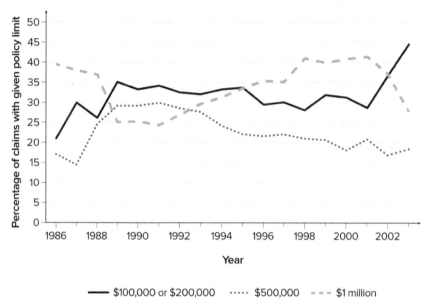

Notes: Per occurrence policy limits by purchase year in nominal dollars for large (>$25,000 [1988$]) paid medical malpractice claims against physicians, 1990–2005 (including duplicates), involving policies purchased over 1986–2003. Percentages do not equal 100 percent because some physicians purchased policies with sizes not shown here.

Source: Based on authors' calculations using the Texas Closed Claim Database.

then fell again. The share of $1 million policies fell sharply in 2002 and 2003—the mirror image of the pattern for policies with nominal limits of $100,000 or $200,000. For all policies, mean nominal limits declined steadily over the period, from $974,000 in 1986 to $619,000 in 2003. Median nominal policy limits also declined, from $750,000 to $500,000.

In real dollars, mean and median policy limits fell substantially more. Figure 5.2 provides data by year on mean real limits for physicians involved in perinatal and non-perinatal cases. From 1986 to 2003, mean real limits fell by 63 percent for perinatal claims and by 51 percent for non-perinatal claims. There were similar declines in median real limits.[69]

As Figure 5.2 shows, since 1991, perinatal physicians have consistently carried less insurance than other physicians, on average, even though they face larger claims—mostly attributable to the large economic damages

# Figure 5.2

## Texas physician real policy limits by purchase year

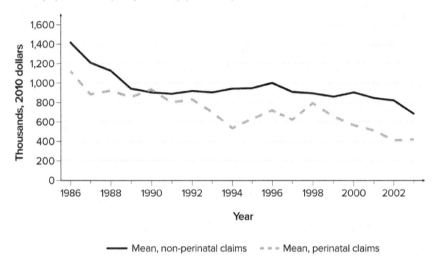

Notes: Mean real per occurrence policy limits by purchase year for large (>$25,000 [1988$]) paid medical malpractice claims against physicians, 1986–2003 (including duplicates), involving policies purchased over 1986–2003, separately for perinatal and non-perinatal claims. We winsorize limits for 14 perinatal and 154 non-perinatal policies with limits greater than $5 million, at $5 million.

Source: Based on authors' calculations using the Texas Closed Claim Database.

associated with the lifetime medical treatment that is often needed following a severe birth injury. In particular, perinatal physicians are less likely to purchase policies with nominal limits of $1 million or more. Over our full sample period, 23 percent of perinatal claims involved these policies versus 42 percent of non-perinatal claims; this difference is highly statistically significant.

We do not have data on insurance policies purchased in other states. The conventional wisdom on standard policy sizes might be more often true elsewhere. But this standard size has not changed, to our knowledge, since at least the 1980s, even though nominal prices have more than doubled since then. This suggests that real policy limits are likely dropping in other states too. If real policy limits fell in other states, this could help explain, at least in part, our finding in Chapter 11 that medical malpractice filings decreased in all states, including those that did not impose damage caps or other tort reforms.

Because real policy limits declined over time and policy limits often cap recoveries, one might expect that real payment per paid claim also declined. In fact, as we reported in Chapter 3, payout per large paid claim was stable. The lack of a time trend in payout per claim could reflect offsetting trends: a rise in real damages, partly attributable to rising medical costs, offset by a decline in real policy limits, which limited payouts. It could also reflect some smaller claims being squeezed out of the medical malpractice system by rising litigation costs, as we discussed in Chapter 3. Other things being equal, this would lead to higher payout per claim for the claims that are still brought.

## POLICY LIMITS AS DE FACTO CAPS ON PAYOUTS

We showed in Chapter 4 that policy limits often act as de facto caps on payouts in tried cases involving all types of defendants. Here we broaden the scope to examine both tried and settled cases—but simultaneously limit our scope and focus only on physicians. We find that even when payments are made above limits, insurers are the principal payers. Thus, the direct financial impact of medical malpractice payouts falls almost exclusively on insurers. That impact is transmitted to physicians primarily through insurers' underwriting, pricing, and monitoring practices.

We begin with summary data. Table 5.1 shows the number of claims with payments by each relevant party—primary insurer, excess insurer, and physician—and the amount paid by each. Primary carriers make most of the payments on malpractice claims. Deductibles aside, 98 percent of claims were resolved with primary carriers' money alone.[70] This includes 129 claims in which primary carriers paid more than limits.

Above-limits payments are rare—they are found in only 3.1 percent of cases. When an above-limits payment is made, a primary or excess insurer often makes this payment. Overall, primary carriers paid $3.7 billion at or below limits and $76 million above limits (2 percent of their total payments); excess carriers paid another $87 million above the limits of the primary insurance policy.

Physician out-of-pocket payments are rare. Deductibles aside, physicians made such payments in only 77 cases over an 18-year period—an

# Table 5.1

Payers, amounts paid, and payment counts, Texas

| Payment source | | | | | Insurer | | Physician out of pocket | |
|---|---|---|---|---|---|---|---|---|
| Primary insurer | Excess carrier | Physician out of pocket | Number of claims | Claims (%) | Amount (millions, 2010 dollars) | Total insurer payments (%) | Amount (millions, 2010 dollars) | Total physician payments (%) |
| Within limits | N | N | 12,005 | 96.95% | 3,557 | 93.93% | 0 | — |
| Above limits | N | N | 129 | 1.04% | 147 | 3.88% | 0 | — |
| Within limits | Y | N | 169 | 1.36% | 50 | 1.32% | 0 | — |
| Above limits | Y | N | 3 | 0.02% | 3 | 0.08% | 0 | — |
| Within limits | N | Y | 67 | 0.54% | 24 | 0.63% | 13.48 | 84.94% |
| Above limits | N | Y | 3 | 0.02% | 2 | 0.05% | 0.26 | 1.64% |
| Within limits | Y | Y | 6 | 0.05% | 3 | 0.08% | 2.03 | 12.79% |
| Above limits | Y | Y | 1 | 0.01% | 1 | 0.03% | 0.10 | 0.63% |
| **Total** | | | **12,383** | **100.00%** | **3,787** | **100.00%** | **15.87** | **100.00%** |

*Notes:* Sources of funds for large paid medical malpractice claims against physicians, 1988–2005 (including duplicates). Physicians also paid deductibles in 350 cases; including 15 claims paid using only a deductible and 2 claims paid using only deductible and excess carrier funds.

*Source:* Based on authors' calculations using the Texas Closed Claim Database.

average of 4.3 cases per year, with no apparent time trend. This is 0.6 percent of cases. The out-of-pocket payments represent only 0.4 percent of all payouts—a total of $16 million.

To determine the frequency of payouts at different fractions of policy limits, we compute payment-to-limit (PTL) ratios for all claims with no payment by an excess carrier. A $500,000 payout on a $1 million policy produces a PTL ratio of 0.5. The PTL ratio equals 1 when payout exactly equals policy limits. Panel A in Figure 5.3 shows the distribution of PTL ratios for all claims against physicians. Panel B shows this distribution for perinatal claims involving patients ages 0–1 months at date of injury, which are more likely to involve large damages. In both charts, the spikes at policy limits are obvious and large. Sixteen percent of all claims, and 32 percent of perinatal claims, have PTL ratios between 0.95 and 1 (including exactly 1.00). Most of these at-limits payouts are at *exact* limits: 14 percent of all payouts and 29 percent of perinatal claims are at exact limits. Figure 5.3 also shows the rarity of above-limits payouts.

## Figure 5.3

### Distributions of payment-to-limit ratios, Texas

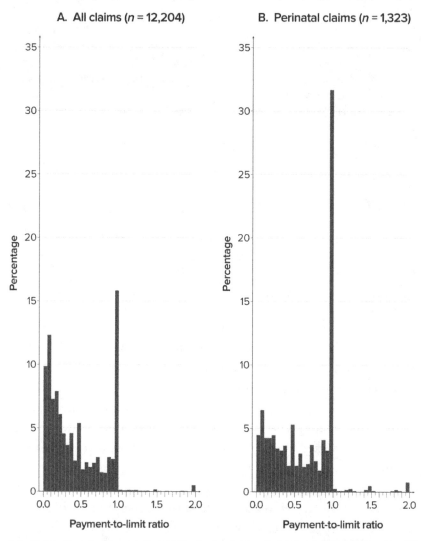

A. All claims (*n* = 12,204)          B. Perinatal claims (*n* = 1,323)

*Notes:* Distributions of payment-to-limit (PTL) ratios for all claims (Panel A) and perinatal claims (Panel B) for large (payout > $25,000 [1988]) paid medical malpractice claims against physicians, 1988–2005 (including duplicates; excluding claims with payments by an excess carrier). Each bar represents a 0.05 increment in PTL. Claims with ratios greater than 1.95 are shown in the single bar at a ratio of 2 at the far right of each graph. The spike at 1.00 covers 0.95 < PTL ≤ 1.00.

*Source:* Based on authors' calculations using the Texas Closed Claim Database.

# Figure 5.4

## Probability of at-limits payment for paid claims by year claim closed, Texas

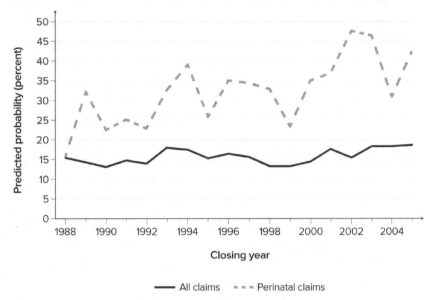

*Notes:* Trends in fraction of payments near policy limits (0.95 < PTL ≤ 1.00) by closing year for large (payout > $25,000 [1988$]) paid medical malpractice claims against physicians, 1988–2005 (including duplicates; excluding claims with payments by an excess carrier). PTL = payment-to-limit.

*Source:* Based on authors' calculations using the Texas Closed Claim Database.

Figure 5.4 displays time trends for the likelihood of an at-limits payout. For all claims, there is no discernible time trend. In contrast, for perinatal claims, there is an upward trend over time. For these cases, the likelihood of an at-limits payment rises from 16 percent in 1988 to 42 percent in 2005. Note that payouts will often be less than damages, even apart from the impact of policy limits. This is especially true for settled cases. The plaintiff's *expected* recovery at trial, which should form the basis for settlement negotiations, equals damages multiplied by probability of liability, which will generally be less than damages. Thus, the percentage of paid claims with damages greater than limits—where physicians accordingly face greater risk of an out-of-pocket payment—is greater than the percentage of claims with at-limits payouts as shown in Figure 5.4.

Perinatal physicians thus face a high risk of a claim with damages greater than limits. Yet, as we show below, perinatal physicians carry less insurance than other physicians and have *reduced* their insurance coverage over time. This suggests that even perinatal physicians do not perceive a large risk of making an out-of-pocket payment. If they did, they might carry higher insurance limits, because, as we show below, the odds of making an out-of-pocket payment fall at larger policy sizes.

It is logical to expect the fraction of claims with at-limits payouts to bear an inverse relationship to policy size. The larger the policy, the less likely it is that damages will exceed the amount of insurance available to cover them. Figure 5.5 confirms this. It includes four panels. Panel A shows a chart similar to Figure 5.3 for policies with limits less than $250,000; Panel B shows a chart for policies with limits from $250,000 to $500,000; Panel C shows results for limits from $500,001 to $1 million; and Panel D shows results for policies with limits greater than $1 million. We report both policy size and payouts in 2010 dollars. For the smallest policies, 38 percent of claims settle at the policy limits. This fraction drops steadily as policy size increases, to only 4.2 percent for policies with real limits above $1 million.

The conventional wisdom has long been that standard physician policy limits are $1 million per occurrence (and often $3 million per policy year). For example, a $1 million/$3 million policy is the level used by *Medical Liability Monitor* for its annual malpractice insurance rate surveys, conducted since 1991.[71] That convention is not the norm in Texas; we discuss actual policy sizes below. If it were, then the likelihood of an at-limits payout, and thus the risk to physicians of an out-of-pocket payout, would be much lower, and haircuts to plaintiffs would also be much lower. This offers further evidence that physicians are not very worried about the risk of making personal payments.

## PHYSICIAN OUT-OF-POCKET PAYMENTS

We focus in this section on cases in which physicians made out-of-pocket payments. The most striking feature of these payments is their rarity— only 77 over the 18 years from 1988 to 2005. Moreover, many of

# Figure 5.5

## Payment-to-limit ratios for different real policy limits, Texas

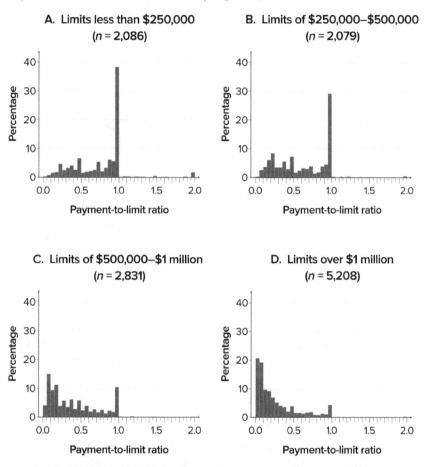

A. Limits less than $250,000
(*n* = 2,086)

B. Limits of $250,000–$500,000
(*n* = 2,079)

C. Limits of $500,000–$1 million
(*n* = 2,831)

D. Limits over $1 million
(*n* = 5,208)

*Notes:* Distributions of payment-to-limit ratios for four different ranges of real policy limits for large (payout > $25,000 [1988$]) paid medical malpractice claims against physicians, 1988–2005 (including duplicates; excluding claims with payment by an excess carrier). Each bar represents a 0.05 increment; claims with ratios > 2 are shown as equal to 2.

*Source:* Based on authors' calculations using the Texas Closed Claim Database.

these payments were relatively small: 43 payments were $100,000 or less. Of the remainder, 15 were $100,000–$250,000, and 19 were more than $250,000. The mean (median) payment was $206,000 ($62,000). Figure 5.6, Panel A, shows the number of out–of–pocket payouts in different size ranges. There was no discernible time trend in payout size.

# Figure 5.6

### Physician out-of-pocket payments, Texas

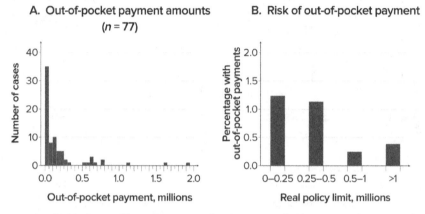

A. Out-of-pocket payment amounts ($n = 77$)

B. Risk of out-of-pocket payment

*Notes:* Panel A: Distribution of the 77 physician out-of-pocket payments for large (payout > $25,000 [1988$]) paid medical malpractice claims against physicians, 1988–2005 (including duplicates). Panel B: Percentage of paid claims with physician out-of-pocket payments for cases with real policy limits in indicated ranges.
*Source:* Based on authors' calculations using the Texas Closed Claim Database.

One might expect physicians with lower policy limits to face a higher risk of an out-of-pocket payout. We confirm this in Figure 5.6, Panel B. An out-of-pocket payment occurs in 1.2 percent of cases with policy limits less than $250,000 (26 of 2,113) but only 0.3 percent of cases with policies greater than $500,000 (27 of 8,139). Yet, even the physicians who choose low limits (under $250,000) are quite unlikely to make an out-of-pocket payment.

Tom Baker has developed a "blood money" hypothesis that plaintiffs are more likely to seek an out-of-pocket payment when physicians carry "too little" insurance.[72] When we consider only claims with PTL ratios greater than 0.9 (60 of the 77 out-of-pocket payments), however, we find no statistically significant correlation between policy size and the likelihood of such a payment. This suggests that the higher rate of out-of-pocket payments for physicians with lower policy limits is driven by the greater likelihood that damages exceed limits, rather than by Baker's blood money story.

The low risk of an out-of-pocket payment, even with low policy limits, implies that carrying low limits could be a sensible strategy for many physicians. The higher risk of an out-of-pocket payment if a claim is made will be offset by a lower medical malpractice insurance premium. Smaller policies may also make physicians less attractive targets for lawsuits. Because recoveries rarely exceed policy limits, low limits may act like damage caps, making cases less profitable for attorneys and, therefore, less likely to be brought. For the cases that are still brought against low-limits physicians (with limits less than $250,000), the average out-of-pocket payment across all large paid claims is $3,135 for physicians. Given that the annual risk of a large paid claim is far below one, low-limits physicians will likely save more than this over time through lower premiums. For all other physicians, the average payment is under $1,000.

Perinatal cases accounted for 11 percent of paid claims but generated 22 percent of out-of-pocket payments (17 of 77). Yet the higher risk of an out-of-pocket payment for perinatal claims is apparently insufficient to persuade perinatal physicians to carry higher limits than other physicians. An alternative possibility is that doctors who face perinatal claims would purchase larger policies if insurers would let them, but insurers, who know that policy limits (implausible, at least up to $1 million) cap payouts, may refuse to sell larger policies in an effort to contain their losses.

## DISCUSSION

### Out-of-Pocket Payments by Physicians

When physicians campaign for tort reform, the risk of personal bankruptcy attributable to uninsured exposure to medical malpractice claims ranks high on their list of complaints. They often contend that a single claim can wipe out the wealth a doctor accumulates over an entire career. The reality is quite different. Out-of-pocket payments are rare, and they rarely threaten physicians' financial solvency. Policy limits usually act as a de facto cap on recoveries. As a result, many payouts stack up at policy limits. Even when plaintiffs recover more than policy limits, insurers are the primary payers. (We discussed in Chapter 4 the legal rules and bargaining dynamics that can produce this result.) These findings even hold true for so-called bad baby cases, despite the fact that perinatal physicians tend to face higher damages, yet carry smaller policies than other doctors.

Texas is a large state, averaging around 30,000 active practicing physicians during the period we studied.[73] Yet physicians made only about four out-of-pocket payments per year. Thus, an average physician faced an annual risk of having to make an out-of-pocket payment of only about 0.01 percent. Many of those payments were relatively small, less than $100,000—enough to hurt but not likely to be a bankrupting amount. Many physicians could reduce their risk further by carrying $1 million policy limits, but they choose not to do so. To be sure, the low risk of an out-of-pocket payment may to some extent be specific to Texas, which has pro-debtor insolvency rules, including an unlimited homestead exemption. Out-of-pocket payment risks could be higher in other states.

Although some out-of-pocket payments were large, few were catastrophic. Defining "disaster" as a payment exceeding $250,000, disaster struck 19 times in 18 years—an annual risk of 0.003 percent for all physicians—and even less for physicians with $1 million policy limits. We discussed outcomes following a plaintiff verdict at trial in Chapter 4, and we find that even when the plaintiff wins an above-limits verdict, an out-of-pocket payment remains a rare event.

### Policy Limits

Texas physicians with paid malpractice claims often carried less than the supposedly standard $1 million per occurrence policy limits, and their real limits declined by more than 50 percent over our sample period. In 2003, the median policy had $500,000 nominal limits. We have not studied the factors that might explain this fall in real policy limits. One possibility is that many doctors purchase the minimum amount of coverage needed to obtain hospital privileges, or perhaps the amount that their peers purchase. Unless these minimums rise with inflation, real policy limits will degrade. Another is that physicians have learned over time that they can purchase smaller, cheaper policies and still face a very small risk of an out-of-pocket payment. The burden of those lower limits may fall largely on plaintiffs who suffer uncompensated harm because it is not feasible to collect above policy limits. This is a special concern for perinatal claims. The decline in real policy size coincides with, and likely contributes to, an increasing tendency for perinatal claims to stack up at policy limits.

## CHAPTER 6

# DEFENSE COSTS

## OVERVIEW

Controlling for payouts, real defense costs in medical malpractice cases rose by 5 percent per year over 1988–2005. These costs roughly doubled over this period and rose much more rapidly than defense costs for other types of personal injury claims. Yet real hourly rates for personal injury defense lawyers were flat. Defense costs in medical malpractice cases correlate strongly with payouts, the presence of multiple defendants, the stage at which a case is resolved, and case duration. Mean duration declined over time; otherwise, defense costs may have risen still faster.

Insurer reserving practices raise some puzzles relative to how we would expect insurers to behave. Initial "expense" reserves predict only a very small fraction of actual defense costs. And medical malpractice insurers should have reacted to the sustained rise in defense costs by adjusting their expense reserves, either in real dollars or as a fraction of their reserves for payouts, but failed to do so. Thus, expense reserves declined substantially relative to defense costs. The tort system is also a very expensive way to transfer resources from defendants to plaintiffs. We estimate that it costs $1.33 in legal fees and other expenses to deliver $1 to negligently injured plaintiffs.

## INTRODUCTION

In this chapter, we study the costs that insurers incur to defend against medical malpractice claims, how those costs changed over time, and how insurers establish reserves for those costs ("expense reserves"). We focus on total defense costs, which are primarily composed of legal fees but also include "other expenses" (mostly fees paid to expert witnesses). Our principal findings are as follows. Unless otherwise specified, defense costs are those on the primary report and amounts are per case.

- Defense costs
  - Defense costs rose 5 percent per year, controlling for payout. In 1988–1990, defense costs averaged 8 percent of total payout; by 2003–2005, this percentage had risen to 17 percent.
  - The rate of increase in defense costs in medical malpractice cases is much higher than for other types of personal injury.
  - Insurers' defense costs rise with exposure (a measure of expected damages, before accounting for the effect of defense spending to limit those costs), the presence of multiple defendants, the stage at which the case is resolved, and case duration.
  - We did not find evidence to support a number of possible explanations for rising defense costs, including rising payouts, rising exposure, rising hourly rates for defense counsel, longer case duration, and more cases going to trial. Defense counsel must be devoting more hours per case, but why they are doing so is unclear.
- Insurer reserving practices
  - Insurers' initial expense reserves are a surprisingly poor predictor of eventual defense cost. Using basic case information (year, plaintiff age, employment status, type of harm), we can predict much more of the variation in defense costs than is predicted by initial reserves.

- During our sample period, per case defense costs more than doubled, yet medical malpractice insurers modestly *decreased* their initial expense reserves. In contrast, insurers for other lines of coverage responded to increases in defense costs by increasing their reserves.

The principal surprises in this research are the strong long-term rise in medical malpractice defense costs and the poor job that malpractice insurers do in estimating expense reserves, in using case-level information, and in adjusting their estimates to reflect the long-term rise in defense costs. At the same time, our findings on how insurers defend cases are consistent with sensible insurer behavior. For example, insurers invest more to defend cases with larger exposure and more defendants, and they spend more on cases that progress further in the litigation process and last longer.

## LITERATURE REVIEW

Estimates of the overall cost of medical malpractice litigation, including legal fees and expenses for plaintiff and defendant, plus insurers' administrative costs, typically exceed 50 percent of the total premium dollars collected by medical malpractice insurers. However, these estimates are often partly or entirely anecdotal. Studies frequently use different definitions of the sample, the numerator, and the denominator. When the original source permits, we report estimates of total *direct* defense costs (legal fees plus other out-of-pocket costs) as the numerator, and total claim costs (defense costs plus payout) as the denominator. We lack data on insurers' indirect costs.

*Snapshots of defense costs for closed paid claims.* Studdert and others found that total direct defense costs were 19 percent of payouts, and 16 percent of the sum of payout and defense costs, for 1,452 claims from five liability insurers over 1984–2004.[74] Vidmar and others found that defense costs in Florida over 1990–2003 were 14 percent of the sum of payout and defense costs.[75] The Bureau of Justice Statistics found that median allocated loss adjustment expenses (which insurers call ALAE) for claims settled before trial during 2000–2004 were 14 percent of total claim costs in Missouri, 19 percent in Florida, and 24 percent in Texas.[76] Note that ALAE is a broader measure than direct defense costs—it also includes the insurer's estimate of internal costs that can be assigned to specific cases. These studies do not analyze the factors that affect these costs.

*Time trends.* Several studies find rising defense costs. Carroll, Parikh, and Buddenbaum find rising ALAE, relative to payouts. ALAE as a percentage of payouts rose from 24 percent in 1985 to 45 percent in 2008.[77] A 2005 state of Washington study found a 3.8 percent real increase for all claims over 1995–2004, with a 5.8 percent annual rise for paid claims.[78] The Congressional Budget Office reported in 2004 that medical malpractice defense costs had been increasing over the prior two decades but provided no details.[79]

But two other studies are mixed. For Florida, Vidmar and others found mean defense cost for paid claims declined during 1990–2003 by an average of 2.8 percent per year, but mean defense cost in claims with no payout rose by 3.1 percent per year over 1990–1997.[80] And Kessler reports that ALAE in medical malpractice cases declined from 24.7 percent of incurred losses plus loss adjustment expenses in 1992 to 23.4 percent in 2002.[81]

*Reserves for defense costs.* We assess below how well insurers do in establishing initial expense reserves. We are not aware of prior work on when these reserves are set or on how well case-level reserves predict case-level spending.

## DATA AND METHODOLOGY

### Medical Malpractice Dataset Limitations

*Defense cost information.* We have information on legal fees and other loss adjustment expenses (e.g., expert witness fees and filing fees). Some cases have legal fees but zero other expenses; for these cases, the legal fees line may include expenses incurred by counsel and included in counsel's bills to the insurer. For reports with zero reported defense costs, the reporting patterns appear to us to be consistent with correct reporting rather than missing data.

*Initial payout and expense reserves.* The Texas Department of Insurance (TDI) requires insurers to report initial and final case-level reserves for both payout and defense costs. We study only initial reserves here. TDI provides no instructions on when the initial reserve should be established. Industry participants advised us that their practice could well vary, both across insurers and for different claims adjusters who work for the same insurer. We study only case-level reserves. Insurers can also establish overall reserves, not those tied to specific claims. We have no data on those reserves.

In 923 medical malpractice reports (6.1 percent of 15,065 claims), the indemnity reserve—the amount reserved for future payout—exactly equals the payout. In 343 of these, the indemnity reserve equals policy limits, and the insurer might plausibly have first reserved and then eventually paid the policy limits. But in the other 580 cases, the indemnity reserve is not equal to the policy limits. Insurers might sometimes be able to settle for the exact amount they reserve, but it seems likely that in many of these cases, the insurer never set an initial indemnity reserve and instead reported an initial indemnity reserve equal to the final payout once the final payout was known. In another nine cases, defense costs were positive and the expense reserve exactly equaled reported defense costs. We exclude these 589 cases from regressions that use indemnity reserves or expense reserves as a variable.

*Analysis of reserves.* Generally in this book, we sum payouts and defense costs across "duplicate" reports that relate to the same claim. When we study reserves, we adopt a different approach because reserves are insurer specific. We therefore compare each insurer's reserves to the amounts paid for a particular defendant, whether by the defendant, the primary insurer, or an excess insurer. Excess insurers usually rely on primary insurers to defend cases and typically do not engage separate counsel.

### Defense Attorney Hourly Rate Information

Since 1989, the Texas State Bar has conducted periodic surveys of hourly rates and other billing practices for Texas lawyers. We rely on these surveys to determine median hourly rates from 1989 to 2005. The state bar surveys contain aggregate information for the entire period and information by specialty, including personal injury defense counsel, for 1994–2005.

## WHAT FACTORS PREDICT DEFENSE COSTS IN MEDICAL MALPRACTICE CASES?

Table 6.1 provides summary statistics for the large paid medical malpractice claims in our dataset. Almost 97 percent of cases involve positive defense costs. The mean (median) defense cost per large paid claim over the entire time period is $71,000 ($47,000).

A central finding of this chapter involves the rapid rise in defense costs, even though payouts show no time trend (see Chapter 3). Figure 6.1 provides an initial visual picture. Both defense costs and the ratio of defense costs to payout more than doubled.

## Table 6.1

Summary statistics for defense costs in medical malpractice cases, Texas

| Cases | 15,065 | |
|---|---|---|
| Zero defense costs (percentage of cases) | 528 (3.5%) | |
| Positive defense costs (percentage of cases) | 14,537 (96.5%) | |
| | **Mean** | **Median** |
| Defense cost | $71,000 | $47,000 |
| Expense reserve (for defense costs) | $19,000 | $12,000 |
| Total payout | $584,000 | $243,000 |
| Indemnity reserve (for payout) | $118,000 | $59,000 |
| Expense reserve/indemnity reserve | 53% | 27% |
| Defense cost/payout by this insurer | 46% | 23% |
| Aggregate (defense cost/payout) | 21% | |
| Aggregate (outside counsel expense/total counsel expense) | 92.9% | |

*Notes:* Summary data for large (payout >$25,000 [1988$]) paid medical malpractice claims over 1988–2005. Total payout is by all defendants. Defense cost/payout by this insurer excludes cases with zero payout by that insurer. When computing the ratio of expense reserve to indemnity reserve, we exclude 2,679 cases with expense reserve or indemnity reserve of $1,000 or less or with very low or very high ratios of expense reserve to indemnity reserve—expense reserve/indemnity reserve less than 0.02 or greater than 50. Monetary amounts are in 2010 dollars.

*Source:* Based on authors' calculations using the Texas Closed Claim Database.

# Figure 6.1

## Time trends in medical malpractice defense costs, Texas

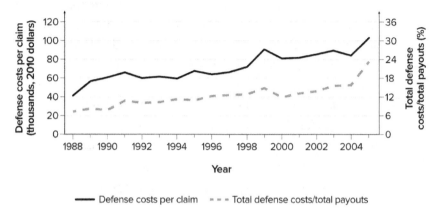

Defense costs per claim ■ ■ ■ Total defense costs/total payouts

*Note:* Mean annual defense cost per claim and annual ratio of total defense costs to payout by all defendants, for large (payout >$25,000 [1988$]) paid medical malpractice claims with positive defense costs over 1988–2005.

*Source:* Based on authors' calculations using the Texas Closed Claim Database.

We used regression analysis to explore which factors predict defense spending. Our principal results are the following:

- *Year.* Without control variables, the rise in defense costs is 4.7 percent per year. This implies a 129 percent increase in defense costs over our sample period. The annual rise is 5 percent if we control for payout and other claim and outcome characteristics, implying a 141 percent increase over our sample period.

- *Payout.* A 1 percent increase in payout predicts a 0.29 percent increase in defense costs. Thus, larger cases cost more to defend, but defense costs rise less than proportionately with payout. In effect, legal defense is a task with substantial setup costs but lower marginal cost relative to the insurer's exposure.

- *Duration.* Duration is strongly related to defense costs. Holding resolution stage constant, a 1 percent increase in days open predicts a 0.71 percent increase in defense costs.

- *Resolution stage.* Defense costs rise if a suit is filed (28 percent of the cases that settle before suit is filed have zero defense costs) and rise further if a trial is begun. Cases that are appealed cost more than cases that are tried but not appealed, but this effect disappears once we control for duration.
- *Case complexity.* The presence of multiple defendants is associated with higher defense costs.
- *Type of defendant.* We don't find evidence that defendant type (e.g., physician, hospital, nursing home) affects defense costs. We don't have data on physician specialty, but it is possible that certain specialties will have higher defense costs related to case complexity or the cost of obtaining expert testimony.

Thus, we find that higher defense costs are associated with larger payouts, longer case duration, and the stage at which a case is resolved.

To be sure, some of these factors are jointly determined. In particular, higher payout predicts higher defense costs, yet defendants presumably spend more to defend cases in the hope of paying less, holding constant their "exposure" (potential payout). To separate the positive effect of exposure on defense costs from the negative effect of defense spending on actual payout, we also conducted an instrumental variable analysis, in which we use several instrumental variables to predict exposure. A valid instrument in this context should predict potential payout but be unrelated to the likelihood of success on the merits. We predict potential payout using the natural log of plaintiff age in years + 1, where we add 1 to avoid losing baby cases; a dummy for baby cases; and a dummy variable for whether the plaintiff is employed. Using this approach, we obtain similar results for the yearly increase in defense costs.

## INSURER RESERVING PRACTICES

We also assessed how well insurers' reserves for defense costs predict actual defense costs. It seems reasonable to assume that when they set reserves, insurers know the basic case characteristics that are later included in closed claim reports, plus information unavailable to us, such as physician specialty, injury severity, and other case-specific facts. It is also reasonable to assume that insurers will use past experience to estimate defense costs, perhaps using a regression analysis similar to the one we present below. We might expect the following:

- Variation in expense reserves will have substantial power to predict variation in defense costs and should outperform naive estimates based only on the basic case characteristics that are available in our data.
- The factors that predict defense costs should also predict expense reserves.
- There should be close to a 1:1 relationship between *ln*(defense cost) and *ln*(expense reserve).
- As defense costs rise over our sample period, expense reserves will rise as well.

We find *none* of these things. Expense reserves do a poor job of predicting actual defense costs. The simple factors that predict defense costs in our regressions either do not predict expense reserves or do so with the wrong sign. And during a period in which defense costs more than doubled, average expense reserves *did not change*. A possible explanation for these results is that insurers apply a rule of thumb on the expected ratio of defense costs to payout that is not sensitive to case characteristics and during our sample period did not update this rule of thumb. We asked several medical malpractice insurers whether they use rules of thumb in establishing expense reserves. Most responded that reserves are established on a case-by-case basis, using the information available at the time. One replied that "A very good rule of thumb among medical malpractice insurers is that [defense costs equal] about half of indemnity [i.e., payout]." However, across all claims, we find no evidence that insurers set expense reserves simply as a fraction of indemnity reserves.[82]

### Average Expense Reserves across Cases
Even if medical malpractice insurers do not do well at reserving for defense costs in individual cases, their case-level reserves might still do

# Figure 6.2

## Defense and indemnity reserves over time, Texas

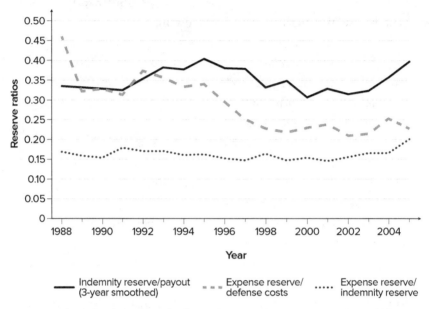

Indemnity reserve/payout (3-year smoothed) — Expense reserve/defense costs — Expense reserve/indemnity reserve

*Notes:* Figure shows three lines: The top line from 1993 on is the three-year smoothed ratio of indemnity reserve to primary insurer payout; the middle line during the same period is the ratio of expense reserve to primary insurer defense cost; and the bottom line is the ratio of expense reserve for large paid medical malpractice claim reports over 1988–2005 to indemnity reserve. For 1990–2005, the smoothed ratio gives weight of 50 percent to current year, 33 percent to prior year, and 17 percent to two years prior; for 1989, the smoothed ratio gives two-thirds weight to 1989 and one-third weight to 1988; for 1988, there is no smoothing. Ratios use annual data, summed over all paid claims for each year.

*Source:* Based on authors' calculations using the Texas Closed Claim Database.

a good job of estimating their aggregate exposure. This is not the case either. Figure 6.2 shows a smoothed three-year average ratio of aggregate indemnity reserves to aggregate payouts (solid line); the ratio of aggregate expense reserves to aggregate defense costs (dashed line); and the ratio of the two aggregate reserves (dotted line).[83]

The ratio of aggregate indemnity reserves to aggregate payouts shows no overall time trend. Nor does the ratio of expense reserves to indemnity reserves, even though, as we have seen, defense costs rose sharply over our sample period. As defense costs increase, the ratio of aggregate expense reserves to aggregate defense costs declines, from an average of 35 percent during 1988–1992 to only 23 percent during 2000–2005.

# Figure 6.3

## Medical malpractice cases: Normalized defense costs and expense reserves, Texas

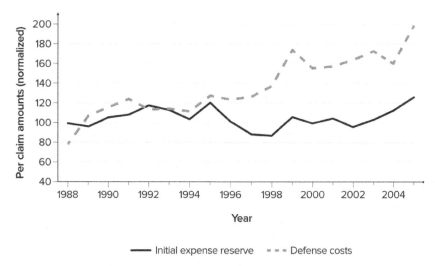

*Note:* Figure shows (solid line) mean per case initial expense reserves for each year and (dashed line) mean per claim defense costs, in each case normalized to 100 over 1988–1990, for large (payout > $25,000 [1988$]) paid medical malpractice cases over 1988–2005.

*Source:* Based on authors' calculations using the Texas Closed Claim Database.

Figure 6.3 shows in a different way the failure of medical malpractice insurers to adjust expense reserves to reflect rising defense costs. It presents mean defense costs and initial reserves by year, normalized to 100 over 1988–1990. Defense costs rise steadily, while reserves are roughly flat. We obtain similar results for medians.

### Expense Reserves for Other Personal Injury Claims

We saw above that medical malpractice insurers did not adjust their expense reserves to reflect increasing defense costs. We also investigated whether insurers updated their reserves as defense costs rose for the other four lines of personal injury claims for which we have data. They do. Figure 6.4 is similar to Figure 6.3. It shows mean per case defense costs and initial reserves for these other types of personal injury cases by year, normalized to 100 over 1988–1990. Defense costs and reserves both rise for non–medical malpractice cases but roughly in parallel. Reserves did fall somewhat behind expenses during 1992–1997,

## Figure 6.4

Non–medical malpractice cases: Normalized mean defense costs and initial expense reserves, Texas

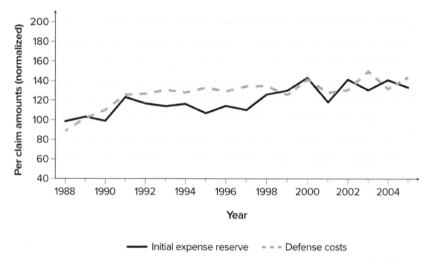

*Note:* Figure shows mean per case initial expense reserve for each year, and mean per claim defense costs, in each case normalized to 100 over 1988–1990, for 65,170 large paid *non*–medical malpractice claim reports in the Texas Department of Insurance dataset of personal injury claims closed from 1988 to 2005.

*Source:* Based on authors' calculations using the Texas Closed Claim Database.

as insurers reduced their per case reserves while expenses gradually rose. But initial reserves caught up in 1998–1999 and remained similar to expenses thereafter.

The ratio of expense reserves to indemnity reserves also rises for auto, general commercial, and multiperil cases and does not change substantially for other professional liability. Yet this ratio falls over time for medical malpractice cases. This only deepens the puzzle: medical malpractice insurers faced a much faster rise in defense costs than insurers for these other personal injury lines. Why then did insurers in other lines adjust their expense reserves, while medical malpractice insurers did not? After all, insurance actuaries, who are responsible for estimating these costs, exist across all lines of insurance and have similar training.

For this puzzle, we simply have no good explanation. But perhaps this puzzle is a piece of the puzzle we explored in Chapter 3, of rapidly rising premiums with no underlying rapid rise in payouts. If medical malpractice insurers—for whatever reason—are not doing a very good job of estimating reserves, and thus likely not doing a good job of pricing their product, then medical malpractice insurance may be more prone to periodic crises, in which insurers discover that they are losing money and react sharply. The industry could swing from underreserving to overreserving—as indeed appears to have occurred in the medical malpractice insurance crisis of the early 2000s.

It would be helpful to have data from more than one insurance crisis to confirm this finding. Unfortunately, in 2015, Texas's legislature decided to shutter the Texas Closed Claim Database (TCCD) effective January 2016. So the data we have are all we are going to get, at least from Texas.

## SIX FACTORS THAT MIGHT EXPLAIN RISING DEFENSE COSTS—BUT DON'T

Why are defense costs rising in medical malpractice cases? There are six plausible possibilities that we can test (at least partially):

- Hourly legal fees might be increasing.
- Payouts might be rising.
- Exposure might be rising, even if payouts are not.
- Insurers might be spending more in an effort to win a larger fraction of cases.
- Cases might be taking longer to close.
- Cases might be resolved at a later procedural stage.

We examine each of these possible explanations in turn.

### Defense Counsel Hourly Rates
Outside counsel expense is the largest component of defense costs. In a simple model, outside counsel expense equals hourly rate multiplied by hours spent. The TCCD contains no information on either subject, but

we were able to obtain data on hourly fees from periodic surveys conducted by the Texas State Bar that cover our sample period. The surveys
were conducted in 1989, 1994, 1996, 2000, 2003, and 2005. We have
median fees for all six iterations of the survey, and mean fees for some
iterations, for both personal injury defense counsel and all counsel.[84]

Table 6.2 reports mean and median hourly rates for personal injury
defense counsel and all counsel, for the six survey years. Real hourly
rates for personal injury defense counsel fluctuated but ended up almost
unchanged in 2005 versus 1989. Thus, a rise in hourly rates cannot
explain the rise in defense counsel cost. There could, of course, be a
divergence over time between the rates that lawyers report on the survey
and the average rates paid by insurers, or between rates charged by
medical malpractice defense counsel and rates for other personal injury
defense counsel. But there is no obvious reason to expect either source
of divergence, and it seems unlikely that these factors can explain more
than a fraction of the increase in defense costs. This leaves more hours
worked as the likely source of most or all of the increase in counsel fees.

# Table 6.2

## Defense counsel hourly rates in Texas, 1989–2005

| Year | Personal injury defense counsel | | | All counsel | | |
|---|---|---|---|---|---|---|
| | Median | Mean | Sample | Median | Mean | Sample |
| 1989 | $104.9 | | | $111.6 | | 1,389 |
| 1994 | $111.8 | $111.0 | 292 | $111.8 | $116.5 | 4,186 |
| 1996 | $94.3 | $103.3 | 478 | $113.1 | $116.1 | 2,300 |
| 2000 | $103.1 | $100.3 | 22 | $120.2 | $135.3 | 1,038 |
| 2003 | $96.4 | | 45 | $128.6 | $144.0 | 2,705 |
| 2005 | $106.0 | $107.2 | 37 | $130.2 | $141.7 | 2,414 |
| Annual increase | 0.06% | −0.31% | | 0.97% | 1.80% | |
| Period covered | 1989–2005 | 1994–2005 | | 1989–2005 | 1994–2005 | |

*Note:* Median and mean hourly fees charges by personal injury defense counsel and by all counsel for
indicated years.

*Source:* Data are from Texas State Bar surveys for indicated years.

Table 6.2 also shows mean and median rates for all respondents. The all-respondents series is less noisy because of larger sample size but likely less representative of personal injury defense counsel. It shows an increase in median fees of about 1 percent per year from 1989 to 2005. Even if this increase also applied to personal injury defense counsel, it would explain only a fraction of the rise in medical malpractice counsel costs.

### Other Factors

*Payouts.* Higher payouts predict higher defense costs, so if payouts increase over time, defense costs should increase as well. However, as we described in Chapter 3, there was no rise during our sample period in per claim payouts on large claims. Thus, rising payouts cannot explain rising defense costs.

*Exposure.* Defense costs and payouts are endogenous. A possible reason why defense costs are rising, but payouts are not, is that exposure is rising, and payouts would have risen if insurers had not increased their defense spending. We have limited ability to test this hypothesis but note that policy limits provide a measure of maximum exposure. If limits were rising, this could predict rising defense costs. However, as we noted in Chapter 5, policy limits for physicians fell over our sample period.

*Fraction of paid claims.* More vigorous defense of claims could lead to a smaller fraction resulting in a payout. However, in unreported regressions, we find no time trend in the fraction of paid claims over 1995–2005—the period for which we have data on the total number of paid claims.

*Claim duration.* We find that longer claim duration predicts higher defense spending. Thus, if duration were rising, this could help explain rising defense costs. We find instead that medical malpractice cases have been closing more quickly over time. Mean (median) days open dropped from 1,030 (913) over 1988–1992 to 894 (787) over 2000–2005. One major Texas medical malpractice insurer advised us that it sought aggressively to close cases more quickly during the 1990s, having observed that doing so reduced defense costs and did not increase payouts.

*Stage of resolution.* As we noted above, defense costs rise if a suit is filed and rise again if a case goes to trial. Thus, a higher proportion of paid claims coming from cases with a lawsuit, a trial, or both could lead to rising defense costs. In unreported regressions we find a modest increase in the fraction of medical malpractice claims resolved after suit was filed and no change in the fraction that involved a full trial. However, the annual rate of increase in defense costs is similar to the overall rate we report above if we limit the sample to cases with suit filed.

## DISCUSSION

### Rising Defense Costs over Time

We find a strong trend over time toward higher defense costs in medical malpractice cases. Defense costs also rise in other types of personal injury cases, but more slowly. Over 1988–2005, real defense costs in medical malpractice cases more than doubled, while defense costs in other types of cases rose by about 27 percent.

For medical malpractice cases, we were able to largely rule out a number of possible causes of the rise in defense costs. Several other explanations are possible. Plaintiffs' lawyers may have selected stronger cases over time or invested more resources in case development, forcing insurers to respond. Two explanations are specific to Texas. Legislation adopted in 1987 encouraged counties to adopt alternative dispute resolution (ADR) through mediation or arbitration, and legislation adopted in 1995 restricted who could be an expert in a medical malpractice case. In unreported regressions we find a substantial increase in the percentage of cases resolved with ADR. One or both of these changes may have contributed to rising defense costs. But other research suggests that the rise in medical malpractice defense costs is national in scope.[85]

The sustained rise in defense costs deserves further attention from researchers and policymakers. Some insurers have complained about rising defense costs but have offered no data and have blamed runaway tort awards. In Texas, at least, that explanation lacks empirical support.

### Insurer Reserves for Defense Costs

Perhaps our most surprising finding is on medical malpractice insurers' reserves for defense costs. Per case defense costs for these cases doubled over our sample period, yet per case reserves were lower at the end of the period than at the beginning. In contrast, per case reserves for cases covered by other types of insurance kept pace with rising defense costs.

Defense costs are an important part of medical malpractice insurers' costs. By 2005, average defense spending for the large paid claims in our sample was roughly 23 percent of payouts. There is evidence from other studies that defense costs in zero-payout cases are roughly 40 to 45 percent of total defense costs across all cases.[86] Allowing for those costs, a reasonable estimate is that defense costs are roughly 33 percent of total payouts and roughly 25 percent of the sum of total payouts plus total defense costs.

The failure of medical malpractice insurers to adjust their reserve estimates to reflect rising defense costs suggests remarkable inattention to a central aspect of their business—reserving accurately for defense costs. "You manage what you measure" is a well-known business adage; for some Texas medical malpractice insurers, this should perhaps be modified to "you manage what you notice." An alternative possibility is that medical malpractice carriers treat initial case-level defense cost reserves much less seriously than other carriers and focus instead on bulk-level or aggregate reserves at the company level. Because aggregate reserves can exceed the sum of case-level reserves, our findings do not imply that medical malpractice carriers failed to adequately reserve for overall defense costs.

### The High Cost of Medical Malpractice Litigation

The tort system is an expensive way to transfer resources from defendants to plaintiffs. Our findings provide information on how expensive the system is. We estimated above that total defense costs likely equal about 33 percent of observed payouts. If we assume that the median plaintiff's legal fees and expenses are 35 percent of payout,[87] then the per case overhead of running the system is around 50 percent.[88] Stated differently, it costs about a dollar in legal fees and expenses for a plaintiff to end up with $1 in his or her pocket.

Insurers also have administrative and other costs, and some defendants may not report their expenses to TDI. A plausible estimate is that insurers' costs are 15 percent of payouts plus defense costs.[89] Including these costs, our estimate is that we are spending $1.33 in overhead, including legal fees on both sides, to deliver $1 to plaintiffs—meaning that injured plaintiffs walk away with roughly 43 cents of every dollar that flows through the medical malpractice liability system.[90]

### Defense Cost Reserves and the Insurance Cycle

We study here defense costs and expense reserves; we do not study indemnity reserves. We have data only for large paid claims, and thus cannot directly assess whether expense reserves are adequate to cover defense costs for all claims. However, insurers' failure to adjust their reserves for an important source of overall cost could contribute to an "insurance cycle" in medical malpractice premiums. In such a cycle, insurers underprice in "soft" markets; then something (perhaps losses in this or another line of insurance, investment returns, or other factors) shocks the market; insurers raise rates to above-equilibrium levels (a "hard" market); insurers then compete their way down to underpricing again; the next shock strikes, and the cycle repeats. The failure by medical malpractice insurers to incorporate readily available case-level information in expense reserves, or to adjust their procedures for setting expense reserves in a timely manner, is consistent with conventional accounts of the insurance cycle. There is reason to believe that the insurance cycle might be especially severe for medical malpractice claims,[91] but this cannot explain why expense reserves have remained stable when they should have risen.

### The Efficiency of Medical Malpractice Litigation

The sustained rise in defense costs implies that our tort system, never a model of efficiency in providing compensation to injured persons, has become worse at this task over time. To be sure, the optimal level of spending on litigation is not known, and higher spending might produce more accurate outcomes or induce greater care.[92] Still, system efficiency (the fraction of defendant spending that ends up in the hands of plaintiffs) is an important measure of tort system performance. By this measure, the medical malpractice liability system has gotten worse over our sample period.

# CONCLUSION

We have explored the factors that influence defense costs in medical malpractice cases. We find a sustained rise in defense costs, with costs more than doubling over our sample period. Defense costs are higher in cases with a suit filed, cases that go to trial, cases with larger potential damages, and cases that last longer. Medical malpractice insurers failed to adjust their reserving practices to reflect the rise in defense costs, in contrast to insurers for other types of personal injury claims.

The reasons for rising defense costs are unclear. We find no evidence to support a number of possible explanations, including rising payouts, rising exposure, rising lawyer hourly rates, claims staying open longer, and cases settling at a later stage. Defense lawyers appear to be billing more hours for working on apparently similar cases, but we do not know the underlying causes for this trend. However, the rise in defense spending is not large enough to explain the medical malpractice insurance crisis that hit Texas during 1999–2003.

# PART TWO

# Mistreating the Problem: The Impact of Tort Reform in Texas

## CHAPTER 7

# THE IMPACT OF CAPPING DAMAGES

## OVERVIEW

In prior chapters, we studied Texas during the period prior to Texas's 2003 cap on non-economic damages, or shortly after that, before the cap should have had a major effect on closed paid cases. In Part Two, we study the effects of Texas's 2003 medical malpractice reforms, of which a cap on non-economic damages was the centerpiece.

In this chapter, we examine the impact of this cap on the number of paid medical malpractice claims and on payouts in the claims that are still brought. Cap adoption dramatically reduced both the number of paid claims and the payouts in the cases that were still brought. Using simulation methods, we also estimate the impact of Texas's damage cap on payouts in cases brought by or on behalf of victims of various types (e.g., elderly victims, unemployed victims, and deceased victims) if, hypothetically, the same claims had been brought. We also use the simulation approach to compare the stringency of the caps adopted by different states and show that details of cap design make a substantial difference in impact on payouts.

## INTRODUCTION

In this chapter, we first examine the effect of Texas's non-economic (non-econ) cap on the number of large (payout > \$25,000 [1988\$])

paid medical malpractice claims and the payout per claim. We find that Texas's damage cap had a major impact, with payout per large paid claim declining by 42 percent (comparing 2008–2010 to 2001–2003) and paid claim rates falling by 60 percent after controlling for population. The combination of large drops in both payout per claim and paid claim rates led to a 77 percent drop in total medical malpractice payouts per capita. Some of the decline in claim rates would likely have happened anyway— we show in Chapter 11 that there was a sustained nationwide decline in medical malpractice claim rates across all states, including "no-cap" states, which lack damage caps. But the drop in claim rates was steeper in Texas than in no-cap states. And lower payout per large paid claim is attributable to the cap; there was no similar decline in no-cap states.

We use a simulation approach to estimate how the non-econ cap affects payout per claim for different demographic groups. We also simulate the effects on payout per claim of the various damage caps adopted by other states. We find the following:

- The non-econ cap has a disparate impact across plaintiff demographic groups, with larger percentage reductions in allowed damages and payouts for death claims, for claims involving victims who were unemployed, and (less clearly) for elderly plaintiffs. The results for unemployed and elderly plaintiffs—two groups that are disproportionately female— make it likely that there was also a disparate effect for women, although we cannot directly test this with our data.

- The damage caps adopted by different states have widely varying estimated effects. The reduction in mean allowed verdict ranges from 32 percent (Wisconsin) to 75 percent (Colorado). Caps on total damages (i.e., not just on non-economic damages) can have a much larger impact than non-econ caps.

- The lack of an inflation adjustment in many state caps means that these caps become stricter over time. For example, the California non-econ cap blocked 65 percent of non-econ damages and 12 percent of payouts when it was adopted in 1975. This rose to 87 percent of non-econ damages and 26 percent of payouts by 2010.

## LITERATURE REVIEW

We summarize here the principal academic studies that examine the effects of non-econ caps on payouts. Most of these payouts come in settled cases. Earlier studies are mixed, but they lean toward finding a post-cap drop in payout per claim. Avraham studies paid claims against physicians reported to the National Practitioner Data Bank (NPDB) with injury from 1992 to 1998, closed by 2005, based on *injury year*.[93] However, only three small states adopted non-econ caps during this period. His results are sensitive to how he handles two additional caps, which were later invalidated: if he includes these states, he finds a near-zero estimated impact; if he excludes them, he finds a 48 percent post-cap drop in payout per claim in *claim-level* regressions, yet a much smaller and statistically insignificant drop in *state-level* regressions. Waters and others use NPDB data over 1991–2003, study the same three cap adoptions using claim *closing year,* and do not find a statistically significant impact of caps on payout per claim.[94]

Yoon studied Alabama's adoption and later judicial invalidation of a cap on non-econ and punitive damages.[95] Adoption reduced mean recoveries by roughly $20,000; after invalidation, damages returned to their pre-cap level.

In our own research, presented in Chapter 11, we use a larger sample of 12 cap adoptions. We allow for the cap effect on claim rates and payouts to phase in over time as pre-cap-adoption cases are closed. We use NPDB data from 1992 to 2012 to compare trends in the 12 "new-cap" states (which adopted caps during 1995–2005) with "old-cap" states that adopted caps during 1975–1985 and "no-cap" states, which never adopted caps. We find that claim rates are declining in all states, but the decline is larger in new-cap states. The difference between new-cap and other states is large and statistically significant. We also find a larger decline in payout per claim in new-cap states.

## EFFECT OF TEXAS'S NON-ECON CAP

What were the actual effects of Texas's non-econ cap? Figure 7.1 shows trends in large paid claims per 100,000 population and payout per claim from 1990 to 2010. Both claim frequency and payout per claim fluctuated

# Figure 7.1

Texas medical malpractice claim rates and payouts: Before and after reform

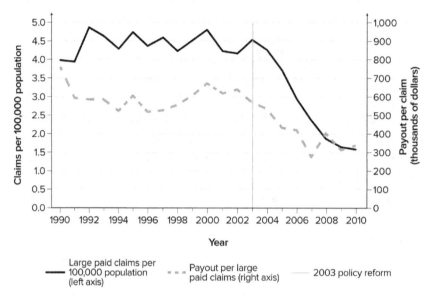

| ── Large paid claims per 100,000 population (left axis) | - - - Payout per large paid claims (right axis) | ─── 2003 policy reform |

*Notes:* Large (payout > $25,000 [1988$]) paid claims per 100,000 population by year for all claimants (left axis), and payout per claim (right axis, in thousands of 2010$), for medical malpractice dataset over 1990–2010. Texas tort reform in 2003 is depicted by vertical line.

*Source:* Based on authors' calculations using the Texas Closed Claim Database.

within a narrow range during the pre-reform period. Both measures fell sharply after Texas adopted a non-econ cap in 2003. Claim frequency fell by 60 percent, comparing 2008–2010 to 2001–2003. Payout per claim dropped by 42 percent (from an average of $608,000 over 2001–2003 to $355,000 over 2008–2010). Payout per capita, which reflects both effects, declined by more than 75 percent.

Other sources also report a large post-reform drop in claims and payouts in Texas. For example, Stewart and others report a drop in surgery-related claims, from 40 suits to 8 suits per 100,000 procedures—an 80 percent drop.[96] The Texas Medical Liability Trust (TMLT), the state's largest malpractice insurance carrier, reported that new claims in 2009 were about half of the pre-reform level despite a larger number of insured physicians.

Unsurprisingly, these dramatic changes in the number of claims and payouts had an impact on medical malpractice insurance premiums.

## Figure 7.2

Texas Medical Liability Trust medical malpractice premiums

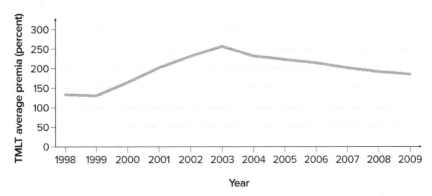

*Notes:* Average medical malpractice insurance rates charged by TMLT for all physicians, 1998–2009, scaled to 1998 = 100. TMLT = Texas Medical Liability Trust.

*Sources:* For 1998–2003, Texas Department of Insurance, "Medical Malpractice Insurance: Overview and Discussion," April 22, 2003; and for 2004–2009, Texas Medical Liability Trust, "TMLT Reduces Rates for Sixth Year Following Texas Tort Reform," September 2, 2008.

Figure 7.2 shows the year-by-year changes in the rates that TMLT charged for medical malpractice coverage. To be sure, by 2009, payouts had fallen to well below pre-cap levels as Figure 7.1 indicates, yet the premiums that TMLT charged remained well above pre-cap levels.

The results in Figures 7.1 and 7.2 make it clear that there was a substantial decline in claim frequency, payout per claim, and medical malpractice premiums during the post-reform period. However, just because something happened after Texas enacted tort reform does not mean that tort reform *caused* that thing to happen. As we discuss in Chapter 11, there was a nationwide trend toward fewer malpractice claims. We need to control for those trends to isolate the impact of the Texas cap. Our back-of-the envelope calculation is that the Texas cap reduced medical malpractice payouts by roughly 50 percent, in addition to the effect that can be attributed to the nationwide decline.

### SIMULATING THE EFFECT OF CAPS ON PAYOUT PER CLAIM

Were the post-reform drops in claim frequency and payout per claim evenly spread across the population, or were some demographic groups hit harder? Texas adopted a non-econ cap that ranges from $250,000 to $750,000, depending on the number and type of defendants. What difference would it have made if Texas had adopted a flat cap of $250,000 or $500,000? The Texas cap is not inflation adjusted; what difference would it make if it were? To answer these questions, we turn to a simulation.

Our simulation uses paid claims from Texas during the pre-reform period to study these questions. We know the breakdown of damages (economic, non-econ, and punitive damages) only for tried cases, but we use that breakdown to impute types of damages to settled cases according to plaintiff demographics. Then we apply the non-econ cap to the actual or imputed non-econ damages and compute the effect of the cap on allowed damages. We then allocate payouts (which we observe) to each category of damages. Because payouts are often less than verdicts (see Chapters 4 and 5), we assume that economic damages are paid first, followed by non-econ damages, punitive damages, and then interest.

We focus on the 350 jury verdicts from the pre-reform period where the jury found for the plaintiff (which we refer to subsequently as "plaintiff jury verdict cases"). Those are the only cases for which we have the breakdown of damages necessary to conduct our analysis. When we focus on those cases, we find that almost half involve awards of non-econ damages below $250,000. If this were known before trial—often, it will not be—Texas's non-econ cap would not affect these cases. At the other end of the distribution, we also find a small number of "blockbuster" cases. The 25 cases with more than $5 million in non-econ awards represent only 7 percent of cases but 47 percent of total non-econ awards. But, as we noted in Chapter 4, for cases with large awards, payouts fall well short of damages, even without a damages cap. Overall, plaintiffs received 49 percent of the "adjusted" (including interest) verdicts. On average, plaintiffs received 72 percent of awarded economic damages but only 36 percent of awarded non-econ damages and 15 percent of punitive damages. An analysis of Texas's non-econ cap needs to take into account that for large awards, the cap is often limiting damages that would not have been paid to begin with.

Our simulation approach has an important limitation. We can use simulation to estimate the effect of damage caps on payouts, *assuming* the same cases would still be brought with or without the cap. But we know that if a cap is adopted, fewer cases will be brought. Unfortunately, we lack a good way to measure or simulate which cases those are.

### How Does the Non-Econ Cap Affect Different Plaintiff Groups?

Critics have argued that non-econ caps have a disproportionate impact on plaintiff groups whose damages are largely non-economic: especially women, the elderly, the unemployed, and the deceased. Prior research is not in consensus on this question.[97] We cannot test whether caps differentially affect women, because we do not have data on the claimant's gender. However, we do have data on age and employment status. Female claimants are less likely to be employed and more likely to be over 65.

Our simulations support a disparate effect of the Texas non-econ cap—and thus non-econ caps more generally—on different plaintiff groups. Table 7.1 shows how the Texas cap affects predicted payouts for several subsamples: death versus nondeath cases; employed versus unemployed plaintiffs; and elderly plaintiffs versus adult nonelderly, children, and babies. Aggregate payouts fall for all groups, but they fall more sharply for elderly plaintiffs and the unemployed and in death cases. This corresponds to these plaintiffs having a higher proportion of non-economic damages (affected by the cap) in their total damages awards, relative to other plaintiffs. The average per case reduction in payout is larger for death versus nondeath cases and for unemployed versus employed plaintiffs; these differences are statistically significant. We discuss medical malpractice claiming by people ages 65 and over in more detail in Chapter 8.

Table 7.1 presents simulation results for tried cases. We conducted similar simulations for settled cases, with similar results. For example, the aggregate payout reduction in settled cases is 24 percent for death versus 15 percent for nondeath cases.

The categories (elderly, unemployed, death cases) with larger drops in payout per claim likely also experience larger drops in claim rates. For example, it is likely that the viability of cases with purely non-economic damages—as is the case for many but not all claims by

## Table 7.1

Differential effects of non-econ cap in tried cases, Texas

| Case type | Age | Number of cases | Aggregate reduction in payout | Mean of per case percentage reductions | |
|---|---|---|---|---|---|
| | | | | Payout | *t*-stat |
| Death | All | 84 | 36% | 23% | 4.05*** |
| Nondeath | All | 266 | 19% | 11% | |
| Unemployed | Nonbaby | 155 | 29% | 17% | 2.23** |
| Employed | All | 164 | 15% | 11% | |
| | Elderly | 52 | 34% | 17% | 1.01 |
| | Adult nonelderly | 236 | 21% | 13% | |
| **All** | Children | 31 | 24% | 16% | 0.71 |
| | Baby | 31 | 22% | 12% | |
| | **All** | **350** | **22%** | **14%** | |

*Notes:* Percentage reduction in aggregate payouts and mean of per case percentage reductions in payouts attributable to non-econ cap for 350 plaintiff jury verdict cases over 1988–2005. Asterisks and bolding in the final column indicate that the difference in the mean per case percentage reduction in payouts is statistically significant. ** and *** indicate statistical significance at the 5 percent and 1 percent levels, respectively.

*Source:* Based on authors' calculations using the Texas Closed Claim Database.

elderly plaintiffs—will be disproportionately affected. Unfortunately, as noted above, we lack a good way to simulate the differential impact of caps on claim frequency for different demographic subgroups.

### The Impact of Cap Design

Across the 31 states that cap damages, there is considerable variation in cap type (non-econ cap, total damages cap, or both) and in cap level. This diversity helps explain why past research has found varying results—and it makes it harder to predict the effect of adopting a particular cap. Our simulation approach lets us study how different cap designs affect estimated payouts against a standardized portfolio of cases. As in Table 7.1, we use the Texas pre–reform cases (both tried and settled).

Table 7.2 shows the predicted effects from our simulation. The results are presented based on the severity of the cap, ranging from most strict (Colorado) to least strict (Wisconsin). We analyze all caps as if they were specified in real 2003 dollars. The ordinal ranking is similar, but not identical, for tried and settled cases.

As Table 7.2 reflects, damages caps vary widely in stringency. At the high-stringency end, Colorado's combination of a $1 million cap on total damages and a $300,000 non-econ cap reduces payouts in tried cases by 59 percent and in settled cases by 36 percent. At the low end, Wisconsin's $750,000 cap on non-econ damages reduces payouts in tried

# Table 7.2

## Simulated effect of state damages caps on payouts

| State | Cap type | Cap level | Decline in mean payout (%) | |
|---|---|---|---|---|
| | | | Tried cases | Settled cases |
| Colorado | Total<br>Non-econ | $1 million total;<br>$300,000 non-econ | 59% | 36% |
| Louisiana | Total | $500,000 plus future medical expenses | 51% | 40% |
| New Mexico | Total | $600,000 plus future medical expenses | 48% | 36% |
| Indiana | Total | $1.25 million | 45% | 27% |
| Virginia | Total | $2 million | 34% | 19% |
| California<br>Kansas<br>Montana | Non-econ | $250,000 | 25% | 21% |
| Texas | Non-econ | $250,000–$750,000, depending on number and type of defendants | 22% | 18% |
| Mississippi<br>North Dakota<br>South Dakota | Non-econ | $500,000 | 18% | 13% |
| Wisconsin | Non-econ | $750,000 | 13% | 9% |

*Notes:* Percentage reduction in mean payouts in tried and settled cases, from applying indicated damages caps to 350 plaintiff jury verdict cases and 14,655 settled cases included in a medical malpractice dataset for 1988–2005. Cap amounts are in nominal dollars; the caps are modeled as if in real 2003 dollars, ordered from the most strict (Colorado) to the least strict (Wisconsin).

*Sources:* For payouts, Texas Closed Claim Database; and for caps, Ronen Avraham, Database of State Tort Law Reforms 5.1.

## Figure 7.3

Effect of total damages versus non-economic caps on payouts, nationwide

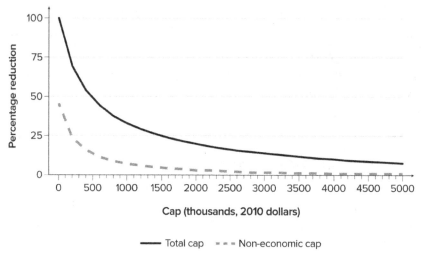

Cap (thousands, 2010 dollars)

—— Total cap    = = = Non-economic cap

*Note:* Simulated percentage reduction in mean payouts due to total damages caps and non-economic caps at indicated levels, for 350 plaintiff jury verdict cases and 14,655 settled cases, included in a medical malpractice dataset for 1988–2005.

*Source:* Based on authors' calculations using the Texas Closed Claim Database.

cases by 13 percent and in settled cases by 9 percent. Caps on total damages have an especially large effect.

In Figure 7.3 we show the predicted effects of caps on total damages and caps on non-econ damages, for cap levels from $0 to $5 million. The graph shows that a $2.6 million total damages cap has roughly the same impact as a $400,000 non-econ cap—each reduces expected payouts across all cases (tried and settled) by around 19 percent. Figure 7.3 also confirms that at all cap levels, total damage caps have a far greater impact than non-econ caps.

### The Impact of Not Indexing a Non-Econ Cap for Inflation

When California adopted the first non-econ cap in 1975, it set the level at $250,000, with no adjustment for inflation. That approach has anchored subsequent debates over non-econ caps.[98] Most caps are not indexed for inflation, so their impact becomes stricter over time. If the California

## Table 7.3

Effect of inflation on allowed non-econ damages and payouts

|  | Percentage of non-econ damages disallowed | Percentage reduction in payout |
|---|---|---|
| California (1975) | 65% | 12% |
| California (1985) | 77% | 19% |
| California (1995) | 82% | 23% |
| As of 2010 | 87% | 26% |
| **Assumed inflation rate = 3 percent** |  |  |
| 2020 | 90% | 29% |
| 2030 | 92% | 30% |
| 2040 | 94% | 32% |

*Note:* Predicted effect of inflation on disallowed of non-economic damages and reduction in payout due to $250,000 simple non-econ cap in nominal 2003 dollars, for 350 plaintiff jury verdict cases included in a medical malpractice dataset for 1988–2005.

*Source:* Based on authors' calculations using the Texas Closed Claim Database.

non-econ cap had been inflation adjusted, it would have been around $1.1 million in 2016 dollars. Another way of evaluating the impact of not indexing a non-econ cap for inflation is to estimate how the cap's effect on payouts changes over time. Table 7.3 does just that, using actual inflation figures for 1975–2010, and then projecting forward to 2040, assuming a 3 percent annual rate of inflation. In 1975, the year the California non-econ cap was enacted, we estimate that the cap disallowed 65 percent of awarded non-econ damages and reduced mean payouts by 12 percent. By 2040, we estimate the California non-econ cap will disallow 94 percent of non-econ damages and reduce payouts by 32 percent.

## DISCUSSION AND CONCLUSION

### The Effect of Texas's Non-Econ Cap

In Texas, damage caps did the job they were intended to do—they substantially reduced claim rates, payout per claim, and malpractice insurance premiums. In the years after reform, paid claims dropped by

60 percent, and payouts per claim dropped by 42 percent. In combination, this caused per capita payouts to drop by 77 percent. Medical malpractice premiums are reported to have dropped by 50 percent. To be sure, to isolate the effect of the Texas cap on claim rates, it is important to control for preexisting trends. We document in Chapter 11 the nationwide receding tide of medical malpractice litigation. But even controlling for nationwide trends, the Texas cap had a substantial effect on claim rates. Moreover, the receding tide did not discernibly affect payout per claim. Thus the 42 percent post-cap Texas drop in payout per claim can be attributed to the cap. Overall, after controlling for preexisting trends, we estimate that the Texas cap led to roughly a 50 percent drop in total payouts.

### Cap Design

In our simulations, cap design strongly affects payouts. The cap level matters—but so does whether the cap limits all damages or only non-econ damages, and whether it is inflation adjusted. Most prior research has ignored the importance of cap design in assessing the impact of damages caps: often, all damages caps are treated as if they were the same. We find that caps on total damages have a much larger impact on payouts than non-econ caps. We also find that caps that are not adjusted for inflation become substantially stricter over time.

### Disparate Impact of Non-Econ Caps

Prior studies of jury awards found mixed results on whether non-econ caps have a disparate impact on women, the elderly, and children. Our simulation approach allows us to explore the impact of non-econ caps on discrete demographic groups. We find evidence that the non-econ cap has a more severe impact on deceased and unemployed plaintiffs, and perhaps (though less strongly) elderly plaintiffs. We cannot directly study the impact on women because we do not have data on claimant gender, but an effect is likely, given our results for elderly plaintiffs and the unemployed—groups that are disproportionately female. Across all cases, we find meaningful differences in the impact of the Texas cap on payouts, but they are smaller than suggested by some cap critics.[99]

## CHAPTER 8

# MEDICAL MALPRACTICE CLAIMING BY ELDERLY PATIENTS

## OVERVIEW

The elderly account for a disproportionate share of medical spending, but little is known about how they are treated by the medical malpractice system or how tort reform affects them. We study those questions here. We compare paid medical malpractice claims brought by elderly plaintiffs (ages 65 and over) in Texas over 1988–2009 to those brought by adult nonelderly plaintiffs. Over 1988–2003, the rate for elderly plaintiffs' paid claims rose from 20 percent to 66 percent of the adult nonelderly rate, and mean and median payments per claim converged, although elderly plaintiffs, were far less likely to receive large payments. The 2003 Texas reforms interrupted the trend toward convergence. The reforms reduced claim rates and payouts for both groups but disproportionately reduced payouts to elderly claimants.

## INTRODUCTION

The elderly account for a disproportionate share of medical spending. They are also more prone than the nonelderly to be harmed by medical error because they encounter the health care system more often, often have multiple medical conditions and medications, and are more fragile. Yet little attention has been paid to how they are treated by the medical malpractice system or how their medical malpractice claims are affected by tort reform. In this chapter, we focus on medical malpractice claims by elderly claimants and how they differ from claims by adult nonelderly claimants. We exclude nursing home claims, which are brought primarily by the elderly. We also consider how the Texas cap on non-economic (non-econ) damages affected elderly claimants compared to its impact on other claimants.

To compare elderly claimants to nonelderly claimants, we need to adjust for the fact that elderly people use more health care. We do that (imperfectly) by adjusting for the number of hospital inpatient days used by each group. The ratio of elderly to adult nonelderly paid claims per inpatient day rose sharply, from under 20 percent over 1988–1990 to more than 50 percent over 2001–2003, but then fell to 41 percent in 2009. Mean and median payouts to elderly claimants were substantially lower at the beginning of our sample period but rose over time and fully converged with those for adult nonelderly claimants for pre-reform claims, which were not affected by the non-econ cap. The non-econ cap reduced post-reform claim rates and payouts to both groups but affected elderly patients more strongly than adult nonelderly. Our main story is thus "interrupted convergence." Prior to Texas's 2003 tort reform, the patterns for medical malpractice claims with elderly plaintiffs and adult nonelderly plaintiffs were converging. After tort reform, convergence ceased, and to some degree, it reversed. We also find that elderly claimants settle claims faster, are less likely to take cases to trial, and are far less likely to receive "blockbuster" payouts.

## BACKGROUND

### Literature Review

The empirical literature on medical malpractice claiming by the elderly is modest and dated. Sager and others analyzed Wisconsin malpractice claims from 1983 to 1984 and found that elderly patients were less likely to initiate malpractice suits.[100] A 1993 General Accounting Office report on malpractice claims against hospitals from 1986 to 1990 found that Medicare patients accounted for about 32 percent of hospital discharges and 44 percent of inpatient days but made only about 10 percent of claims and received about 10 percent of dollar payouts.[101] Studdert and others found that patients over 75 who suffered medical negligence were less likely to file claims than younger patients.[102]

A similarly small body of work examines how tort reform affects elderly claimants. In 2010, Daniels and Martin provided evidence from a survey of Texas medical malpractice lawyers of a disparate impact of the Texas reforms on the willingness of these lawyers to bring claims on behalf of elderly claimants.[103] Finley studied jury verdicts in three states and found that non-econ caps hit elderly claimants harder than nonelderly claimants,[104] but Studdert, Yang, and Mello found no evidence of a disparate impact in a study of California jury verdicts.[105] No study has examined whether caps differentially affect elderly claimants in settled cases.

### Dataset

In this chapter, unlike the rest of this book, we exclude claims against nursing homes from our sample, because we cannot readily compare these claims by elderly patients to similar claims for the adult nonelderly (we do include 35 claims paid by a physician or hospital that also include a payment by a nursing home). We generally focus on two broad age groups, adult nonelderly claimants (ages 19–64) and elderly claimants (ages 65 and over). For some analyses, we separate elderly claimants into age brackets (ages 65–74, 75–84, and 85 and over).

### Sample Selection Bias

To assess the relative impact of tort reform on elderly claimants versus adult nonelderly claimants, we need enough time to pass after reform so that our sample of post-reform cases will be reasonably representative of all post-reform cases. But we observe cases only when they close, and slow-to-close cases might be systematically different than quick-to-close cases. For example, if cases with larger payouts or more complex cases take longer to close, and if they do so differentially for elderly claimants as compared to adult nonelderly claimants, our post-reform results could be biased if we cut off data collection too soon.

Fortunately, as we discuss below, payout has a negligible association with claim duration. Complexity (proxied by the number and type of defendants in the case) does predict longer duration, but the effect is similar for elderly and adult nonelderly claimants. Overall, we judge that ending the sample period in 2009 is a reasonable compromise, taking into account the risk of sample selection bias (if the post-reform period is too short) and the risk that factors other than tort reform are responsible for the observed effects (if the post-reform period is too long).

## EMPIRICAL RESULTS

### Synopsis

We begin with total medical malpractice payouts. Figure 8.1 shows total payouts per capita for elderly and adult nonelderly claimants. The solid line shows payouts to adult nonelderly claimants; the dotted line shows payouts to elderly claimants. The dashed line shows payouts to elderly

## Figure 8.1

Total per capita payouts to adult nonelderly and elderly claimants, Texas

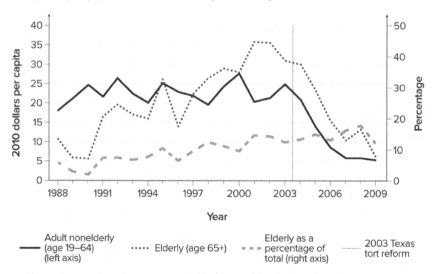

Notes: Total payout per capita by year for elderly and adult nonelderly claimants (left axis), and ratio of elderly payouts/total payout to all plaintiffs (right axis), for non–nursing home, large (payout > $25,000 [1988]) paid medical malpractice claims closed from 1988 to 2009. In this and later graphs, the vertical line between 2003 and 2004 separates the pre- and post-tort-reform periods.

Source: Based on authors' calculations using the Texas Closed Claim Database.

claimants as a fraction of total payouts to all plaintiffs. As one progresses further into the post-reform period, an increasing percentage of cases are affected by tort reform. By 2009, 93 percent of adult nonelderly claims and 89 percent of elderly claims are post-reform.

As Figure 8.1 reflects, per capita payouts to adult nonelderly claimants were roughly flat from 1990 to 2003 but dropped sharply after tort reform, from an average of about $24 per capita over 2001–2003 to just under $6 per capita in 2009.[106] Per capita payouts to elderly claimants increased steadily from about $6 in 1990 to around $36 over 2001–2003 before dropping to under $7 in 2009. As we noted in Chapter 7 and discuss further below, the post-reform drop in payouts per capita comes from a combination of fewer claims and lower payout per claim.

As the dashed line shows, the share of total payouts received by elderly claimants increased from less than 5 percent over 1988–1990 to around 14 percent over 2001–2003 and then was roughly flat through the post-reform period. Thus the rising line for elderly claimants in Figure 8.1 provides graphical support for our overall theme that tort reform interrupted a pattern of convergence between medical malpractice claiming by elderly and adult nonelderly patients.

In unreported regressions, we confirm that prior to the 2003 reforms, the rise in per capita payouts to elderly claimants over time was strongly statistically significant. In contrast, per capita payouts to the adult nonelderly showed no significant time trend. Tort reform affected both groups strongly. From 2003 to 2009, total payouts dropped by 78 percent for adult nonelderly claimants and 80 percent for elderly claimants.

In Table 8.1, we turn from time trends to averages across all years in the dataset. Panel A presents summary statistics on claim frequency and payout by type of paying defendants, as well as the fraction of claims and payouts attributable to elderly plaintiffs. Claims by elderly patients, when made, are disproportionately likely to be against hospitals rather than physicians. This could reflect the conventional wisdom that elderly patients tend not to sue their doctors; the location and intensity of their medical care; or a combination of these factors.

Panel B presents summary information on percentage of population, hospital discharges, hospital inpatient days, and medical spending

# Table 8.1

Summary statistics on large paid claims, Texas

### A. Medical malpractice claims

| Paying defendant | Number of claims | Percentage elderly claimants | Total payout (millions, 2009 dollars) | Percentage paid to elderly |
|---|---|---|---|---|
| Physician | 7,997 | 14.7% | $2,942 | 12.0% |
| Hospital | 1,380 | 34.8% | $627 | 20.5% |
| Physician + hospital | 6,229 | 14.5% | $5,265 | 7.4% |
| Other | 428 | 22.9% | $145 | 23.7% |
| Total | 16,034 | 16.6% | $8,979 | 10.1% |

### B. Medical care use

| Age group | Percentage of population | Percentage of hospital discharges | Percentage of inpatient days | Percentage of health care spending |
|---|---|---|---|---|
| Babies (<1) | 1.7% | 14.7% | 11.3% | 13.4% |
| Children (1–18) | 28.1% | 7.9% | 6.4% | |
| Adult nonelderly (19–64) | 60.3% | 50.8% | 46.8% | 51.6% |
| Elderly (65+) | 10.0% | 26.7% | 35.5% | 35.0% |
| Total | 100% | 100% | 100% | 100% |

*Notes:* Panel A: Number of claims, percentage involving elderly claimants, total payouts, and proportion paid to elderly plaintiffs, for non–nursing home, large (payout > $25,000 [1988$]) paid medical malpractice cases closed from 1988 to 2009. Payouts in millions, 2009 dollars. Panel B: Percentage of population, hospital discharges, hospital inpatient days, and health care spending represented by indicated age groups. Percentages may not sum to 100 percent because of rounding.

*Source:* Based on authors' calculations using the Texas Closed Claim Database.

for different age groups. To assess elderly patients' use of the medical malpractice system, we need to adjust for their use of medical care. Hospital discharges, inpatient days, and medical spending provide different measures of treatment intensity. In this chapter, we rely principally on inpatient days to adjust for health care intensity. But we obtain similar results with the other measures. The elderly account for 10 percent of population, 27 percent of hospital discharges, 35 percent of medical spending, and 36 percent of inpatient days but represent only 17 percent of large paid claims and 10 percent of payouts.[107]

In Table 8.2, we divide the sample into finer age ranges and provide additional detail on claim rates and payout per claim over our full sample period. We define a measure of "claiming propensity" as the ratio of the percentage of large paid claims to the percentage of inpatient days. This ratio is 1 by definition for the whole population. Claiming propensity is 1.36 for adult nonelderly patients but only 0.47 for elderly patients. Among elderly patients, claiming propensity declines with age; it is 0.66 for young elderly patients (ages 65–74), 0.38 for moderate elderly patients (ages 75–84), and 0.25 for those 85 and older. The last two columns in Table 8.2 show a similar but milder pattern for mean and median payout per claim: lower payouts for elderly claimants than

# Table 8.2

## Large paid claims and claiming propensity by age group, Texas

| Age group | Population (%) | Inpatient days (%) | Paid claims (%) | Claiming propensity | Total payout (%) | Payout/claim (in thousands, 2009 dollars) Mean | Median |
|---|---|---|---|---|---|---|---|
| Baby/child (0–18) | 29.7% | 17.7% | 19.9% | 1.13 | 33.5% | $942 | $321 |
| Adult nonelderly (19–64) | 60.3% | 46.8% | 63.5% | 1.36 | 56.4% | $498 | $223 |
| All elderly (65+) | 10.0% | 35.5% | 16.6% | 0.47 | 10.1% | $341 | $195 |
| Young elderly (65–74) | 5.6% | 14.3% | 9.4% | 0.66 | 6.0% | $356 | $210 |
| Moderate elderly (75–84) | 3.3% | 13.9% | 5.4% | 0.38 | 3.2% | $334 | $173 |
| Very elderly (85+) | 1.1% | 7.3% | 1.8% | 0.25 | 0.9% | $291 | $157 |

*Notes:* Percentages of population, inpatient days, and claims; claiming propensity (percentage of claims/percentage of inpatient days); percentage of total payout; and mean and median payout per paid claim for plaintiffs in indicated age ranges, for non–nursing home, large paid medical malpractice cases closed from 1988 to 2009. Percentages may not sum to 100 percent because of rounding. Payouts in thousands, 2009 dollars.

*Source:* Based on authors' calculations using the Texas Closed Claim Database.

for adult nonelderly claimants, with payouts declining with age among elderly claimants.

### Claim Frequency

We turn next to time trends in claim frequency. Figure 8.2, Panel A, shows time trends in the number of large paid claims per 100,000 in each age group from 1990 to 2009, separately for elderly claimants (dotted line) and adult nonelderly claimants (solid line). Claims per 100,000 adult nonelderly persons were roughly flat through 2003 but then declined during the post-reform period, from 4.6 in 2003 to 1.8 in 2009. In contrast, claims per 100,000 elderly increased sharply during the pre-reform period, from 2.4 in 1990 to 9.2 in 2003, before falling to 3.2 in 2009.

In Figure 8.2, Panel B, we compare claim rates for medical malpractice cases to those in the other four lines of personal injury claims included in our dataset. Panel B shows rates for all adults (ages 19+).

## Figure 8.2

### Time trends: Large paid claims per 100,000 population, Texas

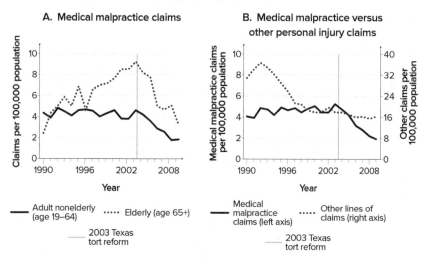

Notes: Panel A: Large paid claims per 100,000 population for elderly and adult nonelderly plaintiffs for non–nursing home medical malpractice cases closed from 1990 to 2009. Panel B: Large (payout > $25,000 [1988$]) paid claims per 100,000 population, separately for medical malpractice cases and other personal injury claims. Vertical line between 2003 and 2004 separates the pre- and post-tort-reform periods.

Source: Based on authors' calculations using the Texas Closed Claim Database.

During the 1990s, claim rates declined for other types of cases, and sharply so through about 1998, but were stable for medical malpractice claims. Over 2000–2003, the trends for the two groups are similar. Post-reform, medical malpractice claim rates dropped sharply, while claim rates for other personal liability claims showed only a modest downward trend. Claim rate trends for other personal injury cases declined over 1997–2009 for adult nonelderly cases but modestly rose for elderly cases.

Claim rates per 100,000 population do not take into account more intensive use of medical care by the elderly. If we control for intensity of use of medical care by adjusting for relative use of hospital inpatient days, the trends are similar, but the claim rate for the elderly is well below the nonelderly rate at all times. The elderly to nonelderly ratio rises from an average of 18 percent over 1988–1990 to an average of 41 percent over 2001–2003 and generally remains in the 40 percent–45 percent range thereafter. We used regression analysis to confirm that, prior to the 2003 reforms, there was a statistically significant rise in elderly claim rates versus no significant trend in adult nonelderly rates.

As Figure 8.2 shows, the 2003 reforms produce a sharp drop in claims for both groups. The percentage drop in claim rates from 2003 to 2009 for the elderly is 65 percent, only slightly larger than the 61 percent drop for the adult nonelderly. But the effective drop for the elderly is likely larger than 65 percent, because their claim rate was rising prior to reform and might well have continued to rise but for reforms.

A caveat is necessary, however. As we discuss in Chapter 11, there was a nationwide trend toward lower claim rates during this period in all states, including no-cap states. This trend likely affected Texas as well; if so, our estimates overstate the impact of reform on claim rates.

### Payout per Claim

We have thus far examined changes over time in claim rates and total payouts. We next consider payout per claim. Figure 8.3, Panel A, presents time trends for mean payouts in medical malpractice cases. We provide separate lines for adult nonelderly and elderly claimants. Over 1988–2003, mean payouts for adult nonelderly claimants were flat or

## Figure 8.3

### Payout per claim: elderly versus adult nonelderly, Texas

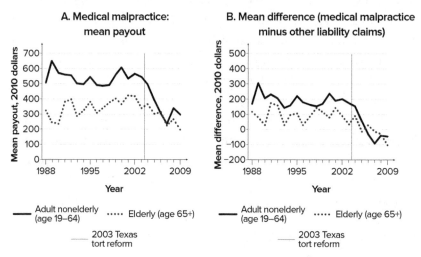

*Notes:* Panel A: Mean payout per claim by year, non–nursing home, large (payout > $25,000 [1988$]) paid medical malpractice cases, closed from 1988 to 2009, separately for elderly and adult nonelderly claimants. Panel B: Differences in mean payout per claim between medical malpractice claims and other large paid liability claims by year, separately for elderly and adult nonelderly claimants. Vertical line between 2003 and 2004 separates the pre- and post-tort-reform periods. Sample is limited to non-duplicate claims.

*Source:* Based on authors' calculations using the Texas Closed Claim Database.

even gently declining, with substantial year-to-year variation. In contrast, mean payouts to elderly claimants were rising, although payouts to elderly claimants remained below the adult nonelderly level. After 2003, payout per claim drops sharply for both groups.

In the initial post-reform years, the gap in mean payout between elderly and adult nonelderly claimants continued to shrink until it was essentially gone by 2006–2007. After that, the elderly and adult nonelderly lines diverged again. This divergence was driven by post-reform claims. Over 2005–2009, there was no discernible difference in mean or median payout on pre-reform claims between elderly and adult nonelderly claimants. In contrast, for post-reform claims, mean and median payouts to adult nonelderly claimants were significantly higher than for elderly patients (mean: $154,000 versus $116,000; $t = 2.96$).

In Figure 8.3, Panel B, we report the *difference* in mean payouts between medical malpractice claims and large paid claims for the other four lines of personal injury claims included in the Texas Closed Claim Database (TCCD), separately for elderly and adult nonelderly claimants. The 2003 reforms affect medical malpractice claims but not the other four lines. Prior to reform, there is no trend for either group. If we look separately at trends for other types of personal injury claims, we find no time trend in payouts for adult nonelderly claimants and a modestly rising trend for elderly claimants, with no change in trend following Texas's 2003 medical malpractice reforms.

Pre-reform, average payouts in large paid claims are larger in medical malpractice cases than for personal injury claims covered by the other four lines of insurance. After reform, average medical malpractice payouts drop sharply relative to those for the other four lines of claims and become smaller than payouts in the other four lines.

We also used regression analysis to study the impact of the 2003 reforms on payout per large paid claim in medical malpractice cases. We use claim-level data, and we know which claims are pre-reform and which are post-reform. Payout per claim dropped for both groups. The drop averaged 37 percent for elderly claimants versus 26 percent for non-elderly. The drops for both groups were statistically significant, as was the extra drop for elderly claimants ($t = 2.05$). This provides additional evidence that the non–econ cap affected elderly plaintiffs more strongly than adult nonelderly plaintiffs.

### Payout per Capita

The combined impact of a sharp drop in claim rates (some of which might have happened without tort reform) and a drop in payout per claim is a very large drop in payout per capita. As Figure 8.1 shows, per capita payouts to the adult nonelderly fell from the mid-twenties prior to reform to about $6 by 2009. Per capita payouts to elderly claimants rose from around $6 at the start of our sample period to the mid-thirties prior to reform, but they have since fallen back to just above their level at the start of our sample period.

## ECONOMIC VERSUS NON-ECONOMIC DAMAGES

Compensatory damages can be either economic or non-economic, and the 2003 tort reforms capped only non-econ damages. Thus, it is worth assessing how the breakdown of damages differs between elderly and adult nonelderly plaintiffs. We know this breakdown for *tried* cases but not for settled cases. We estimate *paid* damages of each type, assuming that payouts are allocated first to economic damages, second to non-econ damages, and third to punitive damages.

Table 8.3, Panel A, reports mean and median per case ratios and the aggregate ratio of paid economic damages to total damages for adult

## Table 8.3

Paid damages by plaintiff age and type of damages, Texas

### A. Paid economic damages: Percentages in tried cases

| Age group | Number of cases | Paid economic damages/total payout | | |
| | | Mean per case ratio | Median per case ratio | Aggregate ratio |
|---|---|---|---|---|
| Adult nonelderly (19–64) | 263 | 47.4% | 37.6% | 56.7% |
| Elderly (65+) | 48 | 35.3% | 22.5% | 25.4% |

*Note:* Mean per case, median per case, and aggregate ratios of paid economic damages/total payout, for 311 non–nursing home, large paid medical malpractice cases involving adult plaintiffs with plaintiff verdicts (290 pre-reform and 21 post-reform cases), closed from 1988 to 2009.

*Source:* Based on authors' calculations using the Texas Closed Claim Database.

### B. Paid damages in tried cases: Amounts

| Age group | Economic damages (thousands, 2009 dollars) | | Non-econ + punitive damages (thousands, 2009 dollars) | |
| | Mean | Median | Mean | Median |
|---|---|---|---|---|
| Adult nonelderly | $444 | $88 | $339 | $135 |
| Elderly | $129 | $66 | $380 | $240 |
| **Ratio: elderly/adult nonelderly** | 29.1% | 76.1% | 111.5% | 178.2% |

*Notes:* Mean and median amounts of paid economic damages and paid (non-economic + punitive damages), for 311 non–nursing home, large paid medical malpractice cases involving adult plaintiffs with plaintiff verdicts, closed from 1988 to 2009. Non-econ = non-economic.

*Source:* Based on authors' calculations using the Texas Closed Claim Database.

nonelderly and elderly plaintiffs. Table 8.3 includes both pre-cap and post-cap cases, but the sample is dominated by pre-cap cases. Across all three measures, economic damages account for a lower proportion of payments to elderly plaintiffs than to adult nonelderly plaintiffs. The difference is greatest for aggregate payouts. Only 25 percent of elderly payouts are attributable to economic damages, compared to 57 percent for the adult nonelderly. Thus, it is not surprising that payouts to elderly claimants are more strongly affected by the non-econ cap, as we found above. The stronger effect of a non-econ cap on payouts to elderly claimants, in turn, explains why one would expect a larger falloff in claim rates for elderly patients than adult nonelderly patients, and a larger falloff for adult non-elderly patients than for babies and children, as we also found above.

In Table 8.3, Panel B, we report payouts in dollars instead of percentages. We report mean and median paid economic damages and means and medians for the sum of non-economic plus punitive damages, separately for adult nonelderly and elderly plaintiffs. The bottom row shows the ratio of the elderly to the nonelderly amount. Mean paid economic damages are much larger for adult nonelderly plaintiffs than for elderly plaintiffs: $444,000 versus $129,000. The difference in median awards of economic damages is smaller ($88,000 versus $66,000) but again favors the adult nonelderly.

The pattern reverses when we study the sum of non-econ and punitive damages. The mean is higher for elderly than for adult nonelderly plaintiffs: $380,000 versus $339,000. Median awards for these damage categories even more sharply favor elderly plaintiffs—the median payout is $240,000 for elderly plaintiffs, versus $135,000 for adult nonelderly plaintiffs. Thus, the lower mean payouts to elderly plaintiffs that we saw in Figure 8.3 are partly explained by lower economic damages. To be sure, attorneys are likely to accept cases with low economic damages only if expected total damages (non-economic + punitive damages) are relatively high. The evidence in Table 8.3, Panel B, is consistent with this selection effect.

## BLOCKBUSTER PAYOUTS

Medical malpractice payouts have a strong positive skew—a limited number of large payouts account for a significant fraction of total payout dollars. We saw in Figure 8.3 that *mean* payouts are substantially lower for elderly than for nonelderly plaintiffs. In contrast, the differences in median payouts to the two groups are smaller, although both differences largely disappear over our sample period. This pattern suggests that elderly claimants are less likely to receive very large payouts. We confirm this by examining the largest ("blockbuster") payouts in our dataset. The top 200 claims are only 1.3 percent of total claims, but they account for 20.2 percent of total payouts.

As Figure 8.4 shows, although the elderly account for 17 percent of all claims (see Table 8.2), they account for only 2 of the largest 200 payouts (1 percent). Both of these cases were pre-cap death cases, which likely had small economic damages (we cannot be sure because both

## Figure 8.4

### Distribution of largest payout claims by age group

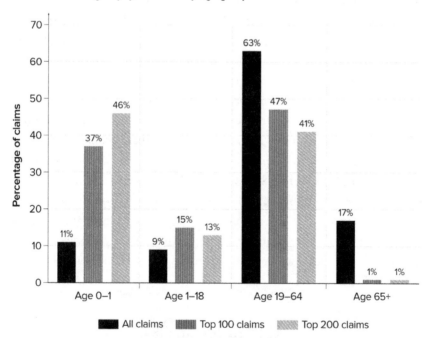

*Notes:* Percentage of all payouts and percentage of top 100 and 200 paid claims made to claimants in indicated age ranges, for non–nursing home, large (payout > $25,000 [1988$]) paid medical malpractice cases closed from 1988 to 2009. Percentages may not sum to 100 percent because of rounding.

*Source:* Based on authors' calculations using the Texas Closed Claim Database.

cases settled before trial). If the non-econ cap had applied during our entire sample period, it is possible that none of the top 200 payouts would have gone to an elderly claimant.

In blockbuster cases, the most common injury is brain damage or spinal cord injuries (140 of the top 200 cases), which often require costly long-term care. The second most common injury is death (24 of the top 200 cases), even though Texas caps economic plus non-economic damages plus pre-judgment interest in death cases at roughly $975,000 (prior to 2003, this cap was per defendant). These findings indicate that blockbuster payouts are primarily going to nonelderly patients who suffer severe injuries.

## CLAIM DURATION AND STAGE OF RESOLUTION

We used regression analysis to examine the impact of the 2003 reforms on claim duration. Duration dropped substantially post-reform, by about 41 percent, for elderly plaintiffs and 28 percent for adult nonelderly plaintiffs. The difference between the two groups was statistically significant ($t = 2.96$). The reasons for the drop in duration are not clear. We can offer only some speculations. Perhaps post-reform, plaintiffs' lawyers avoided complex cases, so the cases they brought closed faster. Tort reform could also have encouraged plaintiffs' lawyers to drop weaker cases (by making them less remunerative); the remaining "strong" cases may have settled more quickly on average. Alternatively, if cases involving elderly plaintiffs are worth less, plaintiffs' lawyers might spend time on them. We cannot evaluate these explanations with our data.

Over our full sample period, elderly claims settled faster than adult nonelderly claims. The mean time from injury to closing was 3.49 years for elderly claimants versus 3.97 years for adult nonelderly claimants—a difference of 0.5 years. The difference in median duration was 0.3 years. Claim duration was shorter for elderly claimants partly because they brought claims more quickly after they were injured and partly because their claims closed faster once they were brought.

We also find evidence of convergence in claim duration. Duration of elderly claims increased by around 1.0 percent per year, relative to

duration for adult nonelderly claims prior to 2003. Thus, for claim duration, similar to claim rates and payout per claim, the story is one of interrupted convergence—claim duration for the elderly was converging on
the nonelderly prior to reform but diverged again after reform.

Finally, we find that elderly claimants were more likely than adult
nonelderly claimants to resolve a large paid claim without a lawsuit and
less likely to take a case to trial. For elderly claimants, the likelihood of
resolution without a lawsuit rose with age.

## DISCUSSION

### Convergence, Interrupted by Tort Reform

We document a pattern of convergence in claim frequency, payout per
claim, and claim duration for elderly versus adult nonelderly claimants
during 1988–2003. After Texas adopted medical malpractice reforms in
2003, including a strict cap on non-econ damages, the convergence on all
three measures stalled and indeed reversed. Tort reform strongly affected
all claimants but had an even greater impact on elderly claimants.

The evidence we present in this chapter indicates that tort reform
had a greater effect on the elderly. We lack the data to study a potential
disproportionate impact on women or the unemployed, but some effect
is likely. The same factors that produce a greater effect for the elderly
should affect these other groups as well. In addition, elderly claimants
were disproportionately likely to be women.

### Why Did Elderly Claims Rise over 1988–2003, before Tort Reform?

Over 1988–2003, we find a 2.5-fold rise in the rate of elderly paid
claims, relative to the adult nonelderly rate. Possible explanations include
(a) greater physician willingness to perform risky procedures on elderly
patients, some of which led to malpractice claims; (b) a cultural shift
toward greater willingness by elderly patients to initiate a claim; and
(c) greater willingness of lawyers to take these claims—perhaps because
an increase in life expectancy made such cases more valuable. We cannot
differentiate among these explanations with our data, and they might
well act synergistically.

### Why Are Elderly Paid Claim Rates Lower than Nonelderly Rates?

Although claims by the elderly increased substantially during our sample period, elderly paid claim rates still remained well below rates for the adult nonelderly, once we adjust for health care intensity. For example, over 2001–2005, the most recent five years that were not heavily influenced by the 2003 tort reforms, the adjusted elderly paid claim rate was only about half of the adult nonelderly rate. Possible reasons include reluctance by elderly patients to bring suit, especially against physicians; lesser familiarity of medical malpractice lawyers with elderly claims; and lower expected damages for many claims. All these explanations seem plausible; we cannot distinguish among them with our data.

### Why Were Elderly per Claim Payouts Smaller—and Why Did Pre-reform Payouts Converge?

Mean and median payouts to elderly and adult nonelderly claimants for claims that were governed by pre-reform rules fully converged by the later years of the period we studied. There remains, however, an almost total absence of very large payouts to elderly claimants. This could reflect lower economic damages among elderly claimants, including a low incidence of high-outlier economic damages. Few elderly claimants will have large lost earnings, and their future medical expenses will often be more modest than those for adult nonelderly claimants because they have shorter remaining lifespans during which to incur these expenses. For the top 200 payments, 70 percent are for brain damage or spinal cord injuries, which often require lifetime care. The present value of that care will be much smaller for elderly claimants than for younger claimants, especially babies.

The relative increase in pre-reform elderly payouts over our sample period could be partly explained by the rising life expectancy of elderly claimants and their greater tendency to still be working.[108] Higher claim rates might also be accompanied by a different mix of elderly claims. We cannot distinguish among these explanations with our data.

### The Value of Elderly Death Claims

An extensive literature estimates the value of a statistical life (VSL). One flashpoint in the debate over the use of VSL has been whether the lives of the elderly should have a lower value than the lives of the young.

Many economists believe that there should be a "senior discount" because the elderly have fewer (and often lower-quality) years of life remaining.[109] Conversely, if the VSL is uniform, that means the value of a life-year is higher for the elderly than for the young.[110] Regulatory attempts to incorporate a senior discount into cost-benefit analysis have been controversial.[111]

What do our data imply about this debate? First, under the pre-reform rules, we find convergence in per claim payouts to elderly and adult non-elderly claimants, both in all cases and in death cases. To the extent there was a "senior discount," it appears to have shrunk. To be sure, we might still find a senior discount if we could control for case mix. Second, the amounts paid in death cases are well below standard VSL estimates for all age groups, indicating systematic undercompensation by the tort system.[112]

## CONCLUSION

At the start of our sample period, controlling for health care intensity, the elderly greatly underclaimed for medical malpractice relative to the adult nonelderly. The elderly paid claim rate, adjusted for intensity of health care use, rose over the first 15 years of our sample period but still reached only about half of the adult nonelderly rate. Paid claims fell sharply after 2003 for all age groups. The trend of rising paid claim rates by the elderly ended, as did the trend toward convergence between elderly and nonelderly claimants.

Per claim payouts to elderly claimants began well below the adult nonelderly level, but for pre-reform cases, they converged fully to the adult nonelderly level by the end of our sample period. However, the 2003 tort reforms reduced per claim payouts for all age groups.

For defendants and insurers, payouts to elderly claimants at the end of the period are a significant portion of total exposure in contrast to the start of our period, when claims by the elderly were much less common. Still, because of lower claiming rates and the differential impact of tort reform on the elderly, the share of medical malpractice payouts to elderly claimants remains well below their share of health care use. And total payouts to elderly claimants, after rising steadily during the pre-reform period, have dropped back to the low levels that prevailed at the start of our sample period.

## CHAPTER 9

# DEFENSIVE MEDICINE? IMPACT ON HEALTH CARE SPENDING

## OVERVIEW

Can tort reform bend the cost curve? Health care providers and tort reform advocates insist the answer is yes. They claim that defensive medicine—unnecessary care provided by hospitals and physicians because of fear of medical malpractice liability—is responsible for hundreds of billions of dollars in wasted health care spending every year. In this chapter, we study whether Medicare spending changed after the 2003 Texas reforms. In Chapter 12, we study the same issue for all nine states that adopted caps on non-economic damages ("non-econ caps") during the third reform wave of 2002–2005.

Tort reform should have a greater impact on physician and hospital incentives in areas where providers face a high level of medical malpractice risk than in areas where risk is lower. We therefore compare Medicare spending trends in Texas counties with high claim rates (high-risk counties) to spending in Texas counties with low claim rates (low risk). Pre-reform, Medicare spending levels and trends were similar in high- and low-risk counties. Post-reform, we find no evidence that spending levels or trends in high-risk counties declined relative to low-risk counties and some evidence of *higher* physician spending in high-risk counties. We also compare spending trends in Texas to national trends and find no evidence of reduced spending in Texas post-reform and some evidence that

Medicare Part B spending (Medicare Part A pays for hospital inpatient care; Part B pays for outpatient care and physician services) *rose* in Texas relative to "control states," which do not have damage caps.

We find no evidence that Texas's tort reforms reduced Medicare spending, as reform advocates claim they will, and some evidence that Medicare Part B (physician-directed) spending rose after reform. In Chapter 12, we find consistent evidence across all nine states that adopted non-econ caps during 2002–2005 of, if anything, *higher* Part B spending following cap adoption—the opposite of the prediction by reform advocates.

## INTRODUCTION

Tort reform can affect health care spending in two distinct ways. It can *directly* lower health care spending by lowering the cost of medical malpractice insurance, which covers indemnity payouts plus defense costs.[113] However, as we discuss in Chapter 11, these direct costs account for only about 0.3 percent of health care spending. Thus, any decline in medical malpractice premiums will have only a minor impact on overall spending.

Tort reform can also affect health care spending indirectly, by reducing the incentive for physicians to engage in "defensive medicine." The true extent of defensive medicine is unclear, but estimates of 4 to 9 percent of total health care spending ($100 billion–$200 billion per year) are common;[114] and one can readily find more extreme estimates.[115] A more balanced estimate by several major health policy scholars is around $45 billion.[116]

Defensive medicine comes in two varieties: "assurance" behavior and "avoidance" behavior. Assurance behavior involves ordering tests and other procedures that do not benefit patients or lack sufficient benefit to justify their costs, with a view to making sure that medical malpractice cases do not arise in the future. Avoidance behavior involves avoiding high-risk patients and risky procedures, again with the same end in mind. In surveys, many physicians believe that both assurance and avoidance behavior are widespread, and they often report engaging in these actions themselves.[117]

Assurance behavior increases health care spending. Avoidance behavior, in contrast, should lower health care spending. Tort reform will plausibly reduce both assurance and avoidance behavior. The net effect of reform on health care spending is thus indeterminate—and will depend on whether tort reform has a larger impact on avoidance behavior or on assurance behavior.[118]

Of course, providers may perform procedures and order tests with limited clinical value for reasons other than liability risk, including economic incentives to provide services, patient preferences for more care (with the costs mostly paid by insurance), the desire to be thorough, local practice norms,[119] concerns about reputation,[120] and risk of professional discipline. If most physicians are inclined to do more for multiple reasons, tort reform could have only a modest impact on spending. Finally, several (but not all) recent studies find evidence that malpractice liability leads to improved quality.[121] Tort reform could cause care quality to decline, which could, in turn, lead to higher spending.

Thus, the impact of medical malpractice risk on overall health care spending is ultimately an empirical question. We examine that question for Texas in this chapter, and for all nine new-cap states in Chapter 12. In this chapter, we compare Texas to national trends, but we also look within Texas. We assess whether health care spending changed after reform in counties with high pre-reform medical malpractice claim rates (high-risk counties), compared to counties with lower pre-reform claim rates (low-risk counties). Our "within-Texas" approach provides a larger sample size and less potential for unobserved differences among states to bias our results.

The core assumption behind our within-Texas analysis is that physicians are sensitive to the *local* risk of a malpractice claim. If so, and if medical malpractice risk is a spur to higher health care spending, then spending within Texas should decline more in high-risk counties, where reform should induce a larger post-reform drop in claim rates than in low-risk counties.

Medicare uses an administered pricing system, with prices largely set on a national basis. These prices are only minimally affected by local medical malpractice risk. Thus, when we study Medicare spending, we are effectively studying whether tort reform changed the *quantity* of medical services provided. Over the long run, in a well-functioning market, providers' savings from lower malpractice premiums should be reflected in lower health care prices and health insurance rates. We cannot assess with our data whether any such change took place in private insurance markets in Texas. But for our research question, which is how tort reform affects physician decisions, the *quantity* of medical services is what we want to measure. Happily, Medicare spending provides such a measure.

To be sure, most medical malpractice claims are brought by the nonelderly (Chapter 8). Ideally, then, if we want to study how tort reform affects health care spending, we should be studying spending among the adult nonelderly population as well, rather than relying only on Medicare data. Unfortunately, those data are not available for the time period we want to study. Thus, like other researchers, we use Medicare data, which is publicly available. We study the issue using data from Medicare Part A and Part B, rather than from Part C (Medicare Advantage) or Part D (prescription medicines). Data are not available for Part C, even though it now covers a substantial fraction of all beneficiaries. And Part D began in 2006, after the tort reforms we study.

Medicare is also a good place to look because its prices are insensitive to medical malpractice risk (so that spending becomes a measure of quantity), but also because it places fewer constraints on providers than most private insurers—leaving more room for defensive practices to affect physician actions. If tort reform does not meaningfully affect Medicare spending, it is unlikely to strongly affect spending by the nonelderly, most of which is covered by commercial health insurance.

So for Texas, what do we find? First, we find no evidence that prior to reform, Medicare spending or spending trends were higher in high-risk counties, nor do we find evidence that the 2003 reforms reduced Medicare spending levels in high-risk counties, in each case relative to low-risk counties. We also find no significant effect of tort reform on spending for imaging and laboratory services, which is widely considered to be the area of medical practice that is most sensitive to liability risk.

Turning from spending levels to spending *trends*, we find no evidence of differing pre-reform trends between high- and low-risk counties and no evidence that reform reduced spending growth rates in high-risk counties. On the contrary, we find some evidence that Medicare Part B spending ("physician spending") trends *rose* in high-risk counties relative to low-risk counties. We find no trend, one way or the other, for Medicare Part A spending ("hospital spending").

We also examine whether spending in Texas as a whole changes relative to states that did not undergo tort reform at around the same time. We find no evidence that the 2003 reforms affected Texas Medicare spending. On the contrary, we find some evidence that physician spending *rose* in Texas after reform, relative to other states.

In sum, we find no evidence that Texas's 2003 tort reforms reduced Medicare spending, and some evidence of higher post-reform spending by Texas physicians who practice in high-risk, generally urban counties. Reform advocates' claim that reform will lower spending by a meaningful amount is not supported by the evidence.

This chapter focuses solely on Texas. But we will see in Chapter 12 that the evidence is similar across all nine states that adopted non-econ caps during 2002–2005. Hospital spending does not appear to change after reform. And for physician-directed spending, the hints of higher spending that we report in this chapter turn into stronger evidence once we look across the new-cap states.

## BACKGROUND

### Literature Review

We focus on studies that rely on state tort reforms as a source of variation in medical malpractice risk. Kessler and McClellan performed the first rigorous studies of the impact of tort reforms on health care spending.[122] Using data on Medicare patients treated for acute myocardial infarction (heart attack) or ischemic heart disease in three years (1984, 1987, and 1990), they initially found that damage caps reduced post-treatment medical spending by 5 to 9 percent without adverse health effects. In a follow-up study, they used a longer time period, controlled for managed care penetration, and found a 4 to 5 percent decline.

In their original 1996 article, Kessler and McClellan observed that *"if our results are generalizable to other medical expenditures outside the hospital, to other illnesses, and to younger patients,* then direct [tort] reforms could lead to expenditure reductions of well over $50 billion per year without serious adverse consequences for health outcomes" (emphasis added). Tort reform advocates relied on Kessler and McClellan's estimate of a 5 to 9 percent drop in spending, adjusted them to reflect the overall rise in health care spending, played down the authors' caveats, and often ignored the smaller estimate in their second article.

More recent studies cast doubt on the generalizability of Kessler and McClellan's results. The Congressional Budget Office (CBO) applied their methods to a broader range of medical conditions and "found no evidence that restrictions on tort liability reduce medical spending."[123] A follow-up CBO study found that states that implemented tort reforms in the 1980s had above-average health care pricing before the 1983 implementation of the Medicare Prospective Payment System, which disproportionately affected states with higher pricing.[124] When CBO corrected for this, it found an estimated drop in Medicare spending after adoption of a non-econ cap of a statistically insignificant 1.6 percent. Sloan and Shadle studied more conditions and more years than Kessler and McClellan and also found insignificant results.[125] Lakdawalla and Seabury found that lower risk predicted modestly lower health care prices, no significant change in health care quantity, and somewhat higher mortality.[126] In Chapter 12, we focus on the effect of third-wave caps, but in the underlying article, we also study the second-wave caps and find no evidence of a significant change in Medicare spending.[127]

Avraham, Dafny, and Schanzenbach measured health insurance premiums for employer-funded health insurance plans representing more than 10 million Americans annually from 1998 to 2006.[128] They found that a non-econ cap reduced premiums for self-funded health plans by 1 to 2 percent but had no effect on premiums for fully insured plans.[129]

Dranove and Gron reported some evidence of avoidance behavior. They found that neurosurgeons cut back on brain surgery, but obstetrician-gynecologist behavior did not change when malpractice premiums rose in Florida.[130]

### Physician Perception and Malpractice Risk

The argument for why tort reform might reduce health care spending is straightforward: if physicians respond to medical malpractice risk by engaging in assurance behavior, tort reform that lowers liability risk will reduce these defensive practices and thus reduce spending. As noted above, this formulation ignores the role of avoidance behavior, which for higher risk leads to lower spending, and of other factors that might influence physician behavior. But it is physicians' perceived liability risk (and not actual risk) that should influence physicians' propensity to practice defensive medicine.[131] Several studies indicate that physicians dramatically overestimate their liability risk. Physician risk perceptions do vary with the level of medical malpractice risk but not nearly as much as they likely should.[132]

## DATA, HYPOTHESES, AND METHODOLOGY

### County-Level Causal Inference Strategy

Most prior studies estimate the effect of medical malpractice reform on health care spending or outcomes using state reforms as an exogenous shock to medical malpractice risk, with state-level spending as the dependent variable. However, state reforms differ substantially. Damage caps vary in what type of damages they apply to (total, non-economic, or punitive), the cap level, and whether the cap varies with the type and number of defendants. Even if one studies only, say, caps on non-econ damages, there are obvious difficulties with treating all caps as identical, yet this is what all previous studies do. In addition, reforms are often bundled, which complicates any attempt to estimate the impact of one particular reform, such as a non-econ cap. There are also only a limited number of state-level reforms, so sample sizes are small.

Our principal methodological innovation is to study a large reform shock to a single state (Texas). We assume that the 2003 Texas reforms reduced local medical malpractice risk more strongly in counties within Texas that had higher pre-reform risk levels. We then look for *intrastate* differences in how the shock to county-level risk affected county-level spending. This approach is attractive because Texas experienced a uniquely large medical malpractice shock, we have county-level data on medical malpractice risk, and that risk varies substantially across counties. We can study roughly 200 Texas counties, which all experienced the same reform, instead of a much smaller number of states, each subject to a different package of reforms.

We make two core causal inference assumptions that we cannot directly test. First, we assume that providers are sensitive to *local* medical malpractice risk, and therefore that providers in high-risk counties will perceive a larger reduction in medical malpractice risk than providers in low-risk counties. One channel through which providers can learn about local risk is malpractice insurance premiums. Suppose that tort reform reduces the likelihood of a medical malpractice claim by 50 percent from its pre-reform level. This might imply a $50,000 drop in annual premiums in a high-risk county, say, from $100,000 to $50,000, but only a $15,000 drop in a low-risk county, from $30,000 to $15,000. A second channel is conversations between doctors about being sued. A similar percentage drop in claim frequency should affect doctors' personal experiences more in high-risk than low-risk counties.

Second, we assume that any other statewide factors that influence health care spending affect high-risk and low-risk counties similarly. This lets us treat the low-risk counties as a control group for the high-risk counties. Our research design, in which all counties are affected by the reforms but high-risk counties are affected more than low-risk counties, is a type of "difference-in-differences" (DiD) design.

We also assume that medical malpractice reform will affect health care spending within a reasonable period of time. The longer the lag, the less confidence one can have that there are not other, unobserved differences that emerge over time between high-risk and low-risk counties. We study lags of up to four years.

We asked physicians, including senior health outcomes researchers, and the proponents of the Texas reforms, about these assumptions. They generally concurred that our assumptions were reasonable and that physicians are likely to be aware of and respond to local risk. Their principal concern was a lag between reform and response, attributable to the "stickiness" of local practice patterns.

## State-Level Analysis

We also study whether tort reform predicts any change in Texas spending levels, or spending trends, relative to other states. This approach is similar to prior DiD studies, except with only a single reform state. The core causal inference assumption for this analysis is that tort reform is the only factor that causes Texas spending to change relative to the control states. Because this assumption is untestable and could easily be wrong, we see our state-level results primarily as a credibility and robustness check on our intrastate analysis.

For the state-level analysis, a key question is to which states we should compare Texas. We use two control groups: (a) the 41 other states that did not undergo major tort reform during our principal 1999–2010 sample period[133] and (b) the 19 other states that do not have caps on non-economic or total damages at all ("no-cap states").[134]

If Texas spending had fallen relative to control states, this would suggest a possible statewide impact of reform not captured by our analysis of county-level variation in risk within Texas. Conversely, if Texas spending remains roughly constant or—as we find—even appears to rise relative to control states, this is consistent with our main intrastate finding that a larger shock to county-level medical malpractice risk does not predict lower post-reform spending, and might predict higher spending.

## Variables

Our main outcome variable is *ln*(Medicare spending)—the natural logarithm of spending per Medicare enrollee. We study separately Part A spending, Part B spending, and total spending. Medicare Part A covers inpatient care in hospitals and hospice care services and can be loosely seen as hospital spending. Medicare Part B covers physician services and outpatient care, including home health, imaging, and clinical laboratory testing, and can be loosely seen as physician-directed spending.

*Medical malpractice risk variables.* Our principal measure of medical malpractice risk is the mean for each county over the five years before reform (1999–2003) of $ln(1 + [\text{no. of claims}/100,000 \text{ population}])$, which we then convert to a standard normal distribution (mean = 0, standard deviation = 1). We use a five-year average because we believe physicians are likely to have a general sense for their risk of facing a medical mal-practice claim but are not likely to change their risk perceptions because of short-term fluctuations in claim rates. We add 1 before taking the natural logarithm of the claim rate to avoid dropping counties with zero claims. Before normalization, this measure has mean = 1.04 and stan-dard deviation = 0.80, so there is reasonable variation between counties. There is also good geographic dispersion in risk—the high-risk counties are not concentrated in one part of Texas.

### Hypotheses

Our hypotheses, based on the defensive medicine literature and on pop-ular views about how physicians respond to medical malpractice risk, are as follows.

*Hypothesis 1: Medical malpractice reform and statewide spending trends.* If medical malpractice risk increases health care spending, then the 2003 reforms will result in lower health care spending in Texas compared to other states that do not adopt similar reforms.

*Hypothesis 2: Medical malpractice risk and county-level spending.* If higher medical malpractice risk increases health care spending, then (subject to possible endogeneity concerns) there should be a positive association between county-level risk and health care spending—perhaps both the level of spending and spending growth rates.

*Hypothesis 3: Medical malpractice reform and county-level spending.* Med-ical malpractice reform will have a greater impact on spending in Texas counties with high pre-reform medical malpractice risk than in low-risk counties, because the reforms will cause a larger drop in risk in high-risk counties.

To preview our conclusions, we find no support for any of these hypotheses. Instead, we consistently find "null results," with reason-ably tight confidence bounds. Where we do find statistically significant results, they have the opposite sign from that predicted. In particu-lar, we find some evidence that Medicare Part B (physician-directed) spending *rose* in Texas after reform, relative to control states (contrary to Hypothesis 1). The higher post-reform spending comes from high-risk counties (contrary to Hypothesis 3).

## MEDICAL MALPRACTICE REFORM AND SPENDING LEVELS

### *Medical Malpractice Reform and State-Level Spending: Initial Evidence*

By any measure, Texas's 2003 tort reforms transformed the medical malpractice liability environment. During the pre-reform period, claim frequency (the number of paid claims per 100,000 Texas residents) and claim severity (defined as payout per capita for all paid claims that closed in a given year) were generally stable (see Chapter 3). After reform, as we discussed in Chapter 7, both claim frequency and payout per claim trended sharply downward, as did medical malpractice insurance premiums. The drop in claim rate was larger in high-risk counties, thus meeting the factual premise for our county-level analysis.

Hypothesis 1 thus predicts a post-reform drop in Texas health care spending relative to other states. We find no evidence of a drop. Figure 9.1 presents the Texas "spending gap" (Texas Medicare spending per enrollee minus Medicare spending per enrollee in comparison

## Figure 9.1

### Texas Medicare spending gap

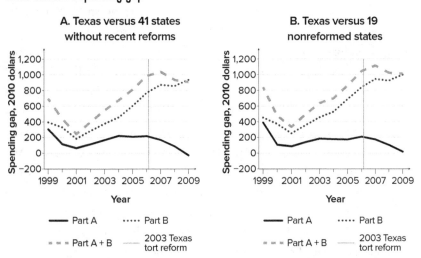

*Notes:* Texas spending gap (Texas minus control group spending per enrollee) for Medicare Part A, Part B, and total Medicare spending. The vertical line separates pre- and post-tort-reform periods.

*Source:* Centers for Medicare and Medicaid Services data on county-level Medicare Part A and Part B spending.

states). We show three lines, for Part A spending, Part B spending, and total spending (the sum of Part A and Part B spending), over 1999–2009. In Panel A, we compare Texas with the broad control group of all 41 U.S. states that did not adopt or repeal damage caps during this period. In Panel B, we restrict the control group to the 19 no-cap states. The Texas spending trend relative to the controls is similar in both panels. The Part A spending gap is small and declines somewhat in 2008 and 2009. The Part B spending gap *rises* substantially beginning in 2002, with no downward "bend" after reform. This is the opposite of the pattern predicted by Hypothesis 1. This is, to be sure, a weak test. Factors other than tort reform surely affect statewide spending trends—indeed, the Texas spending gap is not flat prior to reform. Still, these state-level results suggest that tort reform did not have a large impact on health care spending—at least not a *downward* impact. We return below to the question of whether overall Texas spending *rose* significantly after reform.

### Association between Medicare Spending and Medical Malpractice Risk

We turn next to Hypothesis 2, that health care spending and growth in health care spending will be higher in counties with higher medical malpractice risk. In Figure 9.2, we assess the relationship between medical malpractice risk and *growth* in health care spending. On the *y*-axis, we plot Texas growth in Medicare spending relative to overall U.S. growth in Medicare spending for each county during the medical malpractice insurance crisis period of 1999–2003. We plot medical malpractice risk, measured over the same period, on the *x*-axis. Each dot represents a single county. If Hypothesis 2 were correct, the dots should tend to rise from the lower left part of the graph to the upper right part, and a regression line, fitted to the data, should show a positive slope—indicating a positive relationship between medical malpractice risk and Medicare spending growth. However, it is visually apparent that there is *no* relationship between medical malpractice risk and spending growth; the dots in Figure 9.2 appear to be fairly randomly scattered, with no tendency for higher spending in counties with higher medical malpractice risk. We confirm that visual

## Figure 9.2

### Texas Medicare spending growth versus medical malpractice risk

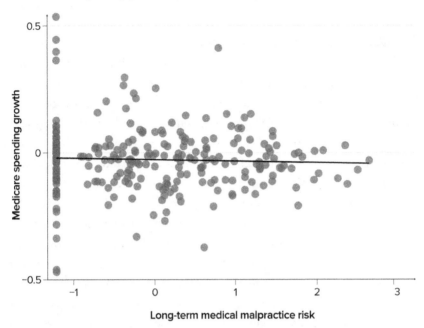

*Notes:* Texas growth in Medicare spending over 1999–2003, relative to overall U.S. growth, calculated as *ln*(relative spending) in 2003 minus *ln*(relative spending) in 1999, versus medical malpractice risk measured over 1999–2003, and regression line showing the relationship between the two. Sample is 254 Texas counties. Slope is −0.006 (*t*-statistic = 0.75).

*Source:* Centers for Medicare and Medicaid Services data on county-level Medicare Part A and Part B spending.

impression in Figure 9.2 by including a fitted regression line based on the data points in the figure. The slope is slightly negative but not statistically distinguishable from zero. Thus, there is no evidence of a significant relationship between county-level medical malpractice risk and health care spending growth.

We also assessed whether there was a relationship between medical malpractice risk and the *level* of health care spending in each county (rather than *changes in spending*, which is what Figure 9.2 is about). To do that, we prepared a scatter plot similar to Figure 9.2, but with spending levels on the *y*-axis instead of changes in spending. After controlling for the urban versus rural nature of the county and for county population, there was no relationship between medical malpractice risk and spending levels.[135]

### Medical Malpractice Reform and County-Level Spending within Texas

We have seen so far that after reform, Texas spending did not fall (and Part B spending may have risen) relative to control states (contrary to Hypothesis 1), and that within Texas, there is no association between medical malpractice risk and either spending growth or spending levels (contrary to Hypothesis 2). It is still possible, however, that reform caused spending to drop in high-risk counties relative to low-risk counties (Hypothesis 3). Yet we find no evidence of that either.

In unreported regression analyses, we find small and statistically insignificant differences in post-reform spending trends between high-risk and low-risk counties. Not only are the differences very small, our estimates are quite precise. For total Medicare spending, the coefficient on a dummy variable for high-risk counties is −0.0004, and the 95 percent confidence interval around our estimate is (−0.010, +0.010). This means that we are 95 percent confident that the true coefficient lies between a −1.0 percent drop in spending and a +1.0 percent rise in spending. We obtain similar results if we weight counties by population to ensure that the results are not driven by smaller, rural counties. We also tried using lags of up to four years to allow for a delayed effect of reform on Medicare spending. There was again no evidence that spending dropped in high-risk counties, relative to low-risk counties.

A common belief is that physicians' ordering of lab tests is especially prone to defensive medicine, because it is easy for doctors to order more tests to avoid the risk of being sued for having "missed something" that a test would have picked up. Consistent with this intuition, Baicker and Chandra found no overall association between insurance premiums and Medicare spending, but they did find an association for the Medicare Part B spending subcategory for "diagnostic, laboratory, and x-ray services."[136] We therefore investigated spending in this subcategory, which we will call "imaging and lab" for short. We found no evidence that reform affected imaging and lab spending in Texas.

### County-Level Analysis: Texas versus Control States

We also conducted a county-level DiD regression analysis.[137] The DiD research design considers counties in Texas as "treated" by the Texas reform. Counties in states that did not adopt damage caps are "controls." We measure the difference in an outcome variable in the treated counties before and after reform and compare this difference to the difference over the same time period in control counties—hence the name "difference in differences." The DiD design assumes that, but for reform, the treated counties would have experienced changes similar to those we observe for the control counties. The difference between the change (if any) in treated counties and the change (if any) in control counties provides an estimate of the true impact of the treatment or reform.[138] In this chapter and in Chapter 12, the outcome variable is health care spending. In Chapter 13, we use DiD analysis to study physician supply.

Using the DiD methodology to study health care spending trends at the county level, we find no statistically significant change in Part A spending. However, Medicare Part B spending in Texas *rises* relative to control states. In regressions with counties weighted by population (so that the results are representative of Texas as a whole), Part B spending in Texas rises by around 6 percent during the post-reform period relative to states without damage caps.[139] Combined Part A and Part B spending rises slightly, but the increase is small, at around 1 percent, and not statistically significant.

Studies that compare spending in a single state (like Texas) to spending in one or more control states have an important weakness. The results could be driven by an unobserved factor that affects Texas spending but not spending in the control states. Thus, the observed post-reform increase in Part B spending in Texas provides some—but only some—evidence that Texas's adoption of a non-econ cap caused the rise in Part B spending. But at a minimum, there is no evidence that spending *fell* after the Texas reforms.

There are a number of reasons why Medicare spending might not fall after the Texas reforms and why it might even rise. First, assurance behavior may often not be driven solely by malpractice risk. Second, assurance behavior may not be strongly affected by even the strong Texas reforms. Perhaps physicians practice defensively because of the mere possibility of being sued, rather than because of actual lawsuit risk. Third, any effect of reform on assurance behavior could be offset by the effect of reform on avoidance behavior. In other words, doctors may have delivered fewer services whose principal function is to reduce liability but more services that expose patients to possible medical injury or simply involve high risks of an adverse outcome. We cannot differentiate between these possibilities with our data.

In Chapter 12, we extend our analysis to include all nine states that adopted damage caps during 2002–2005. We find consistent evidence for higher Part B spending after tort reform across these nine states.

## CASE STUDY OF McALLEN VERSUS EL PASO, TEXAS

What else might affect health care spending, other than medical malpractice risk? A highly publicized 2009 article in the *New Yorker* stressed the role of physician culture in generating high health care spending.[140] The author compared McAllen, Texas, a border town in the Rio Grande Valley with per capita Medicare spending almost twice the national average, to another border area, El Paso, which has similar demographics but Medicare spending close to the national and Texas averages. In 1992, McAllen and El Paso had similar per capita Medicare spending, but after that, spending in McAllen grew far faster (8.3 percent per year versus 3.4 percent per year). By 2011, McAllen was the highest Medicare spending area in the country, knocking Miami into second place. Physicians in McAllen blamed medical malpractice risk and told the author that practicing in McAllen was "legal hell." Can higher medical malpractice risk help explain why spending in McAllen grew so much faster than in El Paso?

Figure 9.3 presents some evidence. Panel A shows physician (Part B) Medicare spending in the McAllen and El Paso Hospital Service Areas (HSAs) for 1992–2007 (we have HSA data only through 2007) and Texas as a whole, in each case divided by U.S. mean spending. There is a striking increase in spending in McAllen. In 1992, McAllen spending on physicians is close to the national norm. By 2007, it is over twice

# Figure 9.3

Medicare Part B spending and medical malpractice risk: El Paso and McAllen compared to Texas

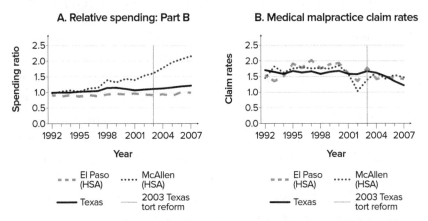

*Notes:* Panel A: Ratio of Medicare Part B spending per enrollee in El Paso and McAllen HSAs, and Texas as a whole, to U.S. Part B spending per enrollee, over 1992–2007. Panel B: Nonnormalized annual medical malpractice risk in El Paso and McAllen HSAs and Texas as a whole, defined as $ln(1 +$ number of claims/100,000 population). Solid vertical lines separate pre- and post-tort-reform periods. HSA = Hospital Service Area.

*Source:* Centers for Medicare and Medicaid Services data on county-level Medicare Part A and Part B spending.

the national norm. Yet spending patterns for Medicare Part A remained similar in McAllen and El Paso, and population health likely remained similar as well.

Panel B shows annual, nonnormalized medical malpractice claim rates. Medical malpractice risk was similar in McAllen and El Paso throughout our sample period, including the period starting in the mid-1990s in which relative Medicare Part B spending soared in McAllen but remained flat in El Paso. Thus, differences in liability risk cannot explain McAllen's sharply rising physician spending.

A comparison of McAllen to El Paso is, of course, an anecdote, not data. Still, the dramatic growth in Part B spending in McAllen suggests that physician culture and practice patterns, including the profit-seeking culture that the author of the *New Yorker* article describes, may be a first-order explanation for observed health care spending trends. The McAllen example and other evidence of large geographic disparities in health care spending suggest that culture is a much more powerful driver of spending than medical malpractice risk.[141]

## DISCUSSION: TEXAS TORT REFORM AND MEDICARE SPENDING

The conventional wisdom is that damage caps reduce health care spending by reducing defensive medicine. But we find that a major shock to medical malpractice risk from Texas's 2003 tort reforms did not reduce Medicare spending (in effect, health care *quantity*), no matter how we slice the data, either in high-risk counties relative to low-risk counties or in Texas relative to control states. On the contrary, we find some evidence that tort reform might have led to higher Part B spending in urban counties, which tend to have higher malpractice risk. We show in Chapter 12 that the evidence for higher Part B spending becomes stronger when we examine all nine states that adopted damage caps during the third reform wave.

Our data are limited to Medicare, but medical malpractice reform seems less likely to influence treatment intensity for the privately insured, because most private insurers exercise greater oversight over treatment decisions than Medicare does.

After tort reform was enacted, medical malpractice premiums fell by half for the state's largest insurer and likely by similar percentages for other carriers. This would have little effect on Medicare spending. The Medicare payment formula does reflect changes in medical malpractice premiums—but only minimally and with a long lag. A drop in direct costs could have a larger impact on private insurers, but any impact would still involve a small fraction of spending, because medical malpractice premiums are only a small fraction of health care spending (see Chapter 11). Moreover, even if health insurers did reduce reimbursement rates paid to providers, that would not imply a decline in defensive medicine *practices*. If one seeks to estimate how tort reform affects defensive medicine, the quantity measure that is reflected in Medicare spending is the appropriate measure.

In this chapter, we end our analysis in 2009. This allows us to analyze trends and levels of health care spending over a six-year post-reform period. We cannot rule out a longer-term impact of tort reform on

Medicare spending. It is possible that defensive medicine is sensitive to liability risk, but physicians are slow to change their practice patterns. That longer-term impact, if it exists, would be hard to estimate, given the other factors that affect health care spending.

## CONCLUSION

The extent to which physicians actually practice defensive medicine—driven solely by malpractice fears—is unknown. They claim to in surveys, but there is no good way to quantify the amount of defensive medicine that occurs or its cost short of insulating physicians entirely from tort liability. The best available approach, and the one we use here, is to assess how tort reform changes physicians' behavior. The evidence for Texas that we report here is in line with most other studies. As best we can tell, damage caps and other reforms have little effect on overall spending.

Our findings do not indicate that there is no defensive medicine. They do provide evidence that tort reform is not a potent way to reduce health care spending. Even a major shock to Texas medical malpractice risk produced no apparent decline in health care utilization over a six-year period following reform. Indeed, we find some evidence of higher utilization in urban areas, which tend to have higher medical malpractice risk. Our Texas results suggest—and the multistate results in Chapter 12 provide further evidence—that, if anything, tort reform appears to lead to modestly higher health care spending, at least for the Medicare population.

In our view, the accumulation of evidence finding zero or small declines in spending, or even—as we find—a rise in Part B spending, suggests that it is time for policymakers to abandon the hope that tort reform can be a major element in health care cost control.

## CHAPTER 10

# IMPACT ON PHYSICIAN SUPPLY IN TEXAS

## OVERVIEW

What effect does medical malpractice reform have on physician supply? Before Texas adopted medical malpractice reform in 2003, proponents claimed that physicians were deserting Texas in droves. After the reforms were enacted, proponents claimed there had been a dramatic increase in physicians moving to Texas because of the improved liability climate. We find no evidence to support either claim. Physician supply was not measurably stunted prior to reform, and it did not measurably improve after reform. This is true whether one looks at all patient care physicians in Texas, at high-malpractice-risk specialties, or at rural physicians.

## INTRODUCTION

The effect of medical malpractice risk on physician supply played a prominent role in the debate over medical malpractice reform in Texas. Proponents argued that physicians were fleeing Texas because of high insurance premiums but would stop leaving if the state adopted reform. After the reforms were adopted, proponents also claimed that the reforms brought large numbers of new physicians to Texas.

In this chapter, we study time trends in the number of active, direct patient care (DPC) physicians in Texas, both pre- and post-reform.

We find no evidence that the number of DPC physicians was declining during the medical malpractice insurance crisis that preceded reform and no evidence that the reforms led to an increase in physician supply.

These and all other statements about physician supply "increasing" or "decreasing" are relative to a baseline in which the number of physicians per capita has been steadily growing, both in Texas and nationally, both before and after reform. Any effect of medical malpractice reform is too small for us to measure. This "non-result" is consistent with other multistate studies, most of which find that state-level medical malpractice reforms increase physician supply modestly, if at all.

We also find no evidence of declining physician supply in high-malpractice-risk specialties. We examine below the three specialties that featured prominently in the 2003 campaign for tort reform—obstetrics and gynecology (ob-gyn), neurosurgery, and orthopedic surgery. These specialists were not fleeing Texas before reform, and their numbers did not surge after reform. In Chapter 13, we study all nine states that adopted damage caps during the third reform wave and a broader range of specialists who face relatively high medical malpractice risk. There we similarly find that tort reform does not lead to higher physician supply.

## LITERATURE REVIEW

Other scholars have examined the extent to which medical malpractice reform influences physician supply. The literature suggests that damage caps can have a small positive impact on physician supply in high-risk specialties and rural areas but are likely to have little effect on statewide physician counts. A review by Kachalia and Mello reports evidence of "modest improvement in physician supply" after adoption of damage caps.[142] But another study by one of the same authors concludes, more equivocally, that research "has not convincingly established what role, if any, liability pressure plays in determining the size of the physician workforce."[143]

We discuss here studies that use difference-in-differences (DiD) research designs. Several researchers studied the second reform wave during the 1980s. Encinosa and Hellinger report that rural counties in states that adopted damage caps had 3.2 percent more physicians.[144]

However, the full results from this study, reported in a web appendix, suggest a near-zero change in urban physician supply and statewide physician counts. Klick and Stratmann use a "triple differences" research design, in which they compare states with and without damage caps, before and after reform, and high-risk versus lower-risk specialties.[145] They report a 6 to 7 percent rise in supply for the 5 specialties with the highest lawsuit risk, and a 3 to 4 percent effect for the 10 highest-risk specialties, relative to the 5 (or 10) lowest-risk specialties, with risk based on payout per paid claim. They found no significant change in overall physician counts. Kessler, Sage, and Becker found that damage caps predict a 3.3 percent increase in physicians per capita three years after reform, with the effect coming partly from greater entry and partly from fewer retirements.[146]

Matsa used a longer period (1970–2000) and studied both the first and second reform waves.[147] He found no effect of damage caps on overall physician supply. (His point estimates were negative but statistically insignificant.) He found a positive and significant increase in physicians per capita in the quartile of counties with the lowest population density, which appeared slowly over time and was statistically significant only 6 to 10 years after reform.

Two recent studies cover the third reform wave, which includes Texas. Helland and Seabury also use a triple differences research design.[148] They find no evidence of an overall increase in physician supply but report an increase in supply for high-risk specialties and, oddly, a decrease for other specialties. In our own research, presented in Chapter 13, we find no evidence of an increase in physician supply, whether for all patient care physicians, high-risk specialties, or rural physicians. In the appendix to the article that forms the basis for Chapter 13, we show that the increase in high-risk specialties that Helland and Seabury report is driven by a combination of (a) bad data for cardiac surgeons in the late 1990s and (b) nonparallel trends in the double differences that underlie their triple difference results.[149]

Thus, for overall physician supply, of six DiD studies, only one—by Kessler, Sage, and Becker—finds a significant increase, but the increase is small (around 3 percent), and it does not control for pre-reform state trends.[150] The evidence on high-risk and rural physicians is also mixed.[151]

Given the mixed results found in these multistate studies, the large effects claimed for Texas by reform advocates would be surprising, if they were real. We show below that they are not real.

Lieber finds evidence that physicians move from counties near state borders in no-cap states to states that adopt damage caps, but also evidence that the physicians who move to cap-adopting states are malpractice prone.[152] This is hardly the outcome that reform advocates might hope for.

Finally, there is one other published study that is specific to Texas. Stewart and others find that after reform, the number of licensed physicians in Texas (whether engaged in patient care or not) increased modestly faster than Texas's population (which we also find—see Figures 10.3 and 10.5), and increased faster after the 2003 reforms than before them.[153] We discuss this study below.

## PHYSICIAN SUPPLY: CLAIMS BY REFORM ADVOCATES

### Pre-reform Claims: Physicians Were Fleeing Texas

During the campaign to convince Texans to amend the state constitution (which had been held to forbid caps on damages), proponents argued that doctors were fleeing Texas and that patients were losing their access to care. For example, a pro-reform brochure warned that doctors were "fleeing Texas, leaving scores of counties with no obstetricians to deliver babies, no neurologists or orthopedic surgeons to tend to the ill." A "flyer printed by the [Texas Medical Association] in English and Spanish and posted in waiting rooms across the state told patients that '152 counties in Texas now have no obstetrician. Wide swaths of Texas have no neurosurgeon or orthopedic surgeon. . . . The primary culprit for this crisis is an explosion in awards for non-economic (pain and suffering) damages in liability lawsuits.'"[154]

### Post-reform Claims: Physicians Are Rushing to Texas

Post-reform, the claim that medical malpractice reform would stop doctors from leaving was replaced by the new claim that medical malpractice reform was bringing many new doctors into the state. In 2006, two prominent reform advocates wrote of an "amazing turnaround" across Texas and asserted that there had been "substantial increases" in several types of specialists.[155] These claims were echoed, extended, and amplified by other reform proponents, including Texas Governor Rick Perry, the executive director of the Texas Medical Board, and federal and state legislators.[156] By 2011, proponents were claiming that medical malpractice reform had made Texas "an enormously popular destination for doctors," and used that claim as an argument in favor of federal medical malpractice reform.[157] Our personal favorite: Texas Governor Rick Perry directly attacked our research in an op-ed published in 2012.[158] For Governor Perry,

> [tort reform] was an overwhelming success. We said if reforms became law, doctors would start working in emergency rooms again, and they have. We said doctors would again choose to treat the most sick and injured patients, and they have. We said more high-risk specialists would be available to treat the public, and they are. We said we would be able to recruit much-needed specialists to our state, particularly in rural areas, and we have.
>
> This was all great news for Texans who needed medical care, as well as the men and women providing it; it wasn't good news for trial lawyers. Therefore, it's not surprising that the trial lawyer lobby will do anything to paint our reforms in a bad light. And that's precisely what prompted a recent report by Charles Silver, a [University of Texas] professor with deep and extensive ties to the trial lawyer industry. His report is a mix of smoke and mirrors and statistical sleight-of-hand, specifically designed to obscure the success story of tort reform in Texas.[159]

Thus, reform proponents repeatedly claimed, in multiple venues and over many years, that Texas's 2003 medical malpractice reforms produced wonderful results, reversing dismal pre-reform trends. If they were right, that would be an important argument in favor of medical malpractice reform. But they were not right. We urge readers to judge for themselves, after reading this chapter, whether we are is using "smoke and mirrors and statistical sleight-of-hand."

## PHYSICIAN SUPPLY: EMPIRICAL REALITY

### *Initial Facts: Licensed and Active Physicians*

Most of the claims that reform increased the number of physicians in Texas are based on reports by the Texas Medical Board (TMB) showing the number of applications it receives, the number of licenses it issues, and the number of doctors in identified specialties by county. Figure 10.1 presents the numbers of applications and licenses reported by TMB for its 2001–2011 fiscal years (ending August 31).

As Figure 10.1 indicates, applications rose moderately in 2004, then substantially in 2006, but were roughly flat since then. Issued licenses increased somewhat later, in 2007 and 2008, and were roughly flat after that. The claims by reform proponents on the number of new doctors entering Texas correspond closely to the number of licenses issued by TMB since the reforms were adopted.

## Figure 10.1

### Medical licenses applied for and granted, Texas

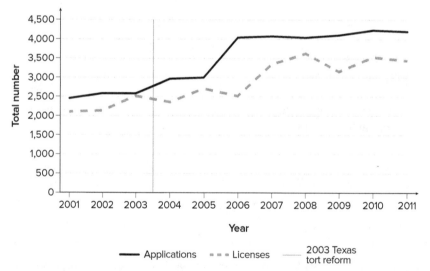

*Notes:* Applications for medical licenses and issued licenses, for fiscal years 2001–2011, reported by the Texas Medical Board. Texas medical malpractice reform in 2003 is depicted by vertical line.

*Source:* Texas Medical Board.

Unfortunately, the number of licenses granted by TMB is a poor measure of growth in physician supply, let alone growth attributable to tort reform. First, data on new licenses (which is what medical malpractice reform proponents have focused on) do not take into account physicians who leave Texas or retire. The number of new licenses, without more information, cannot tell us whether the number of practicing physicians rose, fell, or was unchanged. Second, adding up post-reform licenses, as reform advocates do, effectively assumes that medical malpractice reform deserves the "credit" for every physician who came to Texas after 2003. But physicians came to Texas every year before 2003—and many would have continued to come to Texas even if medical malpractice reform was never enacted.

Third, licensing data do not indicate how many physicians are engaged in patient care. Many licensed physicians are researchers, administrators, or otherwise occupied with nonclinical tasks. A more policy-relevant number is "direct patient care" physicians. TMB does not report that number, but another Texas state agency, the Texas Department of State Health Services (TDSHS) does. We discuss the TDSHS data below.

Finally, credit for the jump in applications in 2006 might belong not to tort reform but to Hurricane Katrina, which struck New Orleans in 2005. Many New Orleans residents, physicians among them, moved to Texas. Some stayed. In a 2010 report, TDSHS suggested that the increase in DPC physicians was "partially due to Hurricane Katrina."[160]

### Which Dataset to Use?

We believe the best Texas data series to use to assess trends in physician supply are the data on DPC physicians developed by TDSHS. TDSHS begins with data from TMB on the number of active physicians in Texas and then adjusts this number to better measure how many physicians are engaged in direct patient care. For example, TDSHS excludes residents and fellows. This is a judgment call, but one that is useful for our research question, which is how medical malpractice reform affects physicians' location decisions. The number of residents and fellows are determined by the number of funded positions in Texas, not by medical malpractice reform.

### Comparing Texas to Itself: Pre-reform versus Post-reform

We first compare Texas to itself—that is, we compare the trends in the number of DPC physicians practicing in Texas pre- and post-reform. Figure 10.2 presents two data series. The top dotted line shows the total number of DPC physicians from 1990 to 2010. The bottom dotted line shows the number of DPC physicians per 100,000 population over the same period. For both lines, we also show solid lines, based on simple regressions over the pre-reform years with available data (1981–2002) of DPC physicians (physicians per capita) on year, Texas real gross domestic product, and a constant term. We use the coefficients from these regressions to predict, based on pre-reform trends, the number of DPC physicians (physicians per capita) over 2003–2011.

As Figure 10.2 shows, the number of Texas DPC physicians grew steadily prior to 2003, both in absolute numbers and per capita. That growth did not stop, or even slow down, during the medical malpractice insurance crisis period (1999–2003).

## Figure 10.2

### Predicted and observed direct patient care physicians, Texas

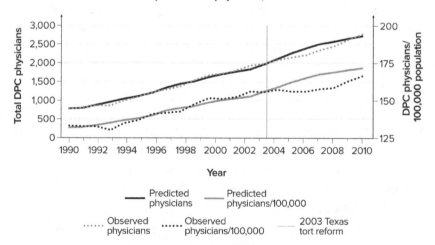

*Notes:* Actual and predicted Texas DPC physicians (left axis) and DPC physicians per 100,000 population (right axis). Predicted lines are based on regression described in text, estimated over 1981–2002. Texas medical malpractice reform in 2003 is depicted by vertical line. DPC = direct patient care.

*Source:* Texas Department of State Health Services.

The growth trend also did not accelerate after reform. Instead, the absolute number of DPC physicians grew at roughly the same rate during the pre- and post-reform periods. Measured on a per capita basis, physician supply fell somewhat *below* the level that we would predict based on pre-reform trends. Thus, the assertion by medical malpractice reform proponents that Texas experienced a pre-reform exodus of physicians followed by a sharp post-reform turnaround is doubly false. There was neither an exodus before reform nor a dramatic increase after reform.

Figure 10.2 also provides reason for caution in interpreting short-term fluctuations in physician supply. Notice that physicians per capita fell over 1990–1993. Whatever the reasons for that decline, medical malpractice litigation is not likely to be one of them; the early 1990s were a quiet period on the medical malpractice front (see Chapter 3).

How was it possible for Texas to issue substantially more licenses after reform, as we saw in Figure 10.1, without a similar increase in DPC physicians per capita? There are a number of reasons. First, there was a lag between medical malpractice reform (2003) and the increase in new licenses (2007). Second, in Figure 10.3 we show the number of DPC physicians, and also the percentage leaving practice during 2000–2009 (we lack data on departures before 2000 or after 2009). The percentage leaving practice rose over 2000–2005 and then fell back to about the 2002 level.

Proponents might argue that the rise in departure rates over 2000–2005 was prompted by a rise in medical malpractice insurance premiums, but the data do not support a large role for malpractice liability. The exit rate rose in 2003, when reform was already on the political agenda, remained high in 2004 and peaked in 2005, well after the reforms were in place. This suggests that other, unknown factors were the principal drivers of physician exit.

The rates of physician arrivals and departures may be related. Departure rates were relatively high in 2003–2005 and peaked in 2005. License applications surged in 2006 (Figure 10.1). This suggests that many physicians who entered practice in Texas were attracted by employment opportunities rather than other factors, such as medical malpractice reform.

## Figure 10.3

Texas statistics on DPC physicians who left practice

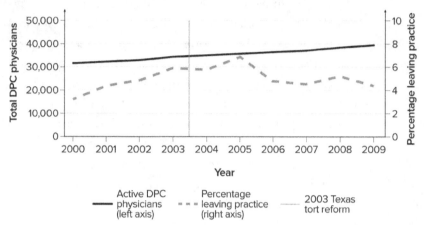

*Notes:* Number of year-end active Texas DPC physicians, and percentage leaving practice each year, for 2000–2009. DPC = direct patient care.

*Source:* Texas Department of State Health Services, *Characteristics of Physicians Who Left Practice in Texas: 2000–2009* (2010), p. 2, Table 1.

Third, the fraction of licensed Texas physicians who are DPC physicians fell from 2002–2010, from about 41 percent to about 39 percent. Thus, a smaller fraction of the newly licensed physicians reported by TMB were becoming DPC physicians.

Fourth, Texas's population was rising. Thus, the total number of new DPC physicians needed to grow to prevent a *fall* in DPC physicians per capita. Moreover, the number of DPC physicians per capita was rising over time, both in Texas (as shown in Figure 10.2) and nationally. We would expect the number of DPC physicians in Texas, and thus the number of new licenses, to grow during the post-reform period to be consistent with this long-term trend.

## TEXAS VERSUS NATIONAL TRENDS

We turn next to how well Texas did in attracting physicians relative to the rest of the United States, both before and after reform. Figure 10.4 shows the number of active, nonfederal, patient care physicians per

# Figure 10.4

## U.S. and Texas trends in patient care physicians

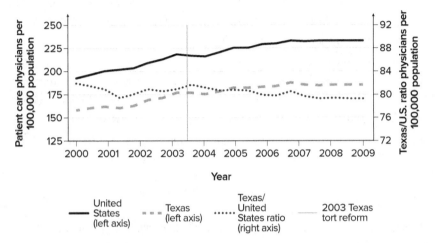

Notes: Texas and U.S. active patient care physicians per 100,000 population, 1990–2010, and ratio of Texas to U.S. physicians per 100,000 population. Texas medical malpractice reform in 2003 is depicted by vertical line.

Source: Area Health Resources Files.

100,000 population, for Texas and for the United States as a whole, from 1990 to 2010.[161] The upward-sloping solid line shows the national average, which rises steadily through about 2006 but flattens out after that. The upward-sloping dashed line shows Texas, which is roughly parallel with the U.S. line. Finally, the sloping dotted line that begins between the other two lines shows the ratio between these two lines—the ratio of Texas physicians to U.S. physicians, each per 100,000 population.

If medical malpractice reform improved Texas's drawing power relative to the rest of the United States, the third line should kink upward after medical malpractice reform. Putting aside short-term fluctuations, which likely reflect data collection issues rather than real changes in physician counts, this line is slightly downward sloping both before and after reform. Here too, there is no evidence that medical malpractice reform measurably increased Texas's appeal to physicians.

An alternative measure of how Texas is doing relative to other states comes from the American Medical Association's (AMA) annual ranking of states based on active patient care physicians per capita. Figure 10.5 presents the AMA rankings from 1997 to 2009 of Texas and four states that were ranked just above or below Texas in 1997: Alabama, Arizona, Arkansas, and Utah. The vertical axis is inverted so that a better (lower) rank appears higher than a worse (higher) one.

If physicians were leaving Texas pre-reform, the state's pre-reform rank should have fallen. Conversely, if medical malpractice reform made Texas more attractive, its post-reform AMA rank should have risen. Texas's ranking did slip pre-reform, from 38th in 1998 and 1999 to 44th in 2003, and it improved slightly post-reform—to 42nd in 2007–2009. But Texas still ranked worse in 2009 than it did during most of the

## Figure 10.5

American Medical Association ranking of Texas and four similarly ranked states on patient care physicians per capita

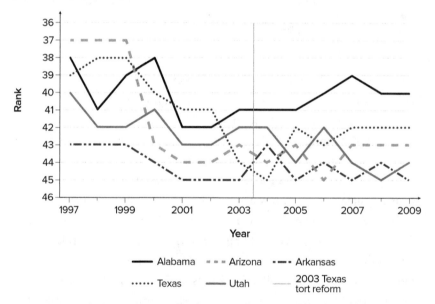

Notes: American Medical Association annual ranking of Alabama, Arizona, Arkansas, Texas, and Utah among 50 states based on active patient care physicians per capita, over 1997–2010. Comparison states are the ones that ranked closest to Texas in 1997. Texas medical malpractice reform in 2003 is depicted by vertical line.

Source: American Medical Association, *Physician Characteristics and Distribution in the United States*, various editions.

pre-reform period. So this measure of relative performance provides at best only mild evidence to support proponents' claims.

Given that Texas was similar to the rest of the United States in trends for patient care physicians per capita in the pre-reform period (Figure 10.4), how can its AMA ranking have improved (Figure 10.5)? The AMA rank reflects Texas's position relative to other states that also have low physician-to-population ratios. During the pre-reform period, Texas fared slightly worse than the average state, yet better than other well-below-average states. Medical malpractice reform could have affected Texas's ranking relative to its peers. But any overall impact was modest. In 1997, Texas was 39th—two spots behind Arizona (37th) and one ahead of Utah (40th). In 2007, Texas was 42nd—one spot ahead of Arizona (43rd) and two spots ahead of Utah (44th). None of these other three states had a non-econ cap in place during this period.

## TRENDS FOR HIGH-RISK SPECIALTIES AND PRIMARY CARE PHYSICIANS

Even if reform had a limited effect on the total number of Texas physicians, it might have had a larger effect on specialties that are at high risk of facing medical malpractice lawsuits. We consider here three specialties that are generally seen as facing high risk (ob-gyn, orthopedic surgery, and neurosurgery) and that figured prominently in the political campaign for tort reform.

Figure 10.6 compares trends in Texas to national trends for these three specialties over 1995–2010. It presents, for each specialty, the Texas-to-U.S. ratio of active patient care physicians per 100,000 population. For ob-gyns, the Texas-to-U.S. ratio dropped over 1995–1997 and was flat thereafter. The ratios for orthopedic surgeons and neurosurgeons were more volatile, which might reflect data collection issues rather than real changes but trend modestly downward, both before and after reform. There is no evidence that tort reform meaningfully affected the number of Texas ob-gyns, orthopedic surgeons, or neurosurgeons, relative to what one would expect based on national trends.

## Figure 10.6

### Changes in physicians in selected specialties, Texas and United States

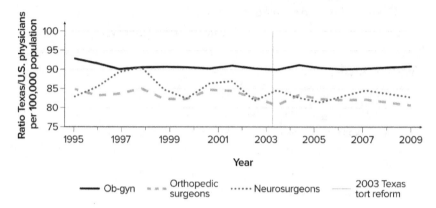

*Notes:* Ratio of Texas to U.S. patient care physicians per 100,000 population in indicated specialties over 1995–2010. Texas medical malpractice reform in 2003 is depicted by vertical line.

*Source:* Area Health Resources Files.

We also checked for evidence of a post-reform change in Texas, relative to national trends, for primary care physicians. The number of primary care Texas physicians per 100,000 population has been nearly constant since 2000. Overall, the Texas-to-U.S. ratio has averaged 85 percent over the last 30 years, with no long-term trend. The ratio increases modestly after reform, but this reflects a drop in primary care physicians nationally, rather than an increase in Texas. To be sure, we cannot rule out the possibility that the Texas ratio would have dropped without reform.

## RURAL PHYSICIANS

Reform advocates argued that rural Texas counties experienced a dramatic inflow of physicians after medical malpractice reform. And, as we noted above, there is evidence from other studies that medical malpractice reform modestly increases the availability of physicians in rural areas.[162]

TDSHS has compared the number of DPC physicians per 100,000 population in urban and rural counties over 1981–2011.[163] Figure 10.7 is

# Figure 10.7

## Direct patient care physicians in urban and rural counties, Texas

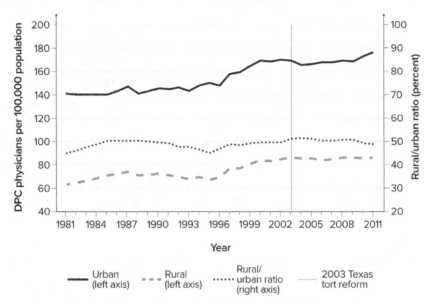

*Notes:* Urban and rural DPC physicians per 100,000 population, and rural to urban ratio in percent, 1981–2011. DPC = direct patient care. Rural/urban ratio = ratio of rural to urban DPC physicians per 100,000 population, converted to percent. Data for missing years are interpolated from adjacent years to compute ratio. Texas medical malpractice reform in 2003 is depicted by vertical line.

*Source:* Texas Department of State Health Services.

adapted from its report and shows separate lines for urban physicians per 100,000 population (top line) and rural physicians per 100,000 population (bottom line). The figure also includes a middle ratio line showing the ratio of rural to urban physicians in Texas per 100,000 population.

As Figure 10.7 indicates, the ratio of rural to urban physicians per capita has not changed much in the past 30 years. There is no evidence of a post-reform upswing. If anything, there was a modest upward trend in this ratio in the pre-reform period, which reversed after reform. We do not suggest that this change in trend is attributable to tort reform, but its existence underscores the point that tort reform is only one factor affecting physician supply.

# DISCUSSION

### Medical Malpractice Reform and Physician Location Decisions

We find no evidence that medical malpractice reform resulted in more physicians choosing to practice in Texas. This is true whether we examine total physicians, high-risk specialties, primary care physicians, or rural physicians. Our results are generally consistent with multistate studies of the relationship between medical malpractice reform and physician supply. Physician supply appears to be primarily driven by factors other than liability risk, including population trends, location of the physician's residency, job opportunities within the physician's specialty, lifestyle choices, and demand for medical services, including the extent to which the population is insured. For some physicians, medical malpractice insurance rates and the risk of being sued may be important factors. But for many physicians, other factors matter more. Medical malpractice reform is not a silver bullet for a state that wants to increase its physician supply relative to its peers.

### Is a Small Effect Surprising?

Is it surprising for a large reduction in malpractice risk to have little or no measurable impact on physician supply? We think not. A downward shock to malpractice risk implies an upward shock to physicians' willingness to supply their services. This change in the supply curve should increase the equilibrium quantity of medical services consumers demand—which means either more physicians or perhaps the same physicians working more hours.[164] But any increase is likely to be modest at best. Direct medical malpractice costs are a very small fraction of health care costs (see Chapter 9). And the demand for many forms of health care is quite inelastic, especially for the large fraction of health care costs that are paid for by others—by insurance companies or the government. Both factors will mute any effect of reform on the equilibrium quantity of health care and thus dampen any increase in the equilibrium supply of physicians, perhaps (as we find) to undetectable levels.

# CONCLUSION

The medical malpractice reform debate has featured extravagant claims about the merits and demerits of damages caps. As we noted in Chapter 7, damages caps can have a dramatic effect on the frequency and cost of malpractice claims, and thus, in the long run, on malpractice premiums. But their broader effects on health care delivery are less clear.

In Texas, medical malpractice reform proponents blamed the absence of a damages cap for Texas's failure to attract physicians and credited adoption of a cap on non-economic damages for an extraordinary increase in the number of physicians. We find no evidence to support either claim. The medical malpractice insurance crisis in Texas did not measurably stunt per capita physician supply in the years leading up to reform, nor did supply measurably improve after reform, relative to other states. This is true whether one looks at the number of Texas physicians in high-malpractice-risk specialties or the total number of active patient care physicians.

# PART THREE

# Mistreating the Problem: A National Perspective on the Impact of Medical Malpractice Reform

## CHAPTER 11

# THE RECEDING TIDE OF MEDICAL MALPRACTICE LITIGATION

## OVERVIEW

We find that the per physician rate of paid medical malpractice claims has been dropping since the early 1990s and by 2012 was less than half the 1992 level. Lawsuit rates, in the states with available data, declined at similar rates. "Small" paid claims (payout < $50,000 in 2011 dollars) have been dropping for this entire period; "large" paid claims (payout > $50,000, a slightly different definition than we used for Texas) have been dropping since 2001. Meanwhile, payout per claim on large paid claims has been roughly flat. Payout *per physician* has been dropping since 2003, and by 2012 was about half the 1992 level. The "third wave" of damage cap adoptions over 2002–2005 contributed to this broader trend. Damage caps reduce both the number of paid claims and payout per claim and thus have a large combined impact on payout per physician. However, there are also large declines in claim rates in states without damage caps.

## INTRODUCTION

In Chapter 7 we examined the impact of Texas's non-econ cap and showed that, during the post-reform period, there were dramatic declines in the number of paid claims and payout per claim. But Texas is not the only state with a damages cap. Currently, 31 states, covering 68 percent of the U.S. population, limit non-econ or total damages in medical mal-practice cases. To what extent is Texas's experience representative? In this chapter, we provide strong evidence that damage caps indeed reduce both the number of paid claims and payout per claim, nationally as well as in Texas. But we also show that there were downward nationwide trends in the number of paid medical malpractice claims even in the 20 states that never had damage caps (no-cap states)[165] and in 19 states that have had these caps for a long time (old-cap states).[166]

In this chapter, we study all 50 states plus the District of Columbia using the National Practitioner Data Bank (NPDB), a national dataset of closed paid claims against physicians and other individual practi-tioners covering 1992–2012. This dataset covers only *paid* claims. We find a large, sustained nationwide drop in paid claims per physician. The national paid claim rate per physician has been dropping for 20 years—as far back as the NPDB data can take us. The decline was gradual during 1992–2001 and principally involved smaller claims, but it accelerated thereafter, and it affected both small and large claims. The drop in paid claims is faster in the 12 "new-cap" states that adopted damage caps during our sample period.[167] But the drops are very large in all states: from 1992 to 2012, paid claims per physician dropped by 57 percent nationally, including 51 percent in the no-cap states, 57 percent in the old-cap states, and 64 percent in the new-cap states.

Payout per physician reflects the combined effect of trends in paid claim rates and payout per claim. Between 1992 and 2001, payout per physician rose somewhat from $7,500 to $8,200. Since then, it has plum-meted by more than 50 percent, to $3,850 in 2012. The national drop since 1992 is 48 percent, including 36 percent in no-cap states, 42 per-cent in old-cap states, and 69 percent in new-cap states.

Thus, since 1992, *all* states have experienced large drops in paid claims per physician and payout per physician. The old-cap states began from a lower baseline for both paid claim rates and payout per claim, which likely reflects their adopting damage caps before NPDB began collecting data. The new-cap states experienced a one-time shift toward fewer claims and lower payout per claim when they adopted caps. Before adopting caps, the new-cap states were similar to no-cap states in paid claim rates and payout per physician. After adoption, they dropped on both measures and became similar to old-cap states.

Finally, we examine how the receding tide affected both medical malpractice premiums and the share of total health care spending represented by medical malpractice payouts. We show that after hitting a peak in 2005, medical malpractice premiums have steadily declined. Total medical malpractice payouts peaked in 2001 and have been steadily declining ever since. As a share of total health care spending, medical malpractice payouts now account for perhaps 0.3 percent—making them a small tail on a very large dog.

## BACKGROUND

### National Trends in Medical Malpractice Premiums

As we saw in Chapter 3, medical malpractice premiums in Texas spiked beginning around 2000–2001. But what about the rest of the country? The best source for information about medical malpractice premiums is the *Medical Liability Monitor* (MLM), which provides information on the average premiums for physicians in three specialties: general surgery, internal medicine, and obstetrics and gynecology, for "standard" policy limits of $1 million per occurrence/$3 million per policy year. Although premiums vary significantly by state and county, we used MLM data to compute overall national average premiums for these three specialties. Figure 11.1 shows the time trends in premiums, with population weighted by county.

Although premiums varied greatly by specialty, the time patterns were very similar. Medical malpractice premiums fell during the 1990s, then rose to a peak in 2005, and have declined steadily since then. In 2016, average medical malpractice premiums were roughly comparable in constant dollars to the levels of the mid-1990s.

We noted in Texas that the spike in medical malpractice premiums in the early 2000s was not sparked by a similar spike in medical malpractice claims or payouts. How about nationally? The dramatic rise in premiums from 2000 to 2005 sparked the third wave of damage cap adoptions over 2002–2005. In states other than Texas, can a "fire" in medical malpractice

## Figure 11.1

Nationwide average medical malpractice premiums by specialty

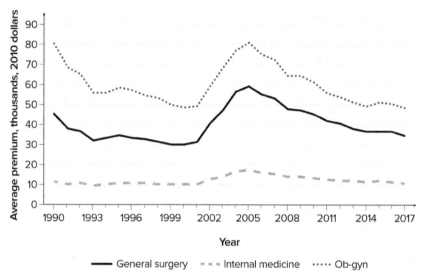

**Year**

General surgery     Internal medicine     Ob-gyn

*Notes:* Premium in thousands of 2010 dollars. Figures are population-weighted by county. Ob-gyn = Obstetrics and gynecology.

*Source: Medical Liability Monitor.*

claiming explain the "smoke" of the dramatic rise in premiums? And did the adoption of caps have a similar effect on claim rates and payouts in Texas and other new-cap states? We study those questions in this chapter.

### National Trends in Medical Malpractice Litigation

Our own work aside, we know of no academic studies of overall national trends in medical malpractice claim rates or payout per physician. An earlier study found no rise in the second half of the 1990s in medical malpractice lawsuits.[168] There are also a few studies involving specific specialties or settings,[169] one study focusing on payout per claim,[170] and one study using data from a single large medical malpractice insurer.[171]

### Effect of Damage Caps on Payouts and Claims

Several studies examine the effect of damage caps on medical malprac- tice litigation, although most do not examine the most recent wave of damage caps, adopted during 1995–2005 in new-cap states. We reviewed several of these studies in Chapter 7.

### Tort Reforms Other Than Damage Caps

We focus in this book on damage caps, but many states have adopted a number of other medical malpractice reforms. Damage caps are often bundled with one or more other reforms adopted at or around the same time. We view our results as estimating the average effect of "serious" reform, where a damages cap is the core element, but often not the only element, of a reform package. That said, there is no evidence that other reforms affect claim rates or payout per claim (the focus of this chapter); spending (the focus of Chapter 12); or physician supply (the focus of Chapter 13). In unreported analyses, we verified that our estimates of the effects of damage caps alone, without controlling for other reforms, would not change appreciably if we controlled for the other principal reforms.[172]

## NATIONAL TRENDS IN CLAIM RATES AND PAYOUTS

### Trends in Claim Rates

Figure 11.2 shows the national trend in paid claims per 1,000 physicians, broken out by payout amount, for 1992–2012. This figure includes four lines, for (a) claims with payout less than $50,000; (b) claims with payout between $50,000 and $250,000; (c) claims with payout of $250,000 or more; and (d) all paid claims. The top line, which shows all paid claims per 1,000 physicians, declines gradually from 1992 to 2001 and then declines more sharply therafter. Over the entire period, paid claims per 1,000 physicians drop by 57 percent.

In contrast, if we look at the other lines in Figure 11.2, we see that the smallest paid claims (i.e., < $50,000) declined over our full sample period from 8.8 claims per 1,000 physicians in 1992 to only 2.4 per 1,000 in 2012. There was a 40 percent decline over 1992–2001 and an additional 54 percent decline over 2001–2012 (a 72 percent overall drop). In contrast, for the other two categories of claims (i.e., $50,000–$250,000 and $250,000+), claim rates were roughly flat through 2001, and then

## Figure 11.2

Nationwide paid claims per 1,000 physicians by payout amount

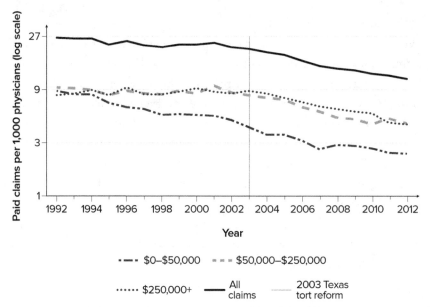

*Notes:* Paid medical malpractice claims (in 2010$) reported to the National Practitioner Data Bank (NPDB) by year, per 1,000 physicians (top line), and claims for indicated payout ranges (< $50,000; $50,000–250,000; and > $250,000) (lower lines), for 1992–2012. Y-axis uses logarithmic scale, so that similar percentage changes will lead to parallel lines. Vertical line at 2001 is illustrative and indicates start of strong receding tide period.

*Source:* National Practitioner Data Bank.

dropped by over 50 percent during 2001–2012. Although not separately shown in Figure 11.2, we find a similar pattern for very large claims (payout > $500,000), which drop by 57 percent over 2001–2012.

Thus, in the first half of our sample period, the modest overall decline in paid claim rates was attributable entirely to a drop in the smallest paid claims. Since 2001, all size categories have shown large declines. The 20-year decline in small paid claims is consistent with these claims being squeezed out of the tort system by rising litigation costs. Defense costs rose much faster than inflation over this period (see Chapter 6).[173] Data on plaintiff-side costs are not available, but if plaintiff-side costs also rose, that could help explain the drop in small paid claims.

One can also use the total paid claim line in Figure 11.2 to calculate a physician's total practice-lifetime risk of a paid medical malpractice claim. In 1992, the rate of 26 paid claims per 1,000 physicians translates into about one paid claim every 40 years (which we treat as a practice-lifetime). By 2012, this rate had fallen by 57 percent, to 11 claims per 1,000 physicians, or about one-half of one paid claim per practice-lifetime.

It is tempting to attribute this decline to the states that adopted damage caps. Instead, the number of paid claims was dropping everywhere—even in states that had never had a damage cap. Table 11.1 analyzes changes in the number of paid claims from 1992 to 2012 for the no-cap, new-cap, and old-cap states.

As Table 11.1 indicates, on average, the number of paid claims dropped by 59 percent in new-cap states and 48 percent in old-cap states over this period—but it also dropped by 51 percent in no-cap states. Among the 20 no-cap states, the drops range from 32 percent (Maine) to 74 percent (District of Columbia).

We do not have a good explanation for why the decline in larger paid claims started in 2001. Indeed, if we analyze trends using injury year, instead of claim closing year, the decline begins two years earlier, in 1999. But there is some irony in the timing of the third wave of medical malpractice reform. That wave was prompted by a rapid rise in

## Table 11.1

Drop in paid claims per physician in no-cap, new-cap, and old-cap states, 1992–2012

| State group | Minimum drop | Maximum drop | Average drop |
|---|---|---|---|
| No-cap | −32% | −74% | −51% |
| New-cap | −34% | −81% | −59% |
| Old-cap | −5% | −72% | −48% |

*Notes:* No-cap = the 20 states that did not have caps on non-economic or total damages during 1990–2010. New-cap = the 12 states, including Texas, that adopted non-economic caps during 1990–2010. Old-cap = the 19 states that had damages caps in place during 1999–2010. The specific states in each group are listed in endnotes 165–167.

*Sources:* For paid claim rates, National Practitioner Data Bank; and for physician counts, American Medical Association annual surveys.

medical malpractice insurance premiums, which began around 1999–
2000, when smaller paid claims were already dropping and just as (with
the benefit of hindsight) the rate of larger new claims was beginning a
sustained decline.

### Trends in Payout per Claim and Payout per Physician

We turn next to time trends in payout per large claim and payout per
physician. Figure 11.3 presents separate lines for mean payout per claim
for claims greater than $50,000 (top line) and mean payout per physician
(bottom line).[174] The top line is flat throughout: payout per large claim
was $416,000 in 1992, was again $416,000 in 2011, and between those
years fluctuated in a narrow range from $400,000 to $440,000.

Payout *per physician* reflects a combination of claim rates and payout per claim. This line is the most relevant for predicting malpractice
insurance premiums. The dashed line in Figure 11.3 shows payout per
physician for all paid claims. Payout per physician was reasonably stable
at around $7,500 from 1992 through 2000, with a bump to $8,200 in
2001. It then dropped rapidly to about $3,900 in 2012. This drop reflects

## Figure 11.3

### Mean nationwide payout per claim and per physician

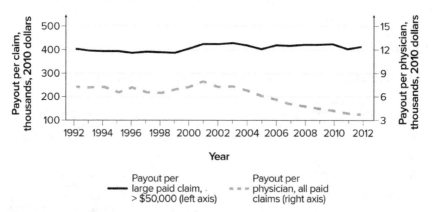

*Note:* Mean payout per claim by year over 1992–2012 for large paid claims (payout > $50,000; left axis),
and mean payout per physician by year (right axis).

*Sources:* For paid claim rates, National Practitioner Data Bank; and for physician counts, American Medical
Association annual surveys.

a declining number of large paid claims, which account for around 98 percent of payout dollars, with roughly stable payout per large claim.

Given the evidence in Figure 11.3 of gently fluctuating payout per physician, why was there a malpractice insurance crisis in the United States during 2000–2005? Payout per physician rose over 1998–2001 but by 2000 had merely returned to the the 1992–1994 average. Only in 2001 did payout per physician exceed that average. This national evidence reinforces a core lesson from Chapter 3: whatever the dysfunctions of the medical malpractice litigation system may be, one must look elsewhere to explain the rapid rise in medical malpractice insurance premiums during this period.

While the causes of the early 2000s crisis in medical malpractice insurance remain unclear, the legislative response is much easier to understand. Physicians are a politically powerful and sympathetic interest group. They faced a genuine crisis in the insurance rates they were paying. From all the anecdotal evidence we know of, physicians believed there must have been a crisis in the medical malpractice litigation system that was causing the insurance crisis. They sought legislative relief, and in many states, they succeeded.

## THE EFFECT OF DAMAGE CAPS: GRAPHICAL EVIDENCE

To what extent are these national trends attributable to damage cap adoptions? To address that question, we compare trends in old-cap, new-cap, and no-cap states. Figure 11.4 contains two panels. Panel A shows trends in large paid claims (payout greater than $50,000) per 1,000 physicians for each group of states, and Panel B shows trends in payout per physician. As Panel A shows, through 2001, claim rates were fairly stable for all three groups of states, with a modest downward trend for old-cap states. Such a relative trend is not surprising, since most caps are not adjusted for inflation and thus become stricter over time. Claim rates were similar for no-cap and new-cap states but were substantially lower for old-cap states, by an average of 25 percent over 1992–2003. From 2001 on, paid claim rates drop in all three groups. The claim rates in no-cap and new-cap states remain similar through 2003. After that, the third wave of cap adoptions begins to affect claim rates, and the new-cap states experience

# Figure 11.4

## Claim trends for no-cap, new-cap, and old-cap states

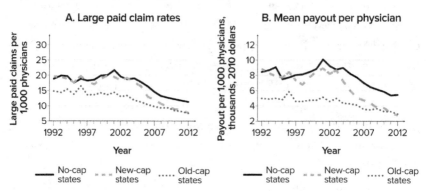

*Note:* Panel A: Large paid claims are for payouts > $50,000.

*Sources:* For paid claim rates, National Practitioner Data Bank; and for physician counts, American Medical Association annual surveys.

an additional drop in paid claims. By 2009, the average claim rate for new–cap states had dropped and become similar to the average for old–cap states. Thus, the large paid claim rate in new–cap states is similar to the rate in no–cap states, *until* new–cap states adopt damage caps, but after which this rate starts to look more like rates in old–cap states.

Panel A provides strong, if partial, evidence that damage caps reduce claim rates. First, through 2003, old–cap states have substantially lower paid claim rates than the other groups. Second, the drop in paid claims in new–cap states relative to other states, beginning soon after these caps were adopted, strongly suggests that damage caps reduce claim rates.

We turn in Panel B to payout per physician, which reflects a combination of paid claim rates and payout per claim. All three groups show no strong trend in the first half of the sample period and a declining trend over roughly the last decade. Payout per physician is similar in new–cap and no–cap states through 2003. In contrast, over 1992–2003, the old–cap states average 41 percent lower payout per physician than the other two groups. Once the new–cap states adopt caps, payout per physician in these states drops rapidly and converges to the old–cap level. This provides further evidence that damage caps have a large effect on payout per physician because of their combined effect on claim rates and on payout per claim.[175]

We also used regression analysis to confirm the effect of damages caps on claim rates, payout per claim, and payout per physician, shown graphically in Figure 11.4. In unreported analysis, we find a fully phased-in damage cap predicts a 27 percent drop in paid claim rates, a 17 percent drop in payout per claim, and a 45 percent drop in payout per physician.

## THE EFFECT OF THE RECEDING TIDE ON MEDICAL MALPRACTICE PREMIUMS

In the long run, medical malpractice premiums should reflect overall time trends in claims and payouts per claim. Even if changes in the tort system do not explain the causes of the premium spike that hit the United States during 2001–2005, the receding tide of medical malpractice claiming should eventually be reflected in insurance premiums. Figure 11.5 analyzes

## Figure 11.5

Nationwide medical malpractice premiums versus payout per physician

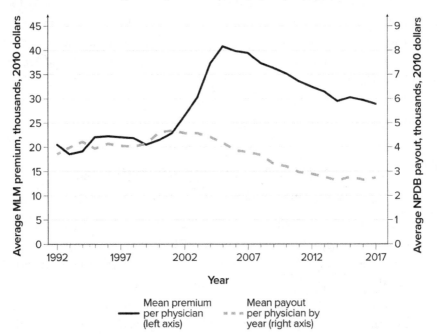

*Notes:* Mean payout per physician by year (right axis) and mean premium per physician (left axis). All figures are in 2010 thousands of dollars. MLM = *Medical Liability Monitor;* NPDB = National Practitioner Data Bank.

*Source: Medical Liability Monitor.*

that issue. In it, we show both data from the *Medical Liability Monitor* on nationwide medical malpractice premiums per physician, and data on payout per physician from Figure 11.3.

Figure 11.5 (like Figure 11.3) shows that payout per physician fluctuated in a narrow range between 1991 and 2000, peaked in 2001, and then began a steady decline before leveling out after 2013. But what about medical malpractice premiums? Nationwide, medical malpractice premiums spiked between 2002–2005—broadly consistent with, though a couple of years later than, the Texas spike, which began in 2000. Since then, nationwide medical malpractice premiums have steadily declined—presumably reflecting the impact of the national receding tide and the additional impact of the damage caps adopted by the new-cap states.

There are two main takeaways from Figure 11.5. First, it confirms that the medical malpractice insurance system is indeed a market that responds (albeit slowly) in predictable ways to changes in inputs and incentives. Second, it confirms that—as we noted for Texas in Chapter 3—in the near to medium term, trends in premiums for medical malpractice insurance can be disconnected from trends in medical malpractice payouts. Payouts by physicians peaked in 2001 and were only moderately higher than in a number of prior years (1991, 1992, 1993, 1995, and 2000), yet insurance premiums rose dramatically beginning in 2002 and kept rising through 2005.

## HOW IMPORTANT IS MEDICAL MALPRACTICE LITIGATION? TOWARD A SENSE OF PROPORTION

Finally, given the receding tide, how does direct spending on medical malpractice litigation compare to overall U.S. health care spending—and how have those figures changed over time? In Figure 11.6, we plot medical malpractice payouts on behalf of physicians as a fraction of overall health care spending on the same graph. A first point to note is that the payout amounts are a small fraction of 1 percent of health care spending. In magnitude, medical malpractice payouts were in the single-digit billions of dollars, while annual health care spending was in the *trillions*.

# Figure 11.6

## National medical malpractice payouts as percentage of total health care spending

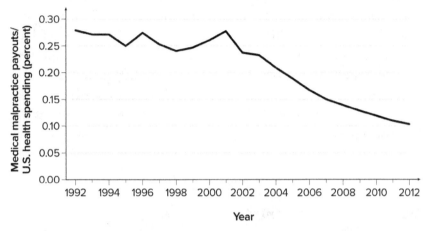

*Note:* Total payouts on medical malpractice claims against physicians reported to National Practitioner Data Bank (NPDB), by year, as a percentage of U.S. national health expenditures.

*Sources:* NPDB; and Centers for Medicare and Medicaid Services National Health Expenditure Data.

Medical malpractice payouts by physicians were fairly constant as a share of overall spending from 1992 to 2001, at around 0.25 to 0.30 percent of overall spending. But starting in 2002, medical malpractice payouts began to drop sharply as a share of spending. By 2012, medical malpractice payouts by physicians had dropped to only 0.11 percent of total health care spending. Given the continuing fall in medical malpractice premiums since then, and the steady rise in health care spending, that level today is below 0.1 percent. Thus, of every $1,000 that we spend on health care, less than $1 goes to plaintiffs who win medical malpractice recoveries from physicians. On a per capita basis, medical malpractice payouts started at $15 in 1992, rose to $18 in 2001, and then fell steadily to under $9 in 2018. Of course, payouts in medical malpractice claims against physicians are only part of the financial cost of medical malpractice liability. A fuller measure would include payouts by other providers, defense costs, and insurer administrative costs. This fuller measure might be roughly triple the physician payouts reported to NPDB—perhaps as much as 0.3 percent of total health care spending.[176] This is still a tiny percentage of health care spending.

Twenty-five years ago, Michael Saks described the medical malpractice liability system as a "mouse with an otherworldly roar."[177] He was referring to the fact that "people have come to overestimate vastly the tort system's vigilance and the magnitude of its sanctions" and suggested that the "tort system achieves what deterrence it does by the unpleasantness of its operation—at least as that is experienced or imagined by defendants." Since Saks wrote, the medical malpractice mouse has shrunk by more than half relative to health care spending. The roar remains, and still influences physicians and legislators, but with less and less mouse behind it.

## DISCUSSION

### Possible Explanations for the Receding Medical Malpractice Tide

The risk to individual physicians of facing a paid malpractice claim has dropped by more than 50 percent since 2001. What might be behind this strongly receding tide? There are a number of possible reasons:

*Tort reform.* Tort reform is part of the story. We find strong evidence that damage caps reduce both paid claim rates and payout per claim. But these reforms cannot explain the strong downward trend in no-cap states, and they can explain only a small part of the similarly strong downward trend in old-cap states.

*Improvements in health care quality.* If the rate of errors dropped, or the errors became more subtle and harder to recover damages for, the rate of malpractice claims should drop as well. Most errors do not lead to claims, but most claims do involve errors, and adverse event rates and malpractice rates are correlated.[178] Unfortunately, although there have been improvements in health care quality in some areas (e.g., a decline in central-line infections in intensive care units), studies of error rates continue to show distressingly high rates, with only limited evidence of systematic improvement in quality.[179] Thus, improvements in health care quality seem unlikely to explain our results.

*Rising litigation costs.* The cost of defending medical malpractice claims is rising over time, as we noted for Texas in Chapter 6. It is plausible that plaintiffs' costs are rising as well—indeed the purpose of some tort reforms is to make lawsuits against physicians harder and more costly to bring as well as less remunerative. For example, requiring an expert report before or soon after a lawsuit is filed and limiting who can be an expert, both increase plaintiffs' litigation costs and exclude claims that can't satisfy these requirements. Caps on contingent fee percentages make large recoveries less remunerative for lawyers. Rising plaintiff litigation costs likely explain some portion of the receding medical malpractice tide, especially the drop in smaller claims over our entire sample period. Increasingly, plaintiffs with smaller claims appear to be unable to find medical malpractice lawyers who are willing to bring their claims.[180]

*More hospital-employed physicians.* There has been a slow, long-term trend toward greater employment of physicians by hospitals. This could induce fewer direct suits against physicians (rather than hospitals) and more settlements in which the hospital pays damages so that the physician won't need to report the settlement to NPDB. This trend, however, can explain only a small part of the observed decline in paid claims reported to NPDB, both because the trend toward hospitals employing more physicians was quite gradual over our sample period and because we find similar drops in lawsuits against all defendants, including hospitals.

*Do hospitals pay so doctors can avoid reporting to NPDB?* Even for physicians who are not employed by hospitals, there are anecdotes about settlements in which the plaintiff sues both the physician and the hospital, and the hospital agrees to make the full payment so that the physician does not need to report the claim to NPDB.[181] If this practice has become more common over time, it could contribute to the overall decline in claims. We know of no national data source on payments by hospitals that would let us assess any changes in prevalence over time. The substitution of hospital for physician as the paying defendant is plausible for small claims and could explain some of the drop in these claims, but it seems less likely for larger claims. At the same time, we looked for evidence of substitution for the three states where we had detailed information on payers—Florida, Illinois, and Texas—and found no evidence of increasing substitution.

*Existence of NPDB and physician willingness to settle.* Physicians must report paid claims to NPDB. This could make them less willing to settle, especially for smaller claims. Without the specter of NPDB reporting, a physician and insurer might agree to settle for modest dollars to get the matter over with. This could contribute to rising litigation costs. But we know of no reason why the NPDB effect should have increased for injuries in 1999 and after.

*Broader decline in personal injury litigation.* Perhaps personal injury litigation as a whole is undergoing a long-term decline. We studied this possibility using the one state (Texas) for which we have detailed data on other types of personal injury claims. These claims were not affected by Texas's 2003 damages cap. We found that claim rates and payouts also declined, although with a different temporal pattern than for medical malpractice.[182] The claim rate per 100,000 population for large paid *non–medical malpractice* personal injury claims dropped by 50 percent between 1992 and 2000, and by a further 13 percent between 2000 and 2009. Payout per capita dropped by 43 percent between 1992 and 2000, and by a further 20 percent between 2000 and 2009. This evidence comes from only one state, but it suggests that there are broader forces at work in the tort system that could affect medical malpractice claims.

### Policy Implications: Deterrence and Compensation

Medical malpractice litigation is intended to deter negligent treatment. However, the evidence on a link between medical malpractice risk and quality is limited.[183] If medical malpractice risk is falling, its deterrent effect is probably falling as well. Medical malpractice litigation is also intended to compensate negligently injured patients. However, the medical malpractice system has long undercompensated most of those who are negligently injured—in part because most negligent errors don't lead to lawsuits, and in part because, as in personal injury litigation generally, severely injured plaintiffs are undercompensated. The receding tide will aggravate these problems as well. This suggests that we should be looking for new mechanisms to motivate health care providers to improve care quality and to improve compensation to those who suffer medically caused harm.

### The Implications of Changing Case Mix

Although mean payout per *large* paid claim did not rise over time, mean payout per claim rose by 2.2 percent per year from 1992 to 2001.

This might suggest that payouts on medical malpractice claims were rising during the 1990s. Indeed, reform proponents often use data on average payouts (not adjusted for inflation, so the increases appear much larger) in exactly this way. But, on closer examination, mean payout rose in the 1990s because small claims largely vanished, not because large claims received larger payouts. Recognizing this change in case mix leads to quite different implications than one would get from simply looking at mean payouts. The focus turns from "what can we do about rising payouts?" to "what can we do about the disappearance of small claims?"

## CONCLUSION

Medical malpractice litigation may once have seemed to physicians like a tidal wave that strongly affected their pocketbooks and sometimes their clinical choices. But for the past two decades, the tide has steadily receded. Tort reform explains only some of this trend. There have also been large, sustained declines in the 20 states that have never adopted damage caps and large declines in states that have long had damage caps (far too large to be explained by the gradually increasing stringency of these caps, which are often not adjusted for inflation).

Adoption of additional damage caps would further expedite the declining trend, but the absolute dollars at stake are modest. As we explain in greater detail in Chapter 14, we estimate that, at most, 0.3 percent of national health care spending is attributable to medical malpractice litigation. Since most states already have caps, a strict damages cap that applied nationwide might save a fraction of this—perhaps 0.1 percent of national health care spending, while leaving more patients to bear the costs of uncompensated injuries. There might be somewhat larger savings from lower health care spending—but our research suggests that there are likely no savings there too (Chapters 9 and 12). For overall health policy, whether damage caps are a good idea or a bad one, they are a *small* idea.

More work is needed to understand why medical malpractice claim rates declined across the board, including in no-cap states. Is this part of a more general decline in personal injury claims? If so, why are personal injury claims declining? Too little is known about how changes in medical malpractice risk affect quality. Some recent research suggests that damage caps may lead to more errors.[184] What happens to health care quality as medical malpractice risk declines, even in states that don't adopt damage caps?

Damage caps are very good for doctors. But their effects on the overall system are small and—if they reduce deterrence—possibly counterproductive. At some point in the future, the medical malpractice tide may return. Until it does, policymakers should look elsewhere for solutions to the problems with American health care.

## CHAPTER 12

# DEFENSIVE MEDICINE IN THE NEW-CAP STATES

## OVERVIEW

Do non-economic (non-econ) caps reduce defensive medicine and thus health care spending? In Chapter 9, we showed that there is no evidence that Texas's non-econ cap reduced spending for in-hospital care (Medicare Part A) and some evidence that spending for outpatient care (Medicare Part B) *rose* after cap adoption—the opposite result from that posited by reform supporters, who often claim that medical malpractice risk drives unnecessary medical spending. In this chapter, we study all nine states that adopted caps during the "third reform wave," from 2002–2005. We find that damage caps have no significant impact on Medicare Part A spending but predict roughly 4 percent *higher* Medicare Part B spending.

## INTRODUCTION

In Chapter 9, we studied whether Texas's adoption in 2003 of a relatively strict damages cap affected Medicare spending. We found no evidence that either spending levels or spending growth were higher in counties with high medical malpractice risk. Nor did we find evidence that after reform, health care spending dropped in high-risk counties relative to low-risk counties. We then compared Texas to other states. We found no significant effect of reform on Part A spending and evidence that Part B spending *increased* after reform.

In this chapter, we extend that Texas-only analysis to cover all nine "new-cap" states, which adopted damage caps during the third reform wave in the early 2000s.[185] We conduct a difference-in-differences (DiD) analysis of spending in the nine new-cap states compared to 20 "no-cap" states, which have no damage caps in place during our sample period (1998–2011). Similar to Chapter 9, we find caps have no significant effect on Medicare Part A spending. (Part A covers payments to hospitals for inpatient care.) Also similar to Chapter 9, we find evidence that Medicare Part B spending *rises* after reform. (Part B covers all Medicare fee-for-service spending except for Part A and prescription drugs, which is Part D; Part C is Medicare Advantage.) We find consistent evidence of higher Part B spending across all nine new-cap states. The rise in Part B spending occurs gradually over a number of years and is strongly statistically significant. We estimate 4 to 5 percent higher Part B spending following cap adoption. The estimated rise in Part B spending is similar, indeed a bit larger, if we compare the new-cap states to both no-cap and old-cap states.[186]

The effect of damage caps on "total" (Part A plus Part B) Medicare spending per enrollee is a blend of the Part A and Part B results. This rise is around 2.0 to 2.5 percent and, across specifications, is either statistically significant or marginally significant.

Some limitations of our study are as follows: Our dataset lets us study only aggregate, county-level Medicare spending per beneficiary, divided into Part A and Part B. Thus, while we provide evidence that Part B spending rises after adoption of damage caps, our data do not let us study why—what do physicians do differently? Second, the control variables in our regression analyses capture county-level demographic characteristics but not health characteristics. Third, we study only the Medicare population with traditional fee-for-service Medicare. There are no available data sources that would let us study the nonelderly or elderly patients who enroll in Medicare Advantage. Fourth, we find a rise in spending only for Medicare Part B, not Part A. This is an odd pattern, which suggests caution in relying on our results as evidence of *higher* spending until confirmed in additional work with patient-level data. At the same time, we provide strong evidence that Medicare spending does not *fall* after cap adoption.

In related work, we extend the results in this chapter in two ways. First, we use national data on paid claims against physicians reported to the National Practitioner Data Bank (NPDB) as a national measure of medical malpractice risk; run county fixed effects regressions over 1992–2014; and find, consistent with the DiD results reported here, that higher paid claim rates predict *lower* Part B Medicare spending, and perhaps, though less clearly, lower Part A spending as well.[187] Second, in a separate study by one of us, we use *patient-level* data for a random 5 percent sample of Medicare recipients and run analyses similar to those reported here, with controls for patient characteristics, including health and either patient or physician fixed effects.[188] With patient fixed effects, the point estimates for post-reform change in spending are positive, similar in magnitude for both Part A and Part B spending, and consistent with the results we report here, but are not statistically distinguishable from no effect. However, that study was only a 5 percent sample of Medicare beneficiaries, and the statistical uncertainty in the estimates is thus much higher than those we report on here.

## BACKGROUND

We review the literature on whether damage caps affect health care spending in Chapter 9. In this chapter, we rely on the same county-level Medicare data as in Chapter 9, over 1998–2011, plus an extensive set of county-level control variables, which we use to control for factors other than tort reform that might affect health care spending. The control variables are the number of active, nonfederal, patient care physicians per 1,000 persons; the percentage of Medicare enrollees who are covered by managed care plans, rather than traditional Medicare fee-for-service (managed care penetration);[189] unemployment rate; median household income; percentage disabled (percentage of Medicare enrollees receiving Social Security Disability Insurance); population; percentage male; percentage in poverty; percentage black; percentage Hispanic; percentage ages 65–74, 75–84, and 85+; and per capita personal income.[190]

## TRENDS IN MEDICARE SPENDING

Figure 12.1 provides an initial graphical analysis of trends in Medicare spending. Each panel shows two lines. Panel A shows results for Part A spending; Panel B is similar but covers Part B spending. In each panel, the upper line shows the ratio of Medicare spending per enrollee in new-cap states to spending per enrollee in no-cap states. Vertical lines show the start and end of the 2002–2005 cap adoption period.

In Panel A, the new-cap to no-cap ratio for Part A spending fluctuates but with no strong trend and no evidence of a change in trend during or after the cap adoption period. The point estimates are similar in 2002 (just before the reform wave) and 2011 (the last data year).

The pattern for Part B spending is different. Part B spending is initially higher in new-cap states than in no-cap states. The gap between new-cap and old-cap states rises during the cap adoption period and is roughly stable after that. The new-cap to no-cap ratio averages

## Figure 12.1

### Relative Medicare spending: New-cap/no-cap versus old-cap/no-cap states

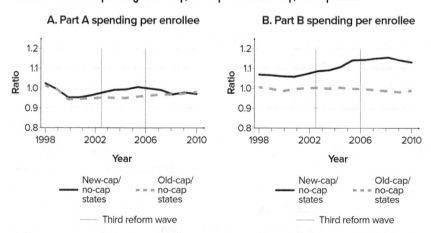

*Notes:* Medicare spending ratios per enrollee for 9 new-cap states and 22 old-cap states, relative to 20 no-cap states, separately for Part A and Part B, over 1998–2011. The specific states in each group are listed in endnotes 165–167. Vertical lines indicate roughly the start and end of the third reform wave period, during which the new-cap states adopt non-economic caps.

*Source:* Centers for Medicare and Medicaid Services data on county-level Medicare Part A and Part B spending.

106 percent during 1998–2001 but rises to an average of 114 percent over 2008–2011.

The bottom lines in the two panels of Figure 12.1 show Part A and Part B spending ratios for old-cap states to no-cap states. We have no reason to expect these lines to be affected by the reforms that take place in *new-cap* states. Thus, these lines are "placebo lines," where we expect to find no effect of reform. The placebo lines are, in fact, fairly flat, for both Part A and Part B spending.

Recall from Chapter 9 that a core DiD assumption is that treatment and control states would have evolved similarly but for the damage cap "treatment." This "parallel trends" assumption cannot be directly tested, but we can use graphs to assess whether Medicare spending trends for new-cap states appear to move in parallel with trends for no-cap states during the pretreatment period. Whether pretreatment trends are parallel is an important credibility check for the parallel trends assumption.

To do so, we construct "leads and lags" graphs, which provides annual estimates of the treatment effect, both before and after cap adoption. To create our graphs, we use a regression model with reforms measured in "event-time" relative to each new-cap state's reform year. Figure 12.2 includes separate leads and lags graphs for Part A, Part B, and total Medicare spending per enrollee. The *x*-axis shows years in event time relative to each state's reform year. The *y*-axis shows the annual coefficients for each year, which can be interpreted as fractional changes in spending per enrollee relative to a base year, which we set as four years before cap adoption. Vertical bars show 95 percent confidence intervals around each coefficient. Year 0 is the year when the reforms were adopted. It can be seen as a partly post-reform year; year +1 is the first full post-reform year.

Consider Panel A, which shows results for Medicare Part A spending. There is some evidence of nonparallel trends, including a rise in spending in new-cap states over years [−7, −5], and then a downward trend over years [−5, −2]. These trends for Part A spending drive similar but milder trends for total Medicare spending in the bottom panel. During the post-reform period, there is no evidence of a trend toward either higher or lower Part A spending. But if we found such evidence,

# Figure 12.2

## Leads and lags graph of Medicare spending per enrollee: new-cap versus no-cap states

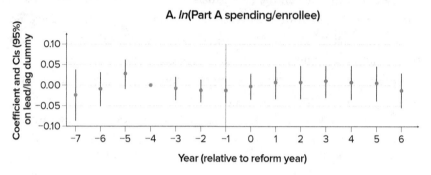

A. *ln*(Part A spending/enrollee)

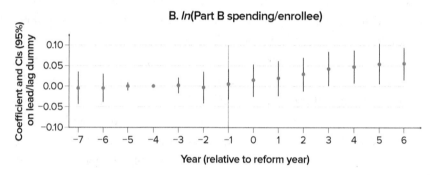

B. *ln*(Part B spending/enrollee)

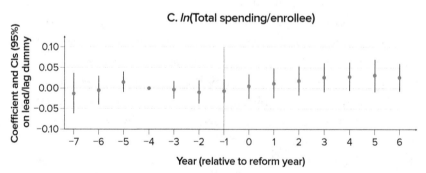

C. *ln*(Total spending/enrollee)

*Notes:* Figures show ratio of *ln*(Medicare spending per enrollee) for 9 new-cap states to *ln*(Medicare spending per enrollee) for 20 no-cap states, separately for Part A spending, Part B spending, and total spending. The specific states in each group are listed in endnotes 165–167. Coefficients are from regressions of *ln*(Medicare spending per enrollee) on leads and lags of a reform dummy variable relative to reform year ($t = 0$), county and year fixed effects, and other control variables. Coefficients are relative to year ($t − 4$) (four years before cap adoption). Regressions are weighted by average number of enrollees in each county over 1998–2011. Vertical bars show 95 percent confidence intervals, using standard errors clustered on state.

*Source:* Centers for Medicare and Medicaid Services data on county-level Medicare Part A and Part B spending.

the nonparallel trends in the pre-reform period would counsel caution in concluding that reform caused that trend.

Panel B of Figure 12.2 shows results for Medicare Part B spending. The annual point estimates are flat and near zero during the pre-reform period. This supports the parallel trends assumption. Spending rises in year 0 (partly a post-reform year) and continues to rise during the post-reform period. The coefficients on point estimates for individual years become statistically significant beginning with year 3 and are around 5 percent in years 4 through 6. While an omitted variable could explain the post-reform rise, this provides evidence that, at least for Part B spending, any reduction in assurance behavior (physicians providing extra treatment because of medical malpractice risk) appears to be outweighed by a reduction in avoidance behavior (physicians avoiding or limiting treatment because of medical malpractice risk).

Combined Part A plus Part B Medicare spending (Panel C) is a blend of the separate trends for Part A and Part B spending. The point estimates are positive in the post-reform period but are not statistically significant.

## DISTRIBUTED LAG REGRESSION RESULTS

We can improve statistical power by combining the post-reform point estimates for individual years, shown in Figure 12.2, during the post-reform period. If we do so, using what are known as "distributed lag" regressions,[191] we estimate a 4 percent increase in Part B spending during the post-reform period, which is strongly statistically significant. In robustness checks in which we use matching methods to ensure that the control counties are similar to the treated counties, the point estimates range from 3 to 5 percent and are statistically significant in all cases. In similar regressions covering total Medicare spending, the estimated post-reform rise is around 2 to 3 percent and is also statistically significant, but not strongly so.

Thus, we find evidence of a statistically significant 4 to 5 percent rise in Part B spending following cap adoption, no significant change in Part A spending, and a 2 percent or so blended rise in total Medicare spending, which is significant in some specifications but not others.

# DISCUSSION

## Will Tort Reform Bend the Cost Curve?

A core policy argument used to support tort reform, especially damage caps, is that caps will reduce "defensive medicine" and thus reduce health care spending. Reform proponents have in mind less assurance behavior. They do not explicitly address the potential for caps to lead to less avoidance behavior as well. Still, point estimates from prior research suggest cost savings—generally in the 2 to 5 percent range—even if many of these estimates are statistically insignificant.[192] This is a small percentage, but for health care, even 2 percent is real money.

We find evidence pointing in the opposite direction. For third-wave damage caps, we find evidence consistent with lower medical malpractice risk leading to *higher* Medicare Part B spending, rather than lower spending. This result could arise if the effect of damage caps in reducing assurance behavior (which should reduce spending) is, on average, outweighed by the effect in reducing avoidance behavior (which can lead to higher post-cap spending). Overall, we estimate a 4 to 5 percent rise in Medicare Part B spending. In the results presented here, and in extensive robustness checks, our estimates for Medicare Part A spending are small, of varying sign, and never statistically significant. Combined Part A and Part B spending appears to rise as well: our point estimates are 2 to 3 percent and are sometimes statistically significant. Thus, at a minimum, we provide strong evidence that tort reform does not *reduce* Medicare spending.

At the same time, we do not observe *why* Part B spending appears to rise after third-wave reforms. Nor do we have a good explanation for why only Part B spending appears to rise. A reduction in avoidance behavior would be likely to affect both Part A and Part B spending. An important avenue for further research involves studying specific clinical decisions using patient-level data, rather than the aggregate, county-level data used in this chapter. Spending may rise for some patients because of less avoidance behavior, yet fall for others because of less assurance behavior.[193] A further area for future research involves investigating post-reform changes in spending for non-Medicare patients.

A further factor is the national trend toward declining medical malpractice risk (see Chapter 11). Whatever impact medical malpractice risk has on physicians' actions, that effect should wane as medical malpractice risk declines.

### A "Credible Interval" for the Impact of Tort Reform on Spending

The political debate over defensive medicine has focused on how much the United States might save on health care if tort reform was enacted. Our results, combined with those from other studies, let us place some bounds on the likely impact of tort reform on spending. Taking the evidence as a whole, we believe that a credible interval for the effect of damage caps in Medicare spending ranges from a 2 percent decline to a 2 percent increase. But any effect has already been realized in the old-cap and new-cap states; a national damages cap would primarily affect Medicare spending in the no-cap states, which account for only about one-third of the U.S. population. We therefore believe that a credible interval for the effect of a national damages cap on national Medicare spending ranges from a 0.7 percent decline to a 0.7 increase. Of course, the American health care system is more than just Medicare, but the effect on non-Medicare spending is likely smaller because private insurers exert tighter control than Medicare on physician decisions. Taking these factors together, we believe that a credible interval for the effect that a national damages cap might have on total health care spending ranges from a 0.5 percent decline to a 0.5 percent increase.

The only careful study with a central estimate that is statistically significant and above this range is the estimate of 4 to 5 percent lower costs for cardiac care in the early Kessler and McClellan study of the effect of the 1980s caps.[194] But there is reason to doubt that this estimate is generalizable beyond cardiac care or that it would apply in the current environment, in which in-hospital spending is a smaller proportion of total Medicare spending.[195] Claims that tort reform can meaningfully bend the health care cost curve, or save hundreds of billions of dollars per year, are simply not plausible.

### Explaining a Null or Nearly Null Result

If even a large shock to medical malpractice risk does not affect health care spending, what are the implications? One possibility is that there may not be much "pure" defensive medicine—medical treatments driven solely by liability risk. If liability is only one of a number of factors that influence clinical decisions, even a large reduction in medical malpractice risk might have little impact on health care spending.

The effects of damage caps on assurance and avoidance behavior could also offset each other. Lower medical malpractice risk could lead some doctors to practice less defensive medicine, yet make them (or other doctors) more willing to offer aggressive medical treatment, especially treatment that is profitable to the doctor but risky for the patient. There could be savings in particular areas of medical practice (cardiac care, perhaps), yet costs in other areas. The physician tendency to do more things, perhaps riskier things, if medical malpractice risk declines might be stronger in urban areas, with more sophisticated physicians. Stated differently, by limiting liability, tort reform might tend to release the brakes that the fear of liability imposes on doctors' willingness to deliver riskier treatments.

Alternatively, the level of defensive medicine may be insensitive to actual liability risk. As we noted in Chapter 9, doctors' level of concern with malpractice risk responds only weakly to tort reform. One survey of Texas physicians reports that since Texas's 2003 tort reform, 31 percent report practicing less defensive medicine, with 64 percent reporting no change and 5 percent reporting an increase.[196] If the highly publicized Texas reforms, followed by a major drop in claim rates and medical malpractice insurance premiums, did relatively little to persuade doctors to practice less defensively, it is unclear what would do so, other than complete abolition of medical malpractice liability. To date, no one has proposed going that far.

## CONCLUSION

Damage caps have long been seen by health policy researchers and policymakers as an easy way to reduce health care costs. We find, in contrast, no evidence that damage caps have reduced health care spending. Instead, we find evidence that states that adopted caps during the third wave of medical malpractice reforms have *higher* post-cap Medicare Part B spending and no evidence that damage caps significantly affect Part A spending.

There is no shortage of plausible first-order explanations for the high cost of U.S. health care. One is physician incentives to provide profitable services. A second is a political system that has been unwilling to impose the sorts of spending limits that are found in many other countries. It has also been unwilling to restrain prescription drug spending in a meaningful way. Little about health care generates bipartisan agreement, but common ground to date is agreement that the elderly are entitled to all the health care their physician wants to prescribe, including access to prescription drugs and medical devices sold at whatever prices drug companies and device manufacturers decide to charge, almost entirely paid for with other people's (i.e., taxpayer) funds.

Politically convenient myths are hard to kill. The myth that defensive medicine is an important driver of health care spending is convenient to politicians who claim to want to control costs but who are unwilling to take the unpopular (with physicians and the elderly) steps needed to do so. It is convenient for health care providers, who prefer lower liability risk and less oversight from the civil justice system. It is also convenient for members of the public to blame lawyers for problems that have complex and difficult roots.

Further research on the effect of damages caps, using patient-level data, would be valuable. Still, one policy conclusion is straightforward: even if one is not convinced that damage caps cause an *increase* in Medicare Part B spending, there is no evidence that limiting medical malpractice lawsuits will bend the health care cost curve toward lower cost. Those interested in a silver bullet that will limit the growth of health care spending should look elsewhere.

## CHAPTER 13

# DOES TORT REFORM ATTRACT PHYSICIANS TO THE NEW-CAP STATES?

## OVERVIEW

In Chapter 10, we studied the effect of Texas's damage cap on physician supply. We turn here to the effect of caps on physician supply in the nine states that enacted damage caps during 2002–2005. Using methods similar to the ones we used in Chapters 11 and 12, we find no evidence that cap adoption led to an increase in patient care physicians. We also find no evidence that cap adoption led to an increase in specialties that face high liability risk (with a possible exception for plastic surgeons) or in rural physicians. Our results for broader groups (all physicians, all high-risk physicians) are a precisely estimated "zero" effect. More concretely, given our data, we estimate that there is only a 2.5 percent chance that there is a true increase in the supply of patient care physicians of more than 1.5 percent and a similar chance of a true decrease of more than 0.9 percent.

## INTRODUCTION

The two principal policy justifications that one often hears for damage caps are that caps will reduce defensive medicine and thus health care spending and that they will attract more physicians to states that adopt caps, especially in specialties such as neurosurgery and obstetrics and gynecology, which face a higher-than-average risk of medical malpractice claims ("high-risk specialties"). We examined the effect of caps on health care spending in Chapters 9 (Texas) and 12 (national results). We examined the effect of caps on physician supply in Texas in Chapter 10, and we report national results in this chapter. As we did in Chapters 11 and 12, we study the nine new-cap states that adopted damage caps between 2002 and 2005, relative to a control group of no-cap states.

In Chapter 9, we studied Texas and found no evidence that cap adoption significantly affects physician supply—overall, for high-risk specialties, or in rural areas. Here we study all nine new-cap states and find similar results across states. With the additional statistical power available from studying nine states, we again estimate a near-zero effect and are able to put tight confidence bounds on that near-zero effect, at least for larger groups of physicians (all patient care physicians or all high-risk physicians). For rural physicians, our point estimates are consistently *negative* across several definitions of which counties should be treated as rural, although not statistically significant. The sole exception to our string of null results is for plastic surgeons. We find some evidence, short of definitive, that plastic surgeon supply increases following tort reform. We also show that all three groups of states—new-cap, old-cap, and no-cap—follow similar trends for physicians per capita prior to reform—the new-cap states were not losing or gaining physicians before reform, relative to other states.

## BACKGROUND

We review the literature on whether damage caps affect physician supply in Chapter 10. All physician counts in this chapter are per 100,000 population.

Our sample period is 1992–2011 for all direct patient care physicians and 1995–2011 for high-risk specialties. As in Chapters 11 and 12, we compare the nine new-cap states to both a narrow control group (20 no-cap states) and a broad control group (20 no-cap states plus 22 old-cap states). We use as control variables median household income; per capita personal income; *ln*(population); and percentage of the population that is male, unemployed, in poverty, black, Hispanic, ages 65–74, ages 75–84, and ages 85+.

## PHYSICIAN SUPPLY OVER TIME IN NEW-CAP, NO-CAP, AND OLD-CAP STATES

As we discussed in earlier chapters, a core difference-in-differences (DiD) assumption is "parallel trends"—the treated and control states would have evolved similarly but for cap adoption. Figure 13.1 provides initial graphical evidence on parallel trends in the three groups of states (new-cap, no-cap, and old-cap). Panel A of Figure 13.1 shows per capita counts for all patient care physicians. Panel B shows counts for physicians in eight specialties that have been found to be at high risk of a medical malpractice lawsuit: neurosurgery, orthopedic surgery, thoracic surgery, general surgery, plastic surgery, gastroenterology, obstetrics and gynecology, and urology.[197]

Figure 13.1 makes several things apparent. First, factors other than medical malpractice risk can have a large effect on physician supply. Indeed, the no-cap states have the highest number of physicians per capita, despite higher medical malpractice risk. The old-cap states have the next highest, and the new-cap states the lowest, both before and after the 2002–2005

## Figure 13.1

### Nationwide physician supply over time

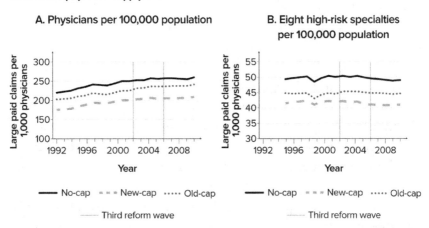

*Notes:* Panel A. Physicians/100,000 population for 1992–2013. Panel B. Physicians in eight high-risk specialties/100,000 population for 1995–2013 (we drop thoracic surgeons for 1995–1999 due to missing data). Both panels: vertical lines in 2002 and 2006 indicate the third reform wave period. The specific states in each group (no-cap, new-cap, and old-cap) are listed in endnotes 165–167.

*Source:* American Medical Association annual surveys.

reform period. Second, overall physician supply is rising in all states—by about 0.5 percent per year. Third, cap adoptions do *not* have a large effect on physician supply. Both for all physicians and for the eight high-risk specialties taken together, there is no visual evidence of a post-cap change in trend for new-cap states relative to other states. For high-risk physicians, the lines for all three groups of states are basically parallel, with no upward tilt for the new-cap states in the post-reform period. In the rest of this chapter we assess more carefully whether there are small effects, not visible in Figure 13.1, or effects for particular specialties.

## RESULTS FOR ALL PATIENT CARE PHYSICIANS

In Figure 13.2, we examine more closely whether damage caps affect the total number of patient care physicians. The lower line shows the ratio of physicians per capita in new-cap states to physicians per capita in no-cap states. This ratio is stable at around 80 percent with little fluctuation over the sample period, 1992–2011. This graph confirms the major takeaways from Figure 13.1. There is no evidence of a post-cap increase in patient care physicians in new cap states. That the new-cap to no-cap ratio is of only about 0.8 shows that factors other than medical malpractice risk have large effects on physician supply.

The top line in Figure 13.2 shows the ratio of patient care physicians per capita in old-cap versus no-cap states. This is a "placebo line." We have no reason to expect that the adoption of damage caps in the new-cap states will affect this ratio. The old-cap to no-cap ratio is around 90 percent overall. This ratio shows a gradual declining trend in the 1990s and an upward trend in the 2000s. Most caps are not inflation adjusted, so they gradually become stricter over time. If cap stringency were an important driver of physician supply, one might expect a gradually rising ratio over the entire period. This is not the pattern we observe.

That the placebo line is *not* flat heightens our concern about attributing post-reform changes in physician supply in new-cap versus no-cap states to the impact of damage caps. In Figure 13.2, if one mixed up which graph involved the new-cap states group and which was a placebo line, damage caps would appear to increase physician supply.

# Figure 13.2

## Nationwide overall physician supply

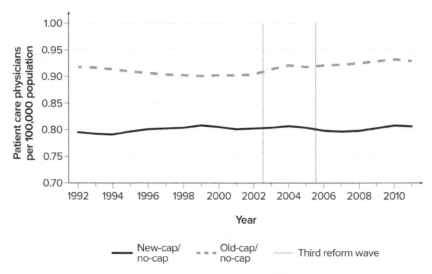

*Notes:* Ratios for 9 new-cap states versus 20 no-cap states, and for 19 old-cap states versus the no-cap states, for patient care physicians per 100,000 population. The specific states in each group (no-cap, new-cap, and old-cap) are listed in endnotes 165–167. Vertical lines in 2002 and 2005 indicate the third reform wave period.

*Source:* American Medical Association annual surveys.

Table 13.1 provides summary statistics on physician counts. We report the average number of physicians in 2000, shortly before the start of the new-cap adoption period, and in 2011, the last year in our sample, and long enough after reform so that the main effects of reform would be likely to have emerged. We report data for all patient care physicians, for the eight high-risk specialties, and for emergency medicine physicians—who are not among the top eight high-risk specialties identified by Jena and others, but who are often thought to face high malpractice risk.[198] We discuss results from this table for all patient care physicians here and results for the high-risk physicians below. Patient care physicians per capita increased by 6.3 percent over this period in new-cap states versus a 6.1 percent increase in no-cap states. The difference is close to zero and is not close to being statistically significant ($t = 0.10$).

Figures 13.1 and 13.2, and the summary data in Table 13.1, do not account for other factors that might affect physician supply. But when

## Table 13.1

Physician supply by specialties, no-cap and new-cap states

| Physician type | Physicians per 100,000 population | | | | | | | |
| --- | --- | --- | --- | --- | --- | --- | --- | --- |
| | 20 No-cap states | | | 9 New-cap states | | | Difference | |
| | 2000 | 2011 | Change (%) | 2000 | 2011 | Change (%) | (new-cap) – (no-cap) | t-stat |
| Patient care total | 244.2 | 259.2 | 6.1% | 196.5 | 208.8 | 6.3% | 0.2% | 0.03 |
| **Top eight high-risk specialties** | | | | | | | | |
| Neurosurgery | 1.8 | 1.9 | 6.4% | 1.6 | 1.7 | 7.6% | 1.2% | 0.09 |
| Orthopedic surgery | 8.1 | 8.5 | 5.5% | 6.7 | 6.9 | 1.7% | −3.8% | 0.46 |
| Thoracic surgery | 1.7 | 1.5 | −15.6% | 1.6 | 1.3 | −18.0% | −2.5% | 0.30 |
| General surgery | 13.7 | 12.7 | −7.1% | 10.8 | 9.9 | −8.7% | −1.6% | 0.24 |
| Plastic surgery | 2.2 | 2.3 | 5.6% | 2.0 | 2.3 | 15.0% | 9.4% | 0.58 |
| Gastroenterology | 4.0 | 4.7 | 17.0% | 3.2 | 3.6 | 14.4% | −2.6% | 0.12 |
| Obstetrics and gynecology | 14.4 | 13.9 | −3.6% | 12.8 | 12.2 | −4.3% | −0.7% | 0.09 |
| Urology | 3.8 | 3.6 | −4.9% | 3.3 | 3.0 | −7.0% | −2.2% | 0.23 |
| **Top eight together** | **49.7** | **49.1** | **−1.2%** | **42.0** | **41.0** | **−2.4%** | **−1.3%** | **0.16** |
| Emergency medicine | 7.5 | 10.5 | 39.2% | 7.0 | 9.0 | 29.0% | −10.3% | 0.53 |

*Notes:* Patient care physicians and physicians in indicated specialties, per 100,000 population, for all no-cap states together and all new-cap states together, in 2000 and 2011, and percentage change from 2000 to 2011. The specific states in each group (no-cap, new-cap, and old-cap) are listed in endnotes 165–167.

*Sources:* For physician counts, American Medical Association annual surveys; and for high-risk specialties, Anupam Jena et al., "Malpractice Risk According to Physician Specialty," *New England Journal of Medicine* 365 (2011): 629–636, https://doi.org/10.1056/NEJMsa1012370.

we conduct DiD regressions with extensive control variables, we get a precisely estimated zero effect for the larger physician groups (all patient care physicians, and all eight high-risk specialties together), consistent with the graphical results in Figures 13.1 and 13.2 and Table 13.1.[199]

In sum, cap adoption does not appear to change overall physician supply. This result accords with prior literature. Some studies find an effect of caps on high-risk physicians or rural physicians, but across studies, there is little evidence of an effect on overall physician supply. Given this prior research, one might say that for total physician supply, we have beaten an already dead horse. Still, in the policy realm, a convincing beating can be valuable, because cap proponents continue to claim that caps are a powerful way to attract physicians.

## RESULTS FOR HIGH-RISK SPECIALTIES

We turn next to high-risk specialties, for which two other studies report some evidence of a post-cap rise in supply.[200] In contrast, we find no such evidence, with the possible exception of plastic surgeons.

### Overall Evidence

Consider first Table 13.1, where we show overall changes in physicians per capita for eight high-risk specialties, individually and together, plus emergency physicians, who are often thought to face high malpractice risk. Over 2000–2011, the number of high-risk physicians shrinks by 2.4 percent in new-cap states—*more* than the 1.2 percent decline in no-cap states. There is more variability for individual specialties, but for seven of the specialties we find a relative decline for new-cap versus no-cap states. The point estimates are positive only for neurosurgeons (at a small and statistically insignificant 1.2 percent) and plastic surgeons (a much larger 9.4 percent increase, albeit still statistically insignificant).

Turning back to graphical evidence, in Figure 13.3 we provide ratios of new-cap states to no-cap and old-cap to no-cap for the eight high-risk specialties taken together. This figure is otherwise similar to Figure 13.2. The roughly flat bottom line compares new-cap states to no-cap states. The ratio of high-risk physicians per capita in new-cap states to high-risk physicians per capita in no-cap states was stable over 1995–2011. The top line is a "placebo" presentation of a similar ratio for old-cap states versus no-cap states. This line also shows no strong trend.

Using regression analysis, we find no evidence of a discernible overall trend after cap adoption—meaning adoption of damage caps does not appear to result in an increase in high-risk specialists.[201]

# Figure 13.3

## Nationwide supply of physicians in high-risk specialties

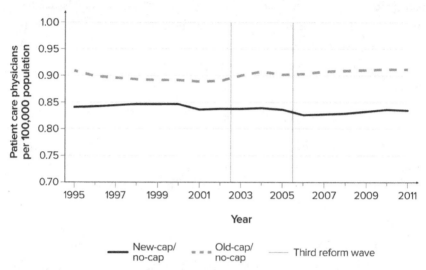

Notes: Ratios for 9 new-cap states versus 20 no-cap states, and for 19 old-cap states versus the no-cap states, for physicians in eight high-risk specialties identified by Jena et al. (2011) per 100,000 population over 1995–2011. The specific states in each group (no-cap, new-cap, and old-cap) are listed in endnotes 165–167. Vertical lines in 2002 and 2005 indicate the third reform wave period.

Source: Anupam Jena et al., "Malpractice Risk According to Physician Specialty," New England Journal of Medicine 365 (2011): 629–636, https://doi.org/10.1056/NEJMsa1012370.

### Evidence for Particular High-Risk Specialties

Even if there is no overall trend for high-risk physicians, there could be specialty-specific trends. In Table 13.1, the largest percentage changes are a relative 10.3 percent drop in emergency physicians in new-cap states over 2000–2011 relative to no-cap states and a 9.4 percent relative rise in plastic surgeons. These are *relative* changes—the number of emergency physicians grew strongly in both groups of states.

We present graphs for emergency physicians and plastic surgeons in Figure 13.4. We find no evidence of a statistically significant rise or fall for the other seven specialties shown in Table 13.1. The graphs are similar to Figures 13.2 and 13.3. They provide "treated-to-control" ratios: new-cap to no-cap states (the bottom lines) and placebo ratios of old-cap to no-cap states (the top lines).

# Figure 13.4

## Nationwide supply of plastic surgeons and emergency physicians

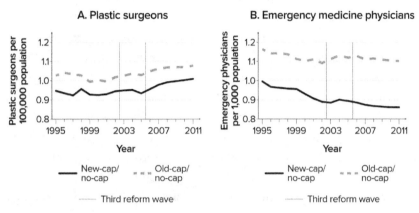

Notes: Ratios for 9 new-cap states versus 20 no-cap states, and for 19 old-cap states versus the no-cap states, for plastic surgeons (Panel A) and emergency physicians (Panel B), in each case per 100,000 population over 1995–2011. The specific states in each group (no-cap, new-cap, and old-cap) are listed in endnotes 165–167. Vertical lines in 2002 and 2005 indicate the third reform wave period.

*Source:* American Medical Association annual surveys.

For plastic surgeons, there is indeed a visible increase in the lower new-cap to no-cap ratio, beginning just after the 2002–2006 cap adoption period. However, there is also a rise in the placebo ratio of plastic surgeons in old-cap states relative to no-cap states. This suggests that the apparent rise in plastic surgeons in new-cap states may not be attributable to the adoption of damage caps. In DiD regression analyses, which assume parallel trends, we nonetheless find a positive and statistically significant effect by cap adoption on plastic surgeon supply of 4 to 6 percent depending on specification. This effect emerges gradually during the post-reform period, which is a plausible time pattern. Taking the evidence on plastic surgeons as a whole, we judge that there is some (but not compelling) evidence that supply rises after cap adoption.

For emergency physicians, Figure 13.4 makes it apparent that the new-cap to no-cap ratio was declining prior to reform, and the decline continued after reform. There is a similar, milder pre-reform decline in the placebo line. There is no evidence that cap adoption caused any change in the new-cap to no-cap ratio.

## PHYSICIANS IN RURAL COUNTIES

One sometimes hears arguments that even if medical malpractice risk does not affect overall physician supply, it reducing this risk may increase physicians' willingness to locate in rural areas, where they often earn lower incomes and so may be more sensitive to medical malpractice insurance premiums. Consistent with this argument, a 2007 study reports evidence of a 3 to 5 percent post-cap increase in "frontier" rural physicians and a 10 to 12 percent rise in frontier specialists—with the "frontier" defined as the quartile of counties with the lowest population per square mile *in 1970*.[202] Another study reports a post-cap increase in rural physicians, averaging 3.2 percent across all rural counties.[203]

We therefore also examined whether third-wave damage caps predict a change in physician supply in rural counties, using the standard U.S. Department of Agriculture division of counties into urban and rural. Figure 13.5 provides our—by now familiar—two main comparisons.

## Figure 13.5

### Nationwide supply of patient care physicians in rural counties

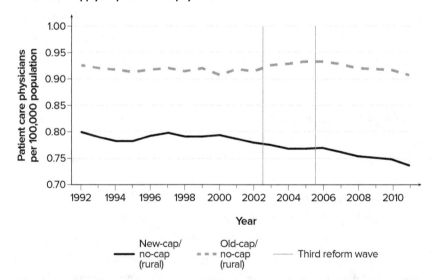

*Notes:* Ratios of patient care physicians per 100,000 population in rural counties over 1992–2011, for 9 new-cap states versus 20 no-cap states and for 19 old-cap-states versus the no-cap states. The specific states in each group (no-cap, new-cap, and old-cap) are listed in endnotes 165–167. Vertical lines in 2002 and 2005 indicate the third reform wave period.

*Source:* American Medical Association annual surveys.

The bottom line shows the ratio of rural physicians per capita in new-cap states to the ratio in no-cap states. The top line is a placebo line, which compares old-cap to no-cap states.

The new-cap states show a steady relative *decline* in physicians per capita, which begins around 1997 and continues during and after the 2003–2006 cap adoption period. There is no post-reform change in the trend line and thus no evidence that caps affect rural physician supply. We also examined trends in the most rural counties, which are comparable to the "frontier counties" measure. We again found no evidence of a post-cap increase in physicians. In DiD regressions, the point estimates were negative (opposite from predicted)—both for all rural counties and for the most rural counties—although the estimates were not statistically significant. Thus we find no evidence that the third-wave cap adoptions helped attract more physicians to rural areas.

# DISCUSSION

### Physicians' Location Choices

Physicians' location decisions simply do not seem to respond very much to damage caps. Perhaps some physicians are strongly influenced by medical malpractice risk, but many more appear to make location choices using other factors. Those factors include the relatively inelastic demand for physician services and the difficulty of relocating. Damage caps will reduce medical malpractice risk and thus medical malpractice insurance premiums, but many physicians may see these premiums as simply one more cost of running a practice, similar to rent, specialized medical equipment, and wages paid to employees. In the medium to long term, changes in malpractice insurance rates should be reflected in the price that physicians can charge for their services. In equilibrium, physicians in high-risk areas should charge more for their services. If (as seems likely) physicians are personally averse to being sued, above and beyond the financial impact through paying for medical malpractice liability insurance, the extra charge to patients could exceed the cost of medical malpractice liability insurance. But the local market for physician services will still clear, with physicians being compensated for bearing medical malpractice risk.

One sometimes hears that even if medical malpractice risk is a secondary factor for most physicians in choosing where to practice, it can matter for older physicians who are considering retirement. We cannot directly assess this claim with our data, but even if for some physicians, damage caps lead to slower retirements, this may not involve many physicians, and, moreover, delayed retirements may reduce new entry, limiting their net effect on supply. We did assess whether cap adoption predicts the number of inactive physicians, which we treat as a proxy for retired physicians. We found no evidence indicating that damage caps predicted a change in the number of inactive physicians.

### Is There an Effect for Plastic Surgeons?

We find hints that the supply of plastic surgeons does respond to cap adoptions. If this effect is real, the greater sensitivity of plastic surgeons to medical malpractice risk would be sensible. Consider cosmetic surgery—a substantial part of overall plastic surgery practice. Most damages are non-economic—and hence strongly affected by a non-economic damages cap. Moreover, a larger proportion of physician charges are paid by patients rather than insurers. Thus, the demand for plastic surgery is likely to be more elastic than for most types of medical care. If so, any drop in provider prices induced by cap adoptions would lead to a larger change in equilibrium demand.

Consider, at the other extreme, obstetrician-gynecologists. Patient demand for delivering babies is likely to be price inelastic. Moreover, most damages are economic—the principal damages in "bad baby" cases are the cost of lifetime medical treatment. Thus, we should not expect a damage cap to lead to much (if any) change in the equilibrium supply of obstetrician-gynecologists.

## CONCLUSION

We find no evidence that physicians' aggregate location decisions are affected by damage caps. We find a precisely estimated zero effect of damage caps on overall patient care physicians and physicians in eight high-risk specialties, taken together. Our estimates for rural physicians and for specific high-risk specialties are less precise because of smaller sample size, but the point estimates from regressions for rural physicians and for most high-risk specialties are *negative*, which is opposite from the prediction of damage cap proponents.

There are some limitations to our approach. We rely primarily on American Medical Association (AMA) surveys to measure physician counts. The survey responses may lag reality. Helland and Showalter provide evidence that physicians may also respond to a decline in medical malpractice risk by working more hours.[204] This result could help explain why damage cap adoptions do not lead to a change in the number of practicing physicians.

It is also important to recognize that even if cap adoption *did* increase physician supply, the effect on social welfare is far from certain. Consider some of the obstacles to determining even the sign of any effect. There is evidence that physicians with poor medical malpractice records are attracted to states that adopt damage caps.[205] If overall demand for physician services is inelastic, then post-reform entry by "bad docs" will presumably lead some good docs to practice elsewhere. Second, if demand is inelastic and caps reduce the incentive for older physicians to retire, that may reduce opportunities for entry by younger physicians. How would that affect the average quality of care? The answer is unknown and could well vary by specialty. Finally, we find some evidence of a post-cap increase in plastic surgeons. Is that welfare enhancing? Opinions on that subject are likely to vary.

But our bottom line is simple: it is time to bury the myth that damage caps have a meaningful effect on physician supply. Despite political rhetoric from cap proponents, other factors are more important in determining where physicians choose to practice.

# PART FOUR

# If Damage Caps Aren't the Answer, What Is?

## CHAPTER 14

# SYNTHESIS: LESSONS AND PATHOLOGIES

This book has covered a lot of territory and presented many facts, figures, and tables. In this chapter, we identify seven key takeaway lessons from our analysis. We then describe several additional pathologies of the U.S. health care and medical malpractice litigation systems that should be considered in accurately diagnosing the medical malpractice problem and designing an appropriate remedy.

## KEY THEMES AND IMPLICATIONS

### *Medical Malpractice Premiums Don't Tell You Much about Claim Rates or Payouts*

The United States has experienced three medical malpractice crises marked by sudden and dramatic liability insurance premium spikes in the past 40 years. The first crisis hit in the mid-1970s, the second in the early to mid-1980s, and the most recent during the early 2000s. These premium spikes caused considerable distress for physicians and triggered lobbying campaigns that have resulted in more than 30 states enacting damage caps, along with a wide variety of less-important reforms.

There is no dispute that these premium spikes occurred. In the medium to long term, malpractice insurance is just one of a number of costs of doing business that should be reflected in health care prices.

But in the short term, prices don't adjust quickly to changes in malpractice premiums. Thus, these spikes impacted physician incomes, especially for higher-risk specialties. The spikes in insurance premiums then receded, and caps contributed to declining premiums. But a key question remains: To what extent were changes in the medical malpractice litigation system—such as an increase in claims and payouts per claim—responsible for these spikes? Reform proponents certainly believed that the "smoke" from rapidly rising premiums was evidence of a "fire" in medical malpractice litigation. Their reforms targeted that presumed fire.

Was there actually a fire? When we examine the performance of the medical malpractice litigation system from roughly 1990 on (the period that our data cover), we find mostly stability, not crisis. There were no notable pre-reform spikes in claims or payouts in Texas or in the other eight states that enacted tort reform during 2002–2005. Thus, changes in the medical malpractice system played only a limited role in whatever caused the premium spikes in the early 2000s.

What about the relationship between the medical malpractice system and the premium spikes during the earlier medical malpractice crises in the 1970s and the 1980s? Unfortunately, there are almost no data on that issue, apart from small studies of individual insurance companies, and our own study of Illinois, where we have data back to 1980. In that study, we find a sharp upswing in paid medical malpractice claims from 1980 to 1985, which roughly leveled off from 1986 to 1993 and has declined steadily since.[206] We also show that payout per claim in Illinois has steadily increased since 1980, but those increases are entirely explained by the virtual disappearance of smaller paid claims and claims involving less severe injuries. The Illinois trends from 1990 on are consistent with the national trends we discuss in Chapter 11. Perhaps, then, the Illinois experience in the early 1980s mirrored a similar national trend. If so, there was a medical malpractice litigation fire in the early 1980s, but not since.

When and if there is a fourth medical malpractice insurance crisis, we should not assume an underlying fire in the medical malpractice litigation system. Instead, we need to be prepared to look elsewhere to find both the causes and the remedies.

### Outlier Jury Verdicts Don't Tell You Much—but Policy Limits Are Crucial

Outlier jury verdicts are where most discussions about the tort system begin and end, and the complaints are always the same. In the words of a medical malpractice defense lawyer, "[t]here's no limit on what jurors can award for pain and suffering, so too often they act like Santa Claus, handing out millions of dollars in cases involving comparatively minor injuries."[207] Stories about runaway jury verdicts are legion. Have you heard about the cases that resulted in jury verdicts of $229 million[208] and $101 million?[209] Or the woman who won a multimillion-dollar verdict when she sued for losing her psychic powers after a CAT scan?[210]

To make sensible policy, we need to leave aside the merits and outcomes of a handful of outlier jury verdicts and consider the bigger picture. First, as we show in Chapter 4, jury trials are quite rare. When there is a jury trial, most of the time the jury finds for the defendant-physician. Finally, in the rare case where there is a jury verdict for the plaintiff, it is just the starting point for determining how much will ultimately be paid. For physicians—and often for hospitals also—their malpractice insurance policy limits act as a functional cap on recovery. The larger the verdict, the more likely and larger the "haircut" the verdict will receive before it is paid.

What, then, are the functional limits on recovery from physicians? The conventional wisdom is that most physicians carry $1 million policy limits. A few states mandate that level of coverage by law. But a million dollars ain't what it used to be. The conventional wisdom about standard limits has not changed since the 1980s. But the real value of $1 million in nominal dollars has fallen over the past 30 years by more than half; $1 million in 2016 dollars is worth around $450,000 in 1986 dollars. Moreover, in states where physicians can carry lower limits, Texas among them, they often carry less than $1 million limits. As we note in Chapter 5, many Texas physicians have policies with much lower limits.

The enormous effect of policy limits—and to a lesser extent, other factors—in constraining payouts when a jury makes a large award means that outlier verdicts don't tell you much about how the medical malpractice litigation system is performing in general. Those who want a better picture of system performance should focus on the less visible parts of the iceberg (the many smaller claims that are settled in the shadow of both the potential jury verdict *and* policy limits), and not its tip (i.e., highly publicized jury verdicts). By that measure, payout per large paid claim has been stable for the past 25 years, even without damage caps.

Of course, these same dynamics apply to settled cases as well. Medical malpractice litigation is mostly about insurers and not really about doctors. Insurers' dollars are the low-hanging fruit, and insurers won't part with them until the doctors they cover are released from (above-limits) liability. When an insurer offers its policy limits in settlement, plaintiffs' lawyers have an easy choice. They can take the (relatively) easy dollars that are on the table now, or they can reject those dollars and take a chance on collecting (relatively) hard additional dollars from a physician after several years of expensive litigation. Because financial considerations weigh in favor of settling, above-limits settlements are rare—and when they occur, they are almost always funded by insurers.

### Physicians Love Damage Caps, for Good Reasons

From a physician's perspective, damage caps are effective. We find strong evidence that damage caps reduce both the number of medical malpractice claims and the payouts in the cases that are still brought. Larger payouts—those above the cap level—are hit the most, as one might expect. Medical malpractice insurance premiums fall as well. Thus, physicians face lower financial costs—and likely lower psychic costs as well. It's no wonder that physicians love these outcomes.

### Damage Caps Don't Reduce Health Care Spending or Attract Physicians

Should anyone other than health care providers love damage caps? The answer to that question turns on how damage caps affect the broader health care system. Do they reduce overall health care spending? Do they attract more physicians to cap-adopting states? The short answer to both questions is no.

We find no evidence that capping damages affects health spending. Defensive medicine—extra spending driven by physicians worried about malpractice liability—surely exists. But either it is immune to the damage cap remedy or, more likely, any effect of caps in reducing spending in some areas is offset by higher spending in other areas. Indeed, we find evidence from Texas (in Chapter 9) and from all nine states that adopted caps in the 2000s (in Chapter 12) that, if anything, damage caps may have "bent the cost curve" *upward*, at least for Medicare Part B spending.

Nor are damage caps an effective way to attract physicians from other states. In Chapter 10, we found no evidence that Texas was losing physicians before it enacted reform in 2003—and no evidence that it saw an influx of physicians after it enacted reform. Here, too, the Texas story is representative of all nine new-cap states, as shown in Chapter 13. We found no evidence that adoption of damage caps led to an increase in physician supply in the cap-adopting states, except maybe for plastic surgeons.

We also find some evidence that damage caps have a disproportionate impact on plaintiffs who are elderly, unemployed, or deceased. And other research suggests that damage caps can result in lower quality of care.

To sum up, we find clear evidence that damage caps are good for physicians but not so good for everyone else. Almost a century ago, H. L. Mencken memorably observed that "there is always a well-known solution to every human problem—neat, plausible, and wrong."[211] Our findings about the effect of damage caps exemplify Mencken's aphorism. The message—caps are good for physicians but have no apparent broader social benefit—emerges clearly from our data.

### Incentives Matter

Incentives matter in medical malpractice litigation. Plaintiffs' lawyers work on contingency. If you take the profit out of medical malpractice litigation, plaintiffs' lawyers will respond by bringing fewer cases and changing which cases they bring. That's what happened in Texas after it adopted a damage cap in 2003. Consider the patients who were victimized by Dr. Christopher Duntsch, a Texas neurosurgeon so awful he was criminally prosecuted, convicted, and nicknamed "Dr. Death": "When Duntsch's patients tried to sue him for malpractice, many found it almost impossible to find attorneys."[212]

We show a similar effect on the volume of litigation in the other eight states that adopted damage caps during 2002–2005. When thinking about damage caps, many people focus on how they affect payouts in particular cases, but a separate, important impact is on the decisions by plaintiffs' lawyers on which cases are still worth bringing.

Incentives also matter when it comes to considering other reforms. The impact of reforms will be the direct result of the incentives that the reforms create. These two simple propositions underlie the reforms we propose in Chapter 15.

### In God We Trust, All Others Should Bring Data

Medical malpractice crises seem to combine the worst elements of a bubble economy and a moral panic. Reform proponents vie with one another to make grandiose claims about the evils of the medical malpractice litigation system and the virtues of proposed reforms. To hear them tell it, the medical malpractice litigation environment is always bad and getting worse. Skeptics are dismissed or attacked. The skeptics, meanwhile, love to blame insurance companies, as if medical malpractice insurance rates are set by some hidden insurance company cartel to maximize profits, entirely insulated from actual payouts. And both sides ignore the periods during which premiums are flat or declining—as has been the case nationally since 2005. Which is getting to be a long time.

Our view is that there is much to be gained by following the advice attributed to W. Edwards Deming: "In God we trust, all others bring data." But if we are going to require all others to bring data, the data have to be available. The data that we use in Parts One and Two of this book only exist because Texas created the Texas Closed Claim Database—the TCCD. But in 2015, the Texas legislature killed the TCCD effective January 2016. Although data were collected for 2013–2015, they have never been released—and the previously available data have been removed from the Texas Department of Insurance (TDI) website, along with all traces that the TCCD ever existed. Florida now stands alone as the only state with a public dataset covering all paid medical malpractice claims.

Similarly, the data that we use in Part Three only exist because the federal government created a database of paid medical malpractice claims—the National Practitioner Data Bank (NPDB). But the federal government took the database offline in 2011, after a newspaper used the NPDB data to publish an article showing that state regulators in Missouri and Kansas were not aggressively pursuing disciplinary sanctions against physicians with multiple paid claims. The NPDB was subsequently put back online, but access is limited to those who promise they will not use the information to identify any individual or entity. Moreover, the NPDB covers only physicians, and there are questions about how complete and accurate it is. Unlike Texas and Florida, the federal government has not put in place any mechanism to police which claims are reported or to check report accuracy. Our updated version of Deming's aphorism would be, "In God we trust, all others bring *audited* data."

### You Can Learn a Lot Just by Watching, but You Have to Watch the Right Things

As Yogi Berra memorably stated, "You can observe a lot just by watching."[213] We believe the same is true of medical malpractice—but it is important to watch the right things and to pay attention to the details. Health care is complicated. Data are crucial, but data are not enough. For medical malpractice reform, advocates on both sides will happily manipulate the data that exist so they appear to favor them, and they will ignore data pointing the other way.

When the third wave of medical malpractice premium spikes hit the United States starting around 2000, physicians were quick to blame the legal system. Nine states, including Texas, responded by adopting the physicians' preferred remedy of a damages cap; many states adopted other reforms as well. Why did all of these states target their treatments on the tort system when the symptoms were manifested in the insurance system?

Connecting the medical malpractice insurance crisis to the medical malpractice liability system seemed logical. Insurance covers liability costs. Because insurance prices were spiking, liability costs had to be spiking as well. The connection seemed especially plausible because the people asserting it were doctors clad in white coats. Appearances matter, and the persons claiming that the liability system was spinning out of control were highly trained professionals in whom the public is accustomed to placing its trust.

Still, why didn't state legislators ask the questions we ask in this book? Such as, was anything dramatic happening to medical malpractice litigation—or only to insurance premiums? Had they done so, they could have uncovered the lesson from Chapters 3 and 11—that there were no spikes in the medical malpractice liability system in Texas or elsewhere that might explain the medical malpractice premium spikes that many states experienced. On the contrary, small claims had been disappearing since 1990, and larger claims were just beginning to tail off as well. But no one looked—or if they looked, they didn't look in the right place.

One also needs to look at the data after adjusting for the right things. For example, our findings on the stability of the medical malpractice litigation system would look very different if we failed to adjust for inflation and changes in population. You get a very different picture of trends in medical malpractice claim rates if you measure claims per physician instead of total claim frequency. More subtly, the way in which the data are analyzed can make a difference. For example, the increase in mean payouts that we quantify for Texas in Chapter 3 is attributable to a disappearance of small claims, rather than an increase in payouts for larger claims. Chapter 11 shows that the same phenomenon is happening nationwide and also that there is a long-term decline in the number of paid medical malpractice claims, even in no-cap states.

Sometimes the choice of measure matters. Chapter 10 shows that you get a different picture about how Texas's non-economic cap affected physician supply if you focus on the number of direct patient care physicians who are actually practicing, rather than the number of new licenses that are issued. And so on.

It is only by analyzing the actual performance of the medical malpractice litigation system that we can know whether it is doing what we want it to—and if not, what the problems actually are. However, if the analysis is not done with scrupulous fairness and due care, the results can easily be misleading. When the analysis is done by those with an axe to grind, skepticism is appropriate.

Conversely, there are several reasons why readers should trust (but verify) our results. First, the core findings in this book have been previously published in top peer-reviewed journals. Second, we have tried to be transparent about what the data can and cannot tell us. Third, the diverse political affiliations of the authors implies that if we did have our own axes to grind, what those axes might be is not apparent.

Health care policy is a lot like health care. If we want to fix a problem, it is critical to diagnose the problem correctly and then prescribe the appropriate remedy. Each of those steps requires good data, handled carefully and without a preconceived opinion on what the outcome should be.

## THE ACTUAL PATHOLOGIES OF MEDICAL MALPRACTICE LITIGATION

Our findings and those of other researchers indicate that the medical malpractice system is not as bad as its critics would have it. With regard to cost, the direct costs of medical malpractice litigation are small, and defensive medicine—at least the part that is reachable through plausible reform—does not seem to drive up health care costs by detectable amounts. Fear of liability also does not seem to scare many doctors away from practicing medicine, except perhaps at a margin too small to show up in the data. The deterrent effect of liability might have some salutary effect on quality as well.

But the medical malpractice litigation system is not performing all that well either. The quality incentives it provides are too weak. Far too many patients suffer medical errors. The system is slow. The average delay between injury and payout is around four years—and longer for cases that go to trial. Moreover, there is no feedback loop, in which past mistakes inform future improvement efforts. Neither settlements nor jury verdicts come with explanations of what the provider did wrong—or, when there is no payout, whether the provider's conduct was exemplary or barely adequate to avoid liability. And when liability is found, many providers believe this is a random lightning strike, from which nothing can be learned, rather than a marker of poor practice. These factors taken together mean that any feedback from the tort system to doctors about the standard of care that is expected of them comes too late and provides too little signal—if, that is, providers believe the signal at all.

The medical malpractice litigation system is also expensive to run and, unfortunately, becoming more so. Plaintiffs' lawyers typically take one-third of any recovery, with out of pocket on top of that. Defense costs account for around 20 percent of every payout dollar in paid cases, and more if we include unpaid claims. If we allow for the overhead costs of insurance, courthouses, and judges, it is costing society more than a dollar to move a dollar to negligently injured plaintiffs.

The medical malpractice system is also prone to underclaiming by the many plaintiffs who are negligently injured but never initiate a claim—either because they don't consider doing so, or because the dollar recovery is too small for a plaintiff's lawyer to take the case. There is surely some overclaiming as well—by those who aren't negligently injured but initiate a claim—but all available evidence indicates that underclaiming is a much larger issue.[214] The tort system is also known to systematically undercompensate the most severely injured plaintiffs— and medical malpractice is no exception. One sign of undercompensation is our finding in Chapter 5 that the biggest verdicts—which usually come in cases with catastrophic injuries—receive the largest haircuts.

On the quality front, the common physician perception that medical malpractice litigation is random is another convenient myth. Some weak cases are brought, but on the whole, the flow of cases into the medical malpractice system is, to a first approximation, a direct function of the frequency and severity of medical injury. When physician groups work in a coordinated fashion to reduce error rates, their malpractice premiums drop.[215] The same is true for hospitals—when rates of preventable adverse events rise or fall, malpractice claims against the hospital rise or fall as well.[216]

Moreover, a considerable body of evidence indicates that the American health care system isn't nearly as safe or as high quality as it should be. According to the Institute of Medicine, medical errors account for roughly 50,000 to 100,000 deaths in the United States every year—making medical error the fifth leading cause of death. Some researchers have estimated even higher death counts.[217] If we included hospital-acquired infections (many of which are preventable), substandard medical care might be the third leading cause of death, behind only heart disease and cancer.[218] Precise estimates are not available, but the annual direct and indirect cost of medical errors and low-quality care is surely in the hundreds of billions of dollars. Thus, whatever safety incentives the liability system does create are too little and often too late.

Finally, the medical malpractice system is perceived by everyone involved as deeply inhumane. Being sued for medical malpractice is probably the worst thing that will happen to most physicians in their professional lives—and even after the medical malpractice tide has receded to well below its high-water mark, most physicians in high-risk specialties can indeed expect to get sued at least once. Cases can drag on for years, and even when a case is resolved in their favor, physicians report they no longer view patients and the practice of medicine with the same enthusiasm.[219]

Damage caps don't do anything about most of these pathologies, and they make some of them worse. So what do we recommend? We turn to that issue in the next chapter.

CHAPTER 15

# REFORM STRATEGIES: TOWARD A BETTER MEDICAL MALPRACTICE SYSTEM

Readers who have made it this far will want to know how we propose to fix the problems we have catalogued. Alas, we have no silver bullets. But, in the words of Professor James Q. Wilson, we close our book with a "few modest suggestions that might make a small difference."[220]

## FIRST STEPS: AGREEMENT ON SEVEN BASIC FACTS

As we noted in the introduction, the late Senator Daniel Patrick Moynihan (D-NY) memorably observed that "everyone is entitled to their own opinions, but they are not entitled to their own facts." For medical malpractice reform, each side approaches the issue with differing perspectives on what the facts are. We believe that reform should begin with agreement on seven basic facts:

- Our medical malpractice system doesn't provide full compensation to negligently injured patients and provides especially poor compensation to those with severe injuries.[221]
- Our medical malpractice system doesn't create appropriate incentives for providers to exercise care.
- Our medical malpractice system is expensive, is time-consuming, and leads to plenty of hard feelings on both sides.

- Damage caps don't fix any of these problems, and they make some worse.
- Premium spikes are real but can be caused by factors internal to the litigation system (e.g., number of claims, payouts per claim, or defense costs).
- Paid claims have declined steadily since 2001, and smaller claims have been largely frozen out of the system.
- Although things can always change, nationally, medical malpractice insurance premiums have been falling since 2005 and are now back to the levels of the mid-1990s.

Those who disagree with these facts should provide empirical evidence supporting their position. If not, their opinions and recommended reforms should be discounted.

## SEVEN SENSIBLE REFORMS

Once we have agreement on the basic facts, we can move to the topic of how to make things better. We propose seven simple reforms.

### No Personal Liability if Physicians Have Reasonable Coverage

We show in Chapter 5 that out-of-pocket payments are rare, but many physicians still believe that they are one malpractice verdict away from bankruptcy. While that widely held but mistaken belief may have some deterrent value, we prefer to recognize the reality that physicians face very low out-of-pocket risk and propose a compromise in which states would allow physicians to eliminate that risk by buying insurance with "reasonable" limits. If physicians accept this trade—and we hope that many will—then injured patients will lose the small chance of a personal recovery from the physician above policy limits, but many fewer will find their recoveries effectively capped by policy limits.

But what minimum level of coverage is "reasonable" for the legislature to require, in exchange for allowing physicians to avoid the risk of personal liability? The level should be sufficient to cover damages in the vast majority of cases, yet one that physicians will still voluntarily purchase. Since at least the 1980s, "standard" coverage has been policy limits of $1 million per occurrence and $3 million per calendar year. But inflation has steadily eroded the real value of that nominal dollar coverage.

One simple approach would be to bring policy limits up to date, perhaps at $2.5 million per occurrence, but with no cap on the number of paid claims per policy year. Very few physicians ever hit the per year limit, so removing it will only minimally affect pricing. For those few who do, our reform puts the onus on insurers to deal with repeat "bad docs," instead of leaving their victims unpaid.

It is hard to predict how much insurance premiums will rise if the per claim limit rises from $1 million to $2.5 million. The amount will depend on state and specialty, and on whether the state has a non-economic (non-econ) or total damages cap in place. We believe, but cannot prove, that most physicians will face only a modest rise in premiums and will find that rise to be a price worth paying to avoid out-of-pocket risk. If so, this reform could do much to solve the problem of policy limits acting as de facto caps on recoveries.

For physicians who purchase qualifying policies, we would propose a hard bar on personal recovery—with an exception perhaps for intentional misconduct (which will be very rare). This will encourage physicians to buy qualifying policies.

### Let Plaintiffs Keep Their Full Damages and Health Insurance Benefits

"Subrogation rights," which enable health insurers and other health care payers to recapture money from medical malpractice payments, should be eliminated. Subrogation complicates and slows down medical malpractice litigation and raises costs.[222] To the best of our knowledge, although we lack hard data, subrogation mostly results in modest payments. Those recoveries come at a substantial cost in additional legal fees, and in further complicating what is already a complex area of litigation, in which smaller claims are increasingly not viable because of the cost of bringing them.

As we note in Chapter 4, it is already hard for severely injured patients to collect full compensation, even for economic damages. Subrogation rights are generally pursued only for cases with large health care costs and further limit compensation for severe injuries. Given the pervasive gap between damages and what severely injured patients collect (Chapter 4), even before they pay a contingency fee to their counsel, patients should be able to keep what they collect.

This idea should have bipartisan appeal, since a version of it was found in the original version of H.R. 1215, the Republican medical malpractice reform bill that passed the House of Representatives in 2017 (but went no further). States could limit subrogation by law; public payers such as Medicare, Medicaid, and the U.S. Department of Veterans Affairs could set an example for private insurers and employers by forgoing the subrogation rights they now have—either in general or at least in the many cases where if subrogation were enforced, plaintiffs would receive a net recovery (after attorney fees) less than their remaining economic damages. In these circumstances, if subrogation is enforced, the plaintiff effectively ends up paying for health care out of personal resources (the damages recovery), instead of having health care costs paid for through insurance, unlike other persons with the same insurance coverage.

The same reasoning should apply to collateral source reform—a reform type sought by physicians to reduce recoverable damages and create a further obstacle to the viability of medical malpractice claims. This reform denies plaintiffs the ability to recover for health care costs paid for by someone else—whether Medicare, Medicaid, or a private insurer. Collateral source reform prevents injured patients from recovering their full economic damages and effectively denies them the benefits of their health insurance. Their theoretical justification, of preventing double recovery, has little basis in actual litigation practice. The real problem is the large number of seriously injured patients who receive a net recovery far below their economic damages, not the tiny number who recover more than their actual economic damages after paying legal fees.

### A No-Fault System for Smaller Claims

Chapters 3 and 11 make it clear that many smaller claims are no longer being filed, most likely because the cost of suing is too high.[223] To address this problem, we believe that states should experiment with a no-fault system for handling smaller claims, say, for cases with economic damages up to $150,000, indexed for inflation. Recovery would be limited to economic damages, but damages would be multiplied by 1.5, so that plaintiffs could still recover their actual economic damages after paying a one-third contingency fee. (Although patients could theoretically bring these claims without a lawyer, we expect that most will choose to use a lawyer.) For plaintiffs who can show medical errors, this approach would substitute the certainty of recovering economic damages after paying the plaintiff's lawyer for the current non-economic damages "lottery." As we find in Chapter 4, on average, non-economic damages correlate strongly with economic damages, but there is no assurance that they will do so in any individual case.

Rather than being handled by judges and juries, claims would be evaluated by a medical review panel, which would determine if medical error was a probable (i.e., more likely than not) cause of the patient's harm. The standard would be medical error, not negligence. The emphasis should be on speed and simplicity. This approach is not perfect, but neither are the alternatives. And the status quo results in no compensation for most patients with small claims.

Prior no-fault systems have foundered because they have sought to compensate for all medical harms. Providers quickly realized that the attraction of avoiding a battle on fault was outweighed by the massive increase in the number of compensable events. Our proposal differs from prior no-fault proposals in that it requires a finding of medical *error* (a concept broader than negligence but much narrower than medical harm) and is further limited to small claims. Both features should reduce costs and help make the proposal palatable. They may even be attractive to providers, many of whom may favor a move away from the quagmire of deciding whether there was negligence as long as payouts do not mushroom. Plaintiffs' lawyers should be supportive because our proposal targets cases they often cannot now afford to take.

### Learning from Our Collective Mistakes

The best way to reduce the number and severity of medical malpractice claims is to reduce the frequency of medical errors. One way to do that is to create a national database of medical errors—some negligent but many not—and then use those data to learn how mistakes can be avoided. In anesthesiology, the one specialty where such a national effort was undertaken, the reduction in medical errors and paid claims was dramatic.[224]

Learning from crashes and near-misses dramatically improved air safety over a period of decades. Learning from medical errors has similar promise. A start should be made by collecting information from large hospitals, which already have systems in place for reporting and analyzing medical errors. This effort could later be expanded to smaller hospitals, larger physician groups, skilled nursing facilities, and nursing homes. The initial focus should be on collecting and systematizing data that already exist, and then using "big data" methods to extract patterns that no one provider now sees.

A parallel effort would draw on the records created by the medical screening panels that exist in a number of states. Researchers could use those data to identify patterns of medical errors and to identify institutions that have figured out how to prevent them from occurring in the first place.

Of course, there will be implementation challenges, including protecting patient privacy and creating incentives for health care providers to report their data and implement best practices as they are developed. But if we want the health care system to learn from its mistakes, we should get started.

### More and Better Data on Malpractice Claims

We need data to learn what works and what does not work in the medical malpractice system. At the core of this book is a dataset from Texas covering 1988–2012. Although the Texas Department of Insurance (TDI) has collected data for three additional years (2013–2015), it seems clear it will never release that information. The Texas legislature enacted a statute canceling TDI's data collection project in 2015, and all the old data have disappeared off the TDI website, along with all reports and records relating to the Texas Closed Claim Database (TCCD). This means that one of the two longitudinal state-level sources of public data on medical malpractice litigation (the other is Florida) is no longer available. This book shows how valuable the Texas dataset was—and the cost of scrapping it.

This book also relies on a less-detailed but national dataset, the National Practitioner Data Bank (NPDB), which covers individual providers. That dataset includes de-identified information on paid claims and privileges and disciplinary actions against physicians. It does not include information on physician specialty, unpaid claims, or paid claims against hospitals, nursing homes, and other institutional providers. Nor does it contain trial outcomes. There is no similar data source for claims against hospitals or other providers. And the Health Resources and Services Administration (HRSA), the federal entity that administers the NPDB, is notoriously gun-shy about the uses that can be made of the data—with some reason, given past physician attacks on the existence of the NPDB. HRSA could disclose additional information (physician specialty is obvious, low-hanging fruit), but it does not, and it is reluctant to allow access to the additional nonpublic information that it does collect.

The obvious solution is more and better data on the performance of the medical malpractice system. One possibility is to expand the NPDB to cover hospitals, clinics, and nursing homes (because HRSA already collects some of the necessary data) and require HRSA to be more forthcoming with the data it already has. Another is for more states to collect more and better data on medical malpractice and make them readily available to researchers and patients.

### More Experimentation

We have spent the better part of the past 45 years debating damages caps as the principal medical malpractice reform strategy. As a result, we haven't devoted nearly enough time to assessing the costs and benefits of other strategies for improving the performance of the medical malpractice system. We need more experimentation, and we should enlist as many health care providers in that process as are willing to participate. For starters, we suggest large-scale, well-designed studies to test the impact of the following ideas:

*Communication and resolution programs (CRPs).* CRPs allow hospitals and other health care entities to voluntarily disclose that a medical error has occurred. Over the past 15 years, CRPs have moved from a few public and academic institutions into the medical mainstream, earning endorsements from the American Medical Association (AMA), the American College of Surgeons, and other professional groups. But CRPs vary in the extent to which they prioritize transparency; assistance to patients, families, and caregivers; timely compensation; and safety improvement. For example, some but not all CRPs proactively offer compensation or free medical treatment rather than waiting for the injured patient to find a lawyer and file suit.

CRPs may complement or substitute for medical malpractice litigation in ways that make patients better off—or they may be a mechanism for "cooling the mark out," by making patients accept the inevitable and go away without making a fuss.[225] Some physicians may prefer CRPs to the deny-and-defend mentality of their predecessors, whose fear of liability normalized the concealment of errors and who seldom engaged with patients or families when care went poorly. But we don't know nearly enough about how CRPs operate, let alone when they work and don't work.

*More organization and enterprise-level responsibility.* The percentage of physicians in solo or small-group practice has plummeted from roughly 90 percent when Medicare was enacted in 1965 to under 25 percent today. Fully 40 percent of physicians are employed by hospitals compared to 25 percent as recently as 2012. Being an employee means that physicians no longer have to write annual checks for liability coverage and need not worry about its price or availability. Physicians who are employed in organized care settings are often backed up by dedicated patient safety officers, patient counselors, and quality-improvement staff. These developments mean that health care organizations are adopting greater de facto responsibility for preventing and addressing medical errors, even though medical malpractice litigation remains focused on individual fault by individual physicians.

Some medical errors come from "bad docs," but many more come from imperfect systems. Given this reality, and the increasing importance of health care institutions in the delivery of care, we suggest experimentation with "enterprise liability," which assigns primary responsibility for injury to the hospital or other health care organization in which physicians work, rather than to the individual physician. Health care organizations that wish to partner more closely with their health professionals might also experiment with "enterprise insurance," which channels liability risk into a single entity. Some of this is happening already, but we know very little about how large health care organizations manage medical malpractice risk.

There is undoubtedly tension between physician control over medical care and enterprise liability, but institutional liability is better aligned with systems-based safety improvement strategies. As noted previously, institutions are more likely to have personnel and processes in place to support both their professionals and injured patients. Enterprise-level responsibility is also more compatible with quality and safety metrics, as well as with alternative payment mechanisms that factor outcomes into financial incentives. Finally, institutional coverage for medical liability is less vulnerable to insurance crises, which tend to heavily burden a few high-risk specialties.

As with CRPs, we don't know nearly enough about how enterprise liability or other forms of organizational and system-level responsibility will operate, let alone when it will work and won't work. Only systematic studies can answer these questions.

*Private contracts.* Tort law is designed to deal with interactions between strangers—but patients and physicians are generally not strangers to one another. Further complications are created by the near-endless multitude of settings in which medical errors and misadventures can occur, and the divergent preferences of budget-constrained patients. It is implausible that all patients want either full liability rights or a cap on non-economic damages at some arbitrary level. Private contracts that meet legislative minimum standards, specify compensation for medical errors, and offer explicit warranties regarding safety are an obvious possible alternative.

Consider, for example, our proposal above for small claims: recovery of 150 percent of economic damages for medical error, but only economic damages. This is scarcely patient unfriendly. Yet a hospital or practice group that wanted to offer this option to patients today cannot do so.

*Safe harbors for evidence-based practice.* Multiple studies have shown that only about 20 percent of medical malpractice claims close with payment. Although there are good reasons to think that the true success rate in serious cases is closer to 50 percent,[226] that is still a large number of claims that cost money and time to pursue and to defend but that do not produce any compensation for the patient. One strategy for reducing such claims is to immunize providers who adhere to evidence-based practice guidelines developed by reputable sources (call these "qualified guidelines").

Indeed, if the trade we propose above—serious minimum physician policy limits in exchange for no personal liability—is not attractive enough to physicians, one could sweeten the pot by also offering, to physicians who buy complying policies, exemption from liability if they can prove by a preponderance of the evidence that they provided care in accordance with qualified guidelines.

There is, to be sure, a risk that physicians would pressure the guideline-writing organizations to write guidelines that do more to protect physicians from liability than to capture actual evidence-based practice. This is a risk we would take, all the more so given the great difficulty plaintiffs currently face in obtaining recoveries when physicians provide guideline-compliant care.

### Better Incentives

Some research indicates that health care providers often earn more revenue when patient harm occurs by billing for the services that are rendered to address the consequences of the harm. That is perverse. Hospitals and other health care providers that cause harm to their patients should bear the costs of fixing the problems that they cause. To induce providers to voluntarily step up, we suggest adding a multiplier of amounts billed to the damages available in a malpractice suit.

Also, many medical errors are not provably malpractice, and relatively few lead to lawsuits. We believe that providers should be barred from charging to fix their own mistakes, negligent or not, and also required to compensate other providers who address their mistakes, or the third-party payers who fund such care, with an administrative procedure to assess when compensation is appropriate.

Moving outside the domain of malpractice policy, we also think it makes sense for the public to collectively bear the costs of certain treatments that are sufficiently cost-effective to justify that treatment.

For example, better diabetes diagnosis and treatment can both improve population health and reduce lifetime medical costs, much of which are publicly borne through Medicare and Medicaid. We think some form of insulin and of first-line diabetes drugs—perhaps not the fanciest, newest form—should be provided free to all who need it—and we would use centralized purchasing with sealed bids to help keep the price low. We would use a similar arrangement for other treatments with sufficient evidence of benefit and multiple providers. Doing so will reduce the frequency of high-risk medical interventions—thereby reducing the frequency of medical malpractice claims.

## REASONS FOR OPTIMISM

We have already noted how the organizational structure of the health care delivery system has changed. The medical malpractice insurance industry is changing as well. Physician-owned mutual companies have long dominated this market segment, particularly after commercial insurers largely abandoned the field. In 1977, these physician-owned entities formed the Physician Insurers Association of America (PIAA). Since then, PIAA and its member companies have leveraged their relationships with state and local medical societies to lobby for tort reforms of the sort we have described in this book. For obvious reasons, this meant that the debate over medical malpractice reform was framed as a dispute between physicians and trial lawyers.

As more physicians have become employees of hospitals and large medical practices, the medical malpractice liability insurance business has adapted to encompass new approaches to risk management. For example, PIAA has rebranded itself as the Medical Professional Liability Association (MPLA), which "represents a full range of entities doing business in the medical professional liability arena," with the list including "[medical professional liability] insurance companies, risk retention groups, captives, trusts, and other entities."[227] MPLA member companies cover doctors, hospitals, dentists and oral maxillofacial surgeons, podiatrists, chiropractors, nurse practitioners, nurse midwives, and nurse anesthetists.

What does this mean? Simply stated, professional processes and market forces appear to have altered the terrain on which the future of medical malpractice policy will be made, in ways that enhance the likelihood that the interests of patients will receive more attention than has previously been the case.

## CONCLUSION

It is unrealistic to expect individual physicians to compensate all the avoidable injuries inflicted by a technologically advanced health care system that costs almost $4 trillion annually. Physicians' earnings are too small a fraction of the revenue flowing through our health care system to insure against the aggregate harm that is produced. Small specialist physician practices have too little capital and diversification to withstand periodic insurance shocks. And punishing individual malfeasance through our malpractice system does little or nothing to encourage the building of safer systems of care.

In response, we have outlined seven modest, sensible reforms that have potential to improve the performance of our medical malpractice system. Doubtless there are other good ideas that we should be trying, which is why our last suggestion is for more experimentation.

## CHAPTER 16

# THREE CONCLUDING POINTS

We conclude with three final points.

First, medical malpractice litigation is slow, expensive, and noisy. That's pretty much what you should expect of a system that relies on adversarial proceedings to resolve disputes. Litigation is slow—no way around it. It is expensive—no way around that either. Some level of noise—some weak cases that win, some good cases that lose, and considerable commotion (i.e., lawsuits filed, experts hired, depositions taken)—is inevitable in any form of adversarial litigation. We can and should seek improvements in all three of these aspects, but we should not expect litigation to magically become fast, cheap, and highly accurate.

Second, medical malpractice crises are big news, but the absolute dollars at stake are small potatoes relative to the health care system as a whole. Even if we use generous assumptions, the medical malpractice system accounts directly for perhaps 0.3 percent of health care spending, and that figure has been declining since 2001. In the overall scheme of things, medical malpractice is a small tail of a very large dog. And tails do not wag dogs.

Finally, if we want to reform the medical malpractice system, we should select reforms that will fix the problems with our medical malpractice system. To do that, we need a clear understanding of the actual performance of that system and an equally clear understanding of the likely effects of the proposed reforms. It is a serious mistake to proceed using a misdiagnosis of the problem, let alone to mistreat the actual problems that our medical malpractice system does have. More of the same (i.e., damage caps, and the rest of the laundry list of conventional tort reforms) won't work. We need to pursue a different way.

# ACKNOWLEDGMENTS

We owe thanks to the individuals at the Texas Department of Insurance (TDI), which oversaw the Texas Closed Claim Database (TCCD), who patiently answered our questions: Vicky Knox, Ken McDaniel, Clare Pramuk, and Brian Ryder. We also owe thanks to Lesley Braun, Abbey Chiodo, Meera George, Celeste Griffin-Churchill, JaeJoon Han, Kevin Kavanagh, Hyun Kim, Katherine Klein, An-Shih Liu, Rachel Miras-Wilson, and Fang Zhang, who worked with us at various points over the past 15 years as research assistants. David Ovadia standardized the Texas data across all chapters and prepared the replication dataset and statistical coding used to generate the figures and tables in Chapters 2–7. Myungho Paik prepared a replication dataset and statistical coding used to generate the figures and tables in Chapters 8–13. We also want to acknowledge Kathryn Zeiler for coauthoring three articles that provided the bases for Chapters 4 and 5.

We owe a special debt to Mark Gentle, who was responsible for designing the TCCD when he was an attorney at the TDI. The breadth of the work we have done is only possible because of his foresight in identifying the specific data fields that insurers had to report to the TCCD.

We received helpful comments from Richard Anderson, Jennifer Arlen, Ronen Avraham, Lynn Baker, Tom Baker, Randy Bovjberg, Frank Chmielewski, Frank Cross, David Dranove, Ted Eisenberg,

Einer Elhauge, Lee Fennell, Stephen Foreman, James Forman, Michael
Frakes, Ted Frank, Craig Garthwaite, Martin Grace, Pierre Grosdidier,
Eric Helland, Lorens Helmchen, Kris Henning, Allison Hoffman, Paul
Keckley, Meredith Kilgore, Greg Klass, Katherine Klein, Jonathan
Klick, Russell Korobkin, Bert Kritzer, Kate Litvak, Russell Localio,
Anup Malani, Howard Marcus, Michelle Mello, John Mikhail, Ed
Richards, Nick Rosencranz, Steve Salop, Max Schanzenbach, Seth A.
Seabury, Catherine Sharkey, Steve Shavell, Frank Sloan, Albert Strunk,
David Studdert, David Vladeck, Louise Weinberg, Martin Wells, and
Tony Yang.

Our work was greatly improved by comments we received when
earlier versions of portions of this book were presented at the American
Enterprise Institute; the Boston University School of Law; the Brooklyn
Law School; the DePaul University College of Law; the Duke Univer-
sity School of Law; the Georgetown University Law Center; Hanyang
University; the Harvard University School of Law; the New York Uni-
versity School of Law; the Northwestern Pritzker School of Law; the
RAND Institute for Civil Justice; the Stanford University School of
Law; the University of California, Berkeley School of Law; the Uni-
versity of California, Irvine School of Law; the University of Chicago
School of Law; the University of Florida Levin College of Law; the
University of Illinois College of Law; the University of Illinois Institute
of Government and Public Affairs; the University of Kansas School
of Law; the University of Michigan School of Law; the University of
Southern California Gould School of Law; the University of Texas
School of Law; the University of Virginia School of Law; the Vanderbilt
School of Law; and the Washington University School of Law.

In like fashion, the work we present in this book was greatly improved
by comments we received at conferences sponsored by AcademyHealth;
the American Law and Economics Association; the American Society of
Health Economists; the American Society of Law, Medicine and Ethics;
the Canadian Law and Economics Association; the Korean Allied Economic Associations; the Korean Association of Health Economics and
Policy; the Korean Law and Economics Association; the Midwest Health
Economics Association; the Midwest Law and Economics Association;

the Robert Wood Johnson Center for Public Health Law Research; and the Society for Empirical Legal Studies.

In non-crisis years, medical malpractice litigation is the red-headed stepchild of health policy. Michael Cannon saw the merit in our book-length treatment of the issue and persuaded the Cato Institute to publish it. We also appreciate the effort of Jalisa Clark, Jason Kuznicki, and Eleanor O'Connor of the Cato Institute in bringing the book to fruition.

Finally, this work would not have been possible without the generous support provided by our respective institutions: Northwestern University (for Black and Paik); the University of Illinois and Georgetown University (for Hyman); the University of Texas (for Sage and Silver); and Hanyang University (for Paik). In addition, our work was supported by the Jon David and Elizabeth A. Epstein Program in Health Law and Policy at the University of Illinois College of Law and by the Center on Lawyers, Civil Justice, and the Media at the University of Texas School of Law. We received no outside funding and thus have no conflicts of interest to disclose.

# NOTES

## CHAPTER I

1. Shirley Svorny, "Could Mandatory Caps on Medical Malpractice Damages Harm Consumers?," Cato Institute Policy Analysis no. 685, October 20, 2011, p. 1, https://www.cato.org/publications/policy-analysis/could-mandatory-caps-medical-malpractice-damages-harm-consumers.

2. David A. Hyman and Charles Silver, "Medical Malpractice Litigation and Tort Reform: It's the Incentives, Stupid," *Vanderbilt Law Review* 59, no. 4 (2006): 1085–1136; and David A. Hyman and Charles Silver, "The Poor State of Health Care Quality in the U.S.: Is Malpractice Liability Part of the Problem or Part of the Solution?," *Cornell Law Review* 90, no. 4 (2005): 893–994.

3. The nine states were Florida, Georgia, Illinois, Mississippi, Nevada, Ohio, Oklahoma, South Carolina, and Texas.

4. Steven R. Weisman, ed., *Daniel Patrick Moynihan: A Portrait in Letters of an American Visionary* (New York: PublicAffairs, 2010).

5. Robert S. Peck, "Tort Reform's Threat to an Independent Judiciary," *Rutgers Law Journal* 33 (2002): 851–56.

6. Bernard S. Black et al., "Medical Liability Insurance Premia: 1990–2016 Dataset, with Literature Review and Summary Information," *Journal of Empirical Legal Studies* 14, no. 1 (2017): 238–54.

7. *New York Trust Co. v. Eisner*, 256 U.S. 345, 346 (1921).

8. See Black et al., "Medical Liability Insurance Premia"; David A. Hyman, "Regulating Managed Care: What's Wrong with a Patient Bill of Rights," *Southern California Law Review* 73 (2000): 221–75; and David A. Hyman, "Convicts and

Convictions: Lessons from Transportation for Health Reform," *Pennsylvania Law Review* 159 (2011): 1999–2042.

## CHAPTER 2

9. The reporting thresholds are not inflation adjusted. Thus some claims that are reported on the Long Form in later years would have been below the Long Form threshold in earlier years. To address this "bracket creep," we limit the sample to cases with payouts of at least $25,000 in 1988 dollars.

10. For these claims, we lack information on the cause of injury, so we rely on the first two criteria to identify medical malpractice claims. We also lack data on plaintiff age.

11. Most jury trials with defense verdicts drop out of the dataset; they will appear only if there is a payout despite the defense verdict. We discuss in Chapter 6 why some payouts are made after defense verdicts.

12. J. J. Prescott, Kathryn E. Spier, and Albert Yoon, "Trial and Settlement: A Study of High-Low Agreements," *Journal of Law and Economics* 57, no. 3 (2014): 699–746.

13. Tom Baker, *The Medical Malpractice Myth* (Chicago: University of Chicago Press, 2005). Baker collects evidence that the percentage of medical injuries that lead to medical malpractice claims is in the low single digits.

14. In three tried cases, where it is clear that the death cap affected the payout for more than one defendant, we apply the cap on a per defendant basis.

15. Prior to 1995, the cap was the greater of $200,000 or four times compensatory damages.

16. For claims where no lawsuit is filed, we do not know for certain whether the cap applies or not. There are relatively few such claims, and our results are not affected by how we handle them.

17. Of the 16,247 cases with a lawsuit filed in our dataset, 1,912 were filed after September 1, 2003. The reforms affect 0.3 percent of cases closed in 2003, 4.1 percent for 2004, 17.1 percent for 2005, 43.7 percent for 2006, 74.8 percent for 2007, 86.2 percent for 2008, 90.2 percent for 2009, and 95.7 percent for 2010.

18. Consumer Price Index (CPI), U.S. Bureau of Labor Statistics, accessed September 16, 2019, https://www.bls.gov/cpi/home.htm#tables. We use annual average CPI.

19. "Population and Housing Unit Estimates," Census.gov, United States Census Bureau, accessed November 30, 2018, http://www.census.gov/popest/. We use midyear estimates of resident population—intercensus estimates for 1991–2009 and postcensus estimates for 2010–2011.

20. "Area Health Resources Files," Health Resources & Services Administration, accessed July 31, 2019, http://www.ahrf.hrsa.gov/.

21. "National Health Expenditure Data," Centers for Medicare and Medicaid Services, U.S. Department of Health and Human Services, accessed April 17, 2018, https://www.cms.gov/Research-Statistics-Data-and-Systems/Statistics-Trends -and-Reports/NationalHealthExpendData/index.html.

22. "Regional Economic Accounts," U.S. Bureau of Economic Analysis, U.S. Department of Commerce, accessed April 9, 2019, http://www.bea.gov /regional/.

23. "Local Area Unemployment Statistics," U.S. Bureau of Labor Statistics, accessed September 16, 2019, http://www.bls.gov/lau/.

24. "Rural-Urban Continuum Codes," U.S. Department of Agriculture Economic Research Service, U.S. Department of Agriculture, accessed August 20, 2019, https://www.ers.usda.gov/data-products/rural-urban-continuum-codes.

25. We obtained reports for 1989, 1994, and 1996 from the State Bar. For 2000, 2003, and 2005, see "Research and Analysis," State Bar of Texas, accessed September 16, 2019, https://www.texasbar.com/template.cfm?section=research _and_analysis.

26. Discharge data through 2008 are available from Inter-University Consortium for Political and Social Research; see "National Hospital Discharge Survey Series," accessed September 16, 2019, https://www.icpsr.umich.edu/icpsrweb /ICPSR/series/43. The original source is "National Hospital Discharge Survey (NHDS)," 1979–2008, National Center for Health Statistics (NCHS), at Centers for Disease Control and Prevention. We obtain the 2009 data from NCHS; see "NHDS—Questionnaires, Datasets, and Related Documentation," Centers for Disease Control and Prevention, accessed November 6, 2015, https://www.cdc .gov/nchs/nhds/nhds_questionnaires.htm. To estimate Texas discharges and inpatient days by patient age, we adjust these data for differences between the Texas age composition and that for the remainder of the Southern region.

27. "Fee-for-Service Data (1998–2007)," Centers for Medicare and Medicaid Services, U.S. Department of Health and Human Services, accessed February 17, 2021, https://www.cms.gov/Medicare/Health-Plans/MedicareAdvtgSpecRateStats /FFS-Data-1998-2007.

28. These data are included in the Area Health Resources Files. See "Area Health Resources Files," Health Resources & Services Administration, U.S. Department of Health and Human Services, accessed July 31, 2019, https://data .hrsa.gov/topics/health-workforce/ahrf. We use the 2014–2015 Release. Data are missing for 2009 and for some specialties in 1997. We interpolate for 2009 and for the missing specialties for 1997.

29. Texas Medical Board, http://www.tmb.state.tx.us/docs/docs; and "County Supply and Distribution Tables—Direct Patient Care Physicians," Texas Department of State Health Services, accessed February 17, 2021, https://www.dshs.state .tx.us/chs/hprc/DPC-lnk.shtm?terms=practicing%20physicians.

30. We obtained the American Community Survey (ACS) from the Integrated Public Use Microdata Series (IPUMS) "U.S. Census Data for Social, Economic, and Health Research." IPUMS USA, University of Minnesota, accessed November 11, 2015, https://usa.ipums.org/usa/. The ACS includes state and occupation, including "Physicians and Surgeons" (code 3060 in the IPUMS version). From these microdata, we generated the number of physicians in each state-year using the appropriate sample weights. Per IPUMS rules, we provide the following citation: Steven Ruggles, Sarah Flood, Sophia Foster, Ronald Goeken, Jose Pacas, Megan Schouweiler, and Matthew Sobek. IPUMS: Version 10.0 [machine-readable database] (Minneapolis: University of Minnesota, 2021), https://doi.org/10.18128/D010.V11.0.

31. "Public Use Data File," National Practitioner Data Bank, U.S. Department of Health and Human Services, accessed September 16, 2019, https://www.npdb .hrsa.gov/resources/publicData.jsp. We drop 1990 and 1991 because there was likely underreporting during this initial period.

32. We use the actual reform year as year 0 (Avraham's spreadsheet treats reforms adopted July 1 or after as occurring the following year). We use Avraham's "regular" Database of State Tort Law Reforms, version 5.1, not his "clever" variant, in which he turns off selected caps with high cap levels.

## CHAPTER 3

33. Yu Lei and Joan Schmit, "Entry and Exit in the Malpractice Insurance Market from 1994 to 2003—Part I," *PLUS Journal* XIX, no. 12 (2006); and Yu Lei and Joan Schmit, "Entry and Exit in the Malpractice Insurance Market from 1994 to 2003—Part II," *PLUS Journal* XX, no. 1 (2007). See also Yu Lei and Mark J. Browne, "Medical Malpractice Insurance Market Entry and Exit: 1994–2006," *Journal of Insurance Regulation* 27, no. 1 (January 2008): 47–71.

34. Lawrence A. Berger, J. David Cummins, and Sharon Tennyson, "Reinsurance and the Liability Insurance Crisis," *Journal of Risk and Uncertainty* 5, no. 3 (1992): 253–72, https://doi.org/10.1007/bf00057882; and Baker, *Medical Malpractice Myth*.

35. Anne Gron, "Price and Profit Cycles in the Property-Casualty Insurance Industry," Department of Economics, Massachusetts Institute of Technology (unpublished manuscript, 1989), mimeo; Anne Gron, "Property-Casualty Insurance Cycles, Capacity Constraints, and Empirical Results" (PhD diss., Massachusetts Institute of Technology, 1990); Anne Gron, "Capacity Constraints and Cycles in Property-Casualty Insurance Markets," *RAND Journal of Economics* 25, no. (1994): 110–27; Anne Gron, "Evidence of Capacity Constraints in Insurance Markets," *Journal of Law and Economics* 37, no. 2 (1994): 349–77, https://doi.org/10.1086/467317; Scott E. Harrington, "Tort Liability, Insurance Rates, and the Insurance Cycle," *Brookings-Wharton Papers on Financial Services: 2004*, no. 1 (2004): 97–138, https:// doi.org/10.1353/pfs.2004.0010; Ralph A. Winter, "The Liability Crisis and

the Dynamics of Competitive Insurance Markets," *Yale Journal on Regulation* 5, no. 2 (1988): 455–500; Ralph A. Winter, "Solvency Regulation and the Insurance Cycle," *Economic Inquiry* 29 (1991): 458–72; Ralph A. Winter, "The Liability Insurance Market," *Journal of Economic Perspectives* 5, no. 3 (Summer 1991): 115–36; and Ralph A. Winter, "The Dynamics of Competitive Insurance Markets," *Journal of Financial Intermediation* 3, no. 4 (1994): 379–415.

36. Baker, *Medical Malpractice Myth*; Katherine Baicker and Amitabh Chandra, "The Effect of Malpractice Liability on the Delivery of Health Care," *Forum for Health Economics & Policy* 8, no. 1 (2005).

37. Black et al., "Stability, Not Crisis: Medical Malpractice Claim Outcomes in Texas, 1988–2002," *Journal of Empirical Legal Studies* 2, no. 2 (2005): 207–59.

38. We do not have data for years prior to 1995.

39. Black et al., "Stability, Not Crisis."

40. Seth A. Seabury, Nicholas M. Pace, and Robert T. Reville, "Forty Years of Civil Jury Verdicts," *Journal of Empirical Legal Studies* 1, no. 1 (2004): 1–25, https://doi.org/10.1111/j.1740-1461.2004.00001.x.

41. Neil Vidmar et al., "Uncovering the 'Invisible' Profile of Medical Malpractice Litigation: Insights from Florida," *DePaul Law Review* 54 (2005): 315–56, https://scholarship.law.duke.edu/faculty_scholarship/1543. Vidmar and others provide supporting evidence indicating rising injury severity for closed paid medical malpractice claims, studying Florida and a 2003 report by the Missouri Department of Insurance.

42. Myungho Paik, Bernard S. Black, and David Hyman, "The Receding Tide of Medical Malpractice Litigation Part 1: National Trends," *Journal of Empirical Legal Studies* 10, no. 4 (2013): 612–38, https://doi.org/10.1111/jels.12021; and Myungho Paik, Bernard S. Black, and David Hyman, "The Receding Tide of Medical Malpractice Litigation Part 2: National Trends," *Journal of Empirical Legal Studies* 10, no. 4 (2013): 639–69, https://doi.org/10.1111/jels.12022.

43. Seabury, Pace, and Reville, "Forty Years of Civil Jury Verdicts."

44. Tom Baker, "Medical Malpractice and the Insurance Underwriting Cycle," *DePaul Law Review* 54, no. 393 (2005): 393–438.

45. American Medical Association, *Medical Liability Reform NOW!* (Chicago: American Medical Association, 2020).

46. Baker, "Medical Malpractice Underwriting Cycle"; and Harrington, "Tort Liability."

47. Stephen Zuckerman, Randall R. Bovbjerg, and Frank Sloan, "Effects of Tort Reforms and Other Factors on Medical Malpractice Insurance Premiums," *Inquiry* 27, no. 2 (1990): 167–82.

48. "Medical Malpractice Insurance: Overview and Discussion," Texas Department of Insurance, April 22, 2003, https://www.tdi.texas.gov/hprovider/documents/sprompt pay.pdf; and Robert P. Hartwig, *Special Report: Earlybird Forecast*

*2003* (New York: Insurance Information Institute, 2003), https://www.iii.org
/article/special-report-earlybird-forecast-2003.

49. Frank A. Sloan and Lindsey M. Chepke, *Medical Malpractice* (Cambridge,
MA: MIT Press, 2008).

50. Baker, *Medical Malpractice Myth*.

51. "Texas Liability Insurance Closed Claim Study," Texas State Board of
Insurance, February 1987.

## CHAPTER 4

52. Brian Ostrom, Roger Hanson, and Henry Daley, "So the Verdict Is in—What
Happens Next? The Continuing Story of Tort Awards in the State Courts," *Justice System Journal* 16, no. 2 (1993): 97–115, https://doi.org/10.1080/23277556.1993.10871173.

53. Thomas H. Cohen, "Medical Malpractice Trials and Verdicts in Large
Counties, 2001," Bureau of Justice Statistics, *Civil Justice Data Brief*, April 18, 2004,
http://www.bjs.gov/index.cfm?ty=pbdetail&iid=784.

54. Cohen, "Medical Malpractice Trials."

55. Two cases that were subject to judgment notwithstanding the jury verdict
also involved punitive damages that exceeded the punitives cap. We treated the
punitives cap as applying *after* judicial oversight.

56. Bernard Black, David Hyman, and Charles Silver, "Settlement at Policy
Limits and Insurer Duty to Settle: Evidence from Texas," *Journal of Empirical Legal
Studies* 8, no. 1 (2011): 48–84; Tom Baker, "Blood Money, New Money, and the
Moral Economy of Tort Law in Action," *Law & Society Review* 35, no. 2 (2001):
274-319, https://doi.org/10.2307/3185404.

57. We caution that single-payer cases are not representative of all cases.
Multipayer cases represent 29 percent of the cases in our sample but 54 percent
of adjusted verdicts and 53 percent of haircuts. The mean adjusted verdict in
multipayer cases is $4.8 million versus $1.7 million in single-payer cases.

58. We treat cases with payout greater than adjusted verdict as having a zero haircut.

59. The amounts and percentages due to caps and remittitur differ from
those discussed earlier, because earlier we considered the full sample, and here we
consider only single-payer cases.

60. We cannot conduct a similar analysis in multipayer cases because we do not have
complete information on policy limits, but remittitur or caps affect 21 of 103 (20 percent)
of multipayer cases, compared to only 31 of 247 (13 percent) of single-payer cases.

61. Black, Hyman, and Silver, "Duty to Settle."

62. "Bringing Justice to Judicial Hellholes," American Tort Reform Association,
2002, http://www.judicialhellholes.org/wp-content/uploads/2010/12/JH2002.pdf;
"AMA: Medical Liability Reaches Crisis in Texas," *Austin Business Journal*, June 20,
2002, https://www.bizjournals.com/austin/stories/2002/06/17/daily36.html.

63. Baker, "Blood Money."

64. There was also one out-of-pocket payment in a 1990 case with adjusted verdict less than limits. This was also the only case in which the physician paid punitive damages out-of-pocket. The insurer paid the economic damages plus interest; the physician paid $150,000 out of a $250,000 punitive damages award.

65. Kathryn E. Spier, "Litigation," in *A Handbook of Law and Economics*, vol. 1, eds. A. Mitchell Polinsky and Steven Shavell (Amsterdam: North Holland, 2005): 259–342.

## CHAPTER 5

66. Texas does not require physicians to maintain medical malpractice insurance, nor does it set a minimum level of coverage, but many hospitals require physicians to provide proof of coverage before they can obtain admitting privileges. In practice, a high percentage of Texas physicians are insured. In 2001, approximately 29,000 physicians purchased medical malpractice insurance. (See "Medical Malpractice Insurance," Texas Department of Insurance.) This is roughly 90 percent of active nonfederal patient care physicians. Many of the remainder had insurance through their employers, as did federally employed physicians. For example, physicians employed by the University of Texas hospital system have insurance through the University of Texas, and emergency physicians who work for an emergency department staffing company will typically carry insurance through the staffing company.

67. Most but not all medical malpractice policies purchased by physicians have a zero deductible. Physicians also paid deductibles in 350 cases involving policies with deductibles, with a mean (median) of $50,000 ($28,000).

68. Stephen C. Yeazell, "Refinancing Civil Litigation," *DePaul Law Review* 51, no. 2 (2001): 183–218, https://doi.org/10.2139/ssrn.315759.

69. In computing means, we winsorize 14 perinatal policies and 154 nonperinatal policies at $5 million.

70. Physicians paid a total of $18 million in deductibles in 350 cases. The mean (median) real deductible was $50,000 ($28,000). Physicians paid deductibles of $100,000 or more in 28 cases, many of which likely involved self-insured retentions for group practices.

71. Robert Quinn, "Medical Malpractice Insurance: The Reputation Effect and Defensive Medicine," *Journal of Risk and Insurance* 65, no. 3 (1998): 467–84, https://doi.org/10.2307/253660.

72. Baker, "Blood Money."

73. The number of "direct patient care" physicians reported by the Texas State Department of Health Services averages around 28,000 annually. American Medical Association annual surveys produce a larger estimate of around 33,000 active practicing physicians.

## CHAPTER 6

74. Troyen A. Brennan, Michelle M. Mello, and David M. Studdert, "Liability, Patient Safety, and Defensive Medicine: What Does the Future Hold?," in *Medical Malpractice and the U.S. Health Care System*, eds. William Sage and Rogan Kersh (Cambridge: Cambridge University Press, 2006), pp. 93–114, https://doi .org/10.1017/cbo9780511617836.007.

75. Vidmar et al., "Uncovering the 'Invisible.'"

76. Thomas H. Cohen and Kristen A. Hughes, *Bureau of Justice Statistics Special Report: Medical Malpractice Insurance Claims in Seven States, 2000–2004* (Washington: U.S. Department of Justice, March 2007), https://www.bjs.gov/content/pub/pdf /mmicss04.pdf.

77. Aaron E. Carroll, Parul Divya Parikh, and Jennifer L. Buddenbaum, "The Impact of Defense Expenses in Medical Malpractice Claims," *Journal of Law, Medicine & Ethics* 40, no. 1 (2012): 135–42, https://doi.org/10.1111/j.1748 -720x.2012.00651.x.

78. Washington State, Office of Insurance Commissioner, *Medical Malpractice Closed Claim Study: Claims Closed from July 1, 1994 through June 30, 2004* (Olympia, WA: Office of the Insurance Commissioner, 2005).

79. "Limiting Tort Liability for Medical Malpractice," Congressional Budget Office Economic and Budget Issue Brief, January 8, 2004, https://www.cbo.gov /sites/default/files/108th-congress-2003-2004/reports/01-08-medicalmalpractice.pdf.

80. Vidmar et al., "Uncovering the 'Invisible.'"

81. Daniel Kessler, "The Determinants of the Cost of Medical Liability Insurance," unpublished article, Stanford University Graduate School of Business, 2006.

82. In a regression of $ln$(expense reserve) on $ln$(indemnity reserve) and a constant term, the coefficient on $ln$(indemnity reserve) is 0.28 ($t = 42.91$). If defense reserves were often set as a fraction of indemnity reserves, this coefficient should be close to 1.

83. We use smoothing to reduce the impact of outlier payments. For 1990–2005, we give 50 percent weight to the most recent year, 33 percent to the prior year, and 17 percent to two years prior. For 1989, we give 67 percent weight to 1989 and 33 percent weight to 1988. For 1988, we give 100 percent weight to 1988.

84. Some caveats: The survey design changed over time, so results for different years may not be comparable. We have no case-level data on hourly rates or know how case characteristics affect choice of counsel (beyond the basic decision to use inside or outside counsel). We have only statewide data on billing rates and no data on alternative billing arrangements. The 2005 report is available online. See State Bar of Texas Department of Research and Analysis, *Hourly Rates in 2005 Report* (Austin: State Bar of Texas Department of Research and Analysis, September 21,

2006), https://www.texasbar.com/AM/Template.cfm?Section=Demographic_and _Economic_Trends&Template=/CM/ContentDisplay.cfm&ContentID=8820.

85. Carrol, Parikh, and Buddenbaum, "Impact of Defense Expenses."

86. A total of 40 percent of defense costs ($30 million out of $76 million) were incurred in zero-payout cases over 1984–2004. They exclude cases with defense spending less than $2,000 from their sample. In Washington State (2005), 46 percent of defense costs were incurred in cases with zero payout over 2000–2004. In Connecticut Insurance Department, *Connecticut Medical Malpractice Closed Claims Report* (Hartford: Connecticut Insurance Department, April 2007), 38 percent of defense costs were incurred in zero-payout cases over 2005–2006. See Brennan, Mello, and Studdert, "Liability, Patient Safety, Defensive Medicine."

87. For evidence supporting this estimate, see David A. Hyman, Bernard S. Black, and Charles Silver, "Economics of Plaintiff-Side Personal Injury Practice," *University of Illinois Law Review* 2015, no. 4 (June 2015): 1563–604, http://dx.doi.org/10.2139/ssrn.1441487.

88. See Brennan, Mello, and Studdert, "Liability, Patient Safety, Defensive Medicine." Studdert estimates plaintiff's legal fees and expenses at 35 percent of indemnity payouts. Similar estimates, which assume that the plaintiff's counsel charges a 33 percent contingency fee, and then adds a bit for expenses, are common. See Lester Brickman, "The Market for Contingent Fee-Financed Tort Litigation: Is It Price Competitive?," *Cardozo Law Review* 65 (2003). The figure in the text for per case efficiency is calculated as follows: (indemnity payout − plaintiff's legal fees)/(indemnity payout + defense costs) = $(1 − 0.35)/(1 + 0.30) = 0.65/1.30 = 0.50$.

89. Kessler, in "Determinants of Cost of Medical Liability Insurance," estimates these costs at 14 percent of incurred costs for indemnity and expenses.

90. The figure in the text for per case efficiency is calculated as follows: (indemnity payout − plaintiff's legal fees)/(indemnity payout + defense costs + overhead) = $(1 − 0.35)/(1 + 0.30 + (0.15 × 1.3)) = 0.65/1.495 = 0.43$.

91. Baker, "Medical Malpractice Underwriting Cycle."

92. Charles Silver, "Does Civil Justice Cost Too Much?," *Texas Law Review* 80 (2002): 2073, http://dx.doi.org/10.2139/ssrn.314964.

## CHAPTER 7

93. Ronen Avraham, "An Empirical Study of the Impact of Tort Reforms on Medical Malpractice Settlement Payments," *Journal of Legal Studies* 36, no. S2 (2007): 183–229, https://ssrn.com/abstract=912922.

94. Teresa M. Waters et al., "Impact of State Tort Reforms on Physician Malpractice Payments," *Health Affairs* 26, no. 2 (2007): 500–509, https://doi.org/10.1377/hlthaff.26.2.500.

95. Albert Yoon, "Damage Caps and Civil Litigation: An Empirical Study of Medical Malpractice Litigation in the South," *American Law and Economics Review* 3, no. 2 (2001): 199–227, https://doi.org/10.1093/aler/3.2.199.

96. Ronald M. Stewart et al., "Malpractice Risk and Cost Are Significantly Reduced after Tort Reform," *Journal of the American College of Surgeons* 212, no. 4 (2011), https://doi.org/10.1016/j.jamcollsurg.2010.12.025. See also Terry Carter, "Tort Reform Texas Style: New Laws and Med-Mal Damage Caps Devastate Plaintiff and Defense Firms Alike," *ABA Journal* 92, no. 10 (2006): 30–36, http://www.jstor.org/stable/27846331; and Stephen Daniels and Joanne Martin, "'It Is No Longer Viable from a Practical and Business Standpoint': Damage Caps, 'Hidden Victims,' and the Declining Interest in Medical Malpractice Cases," *International Journal of the Legal Profession* 17, no. 1 (2010): 59–82, https://doi.org/10.1080/09695951003588923.

97. Lucinda M. Finley studied jury verdicts in California, Florida, and Maryland and reports evidence of a greater impact of damage caps on these groups in "The Hidden Victims of Tort Reform: Women, Children, and the Elderly," *Emory Law Journal* 53, no. 1263 (2004), https://digitalcommons.law.buffalo.edu/journal_articles/198. In contrast, David M. Studdert, Y. Tony Yang, and Michelle M. Mello studied above-cap jury verdicts in California and found no significant differences in the impact of the California cap on women versus men, or elderly plaintiffs versus nonelderly in "Are Damages Caps Regressive? A Study of Malpractice Jury Verdicts in California," *Health Affairs* 23, no. 4 (2004): 54–67, https://doi.org/10.1377/hlthaff.23.4.54.

98. Amanda Edwards, "Medical Malpractice Non-Economic Damages Caps," *Harvard Journal on Legislation* 43 (2006): 213–30.

99. Finley, "Hidden Victims."

## CHAPTER 8

100. Mark Sager et al., "Do the Elderly Sue Physicians?," *Archives of Internal Medicine* 150, no. 5 (May 1990): 1091–93, https://doi.org/10.1001/archinte.1990.00390170119026.

101. U.S. General Accounting Office, *Report to the Chairman, Committee on Finance, U.S. Senate: Medical Malpractice; Medicare/Medicaid Beneficiaries Account for a Relatively Small Percentage of Malpractice Losses* (Washington: U.S. General Accounting Office, August 1993), https://www.gao.gov/assets/220/218311.pdf.

102. David M. Studdert et al., "Negligent Care and Malpractice Claiming Behavior in Utah and Colorado," *Medical Care* 38, no. 3 (March 2000): 250–60, https://doi.org/10.1097/00005650-200003000-00002.

103. Daniels and Martin, "No Longer Viable."

104. Finley, "Hidden Victims."

105. Studdert, Yang, and Mello, "Are Damage Caps Regressive?"

106. Figure 8.1 includes 1988–1989. Known underreporting of claims during those years means that total payouts (the top two lines in the figure) will be low. We include these years in the figure because we have no reason for thinking that the underreporting affects the fraction of payouts made to elderly plaintiffs (the bottom dashed line in the figure).

107. Each of the intensity measures has a time trend, even though the share of total population of people over 65 is nearly constant at 10 percent. All three measures rise for the first half of our sample period and fall in the second half; the decline is steepest for inpatient days.

108. Life expectancy at age 65 was 16.9 years in 1988 and increased to 18.7 years in 2004. See National Center for Health Statistics, *Vital Statistics of the United States, 1988*, vol. 2, sec. 6, *Life Tables* (March 1991), https://www.cdc.gov/nchs/data/lifetables/life88_2acc.pdf; and Elizabeth Arias, "United States Life Tables, 2004," *National Vital Statistics Reports* 56, no. 9 (December 2007), https://grist.org/wp-content/uploads/2009/04/nvsr56_09.pdf. See also "Life Tables," Centers for Disease Control and Prevention, November 7, 2017, https://www.cdc.gov/nchs/products/life_tables.htm. The labor force participation rate for ages 65–74 increased from 15.2 percent in 1986 to 23.6 percent in 2006; for those age 75+, the rate rose from 4.0 percent to 6.4 percent.

109. See W. Kip Viscusi, "The Devaluation of Life," Vanderbilt Law and Economics Research Paper no. 09–14, April 2009, http://dx.doi.org/10.2139/ssrn.1393771; and John D. Graham, "Saving Lives through Administrative Law and Economics," *University of Pennsylvania Law Review* 157, no. 395 (2008): 395–515, https://scholarship.law.upenn.edu/penn_law_review/vol157/iss2/2/.

110. To see the problem, assume a uniform value of a statistical life (VSL) of $5 million for everyone, and compare the value of a life-year for an elderly person with a 10-year expected lifespan to that for a young person with 50 years of expected life. For the elderly person, each life-year would be worth $500,000, compared to $100,000 for the young person. Conversely, if we assume equal values per life-year, the VSL for the young person will be five times that of the elderly person. Young and old people can have the same VSL or the same value per life-year—but not both.

111. See Cass R. Sunstein, "Lives, Life-Years, and Willingness to Pay," *Columbia Law Review* 104, no. 1 (2004): 205–52, https://doi.org/10.2307/4099352.

112. Frank Cross and Charles Silver, "In Texas, Life Is Cheap," *Vanderbilt Law Review* 59, no. 6 (2006): 1875–923. https://scholarship.law.vanderbilt.edu/cgi/viewcontent.cgi?article=1620&context=vlr.

## CHAPTER 9

113. Fred J. Hellinger and William E. Encinosa, "The Impact of State Laws Limiting Malpractice Damage Awards on Health Care Expenditures," *American Journal of Public Health* 96, no. 8 (2006): 1375–81, https://doi.org/10.2105/ajph.2005.077883; Zuckerman, Bovbjerg, and Sloan, "Effects of Tort Reforms"; and Frank A. Sloan, Paula M. Mergenhagen, and Randall R. Bovbjerg, "Effects of Tort Reform on the Value of Closed Medical Malpractice Claims: A Microanalysis," *Journal of Health Politics, Policy and Law* 14, no. 4 (1989): 663–89, https://doi.org/10.1215/03616878-14-4-663.

114. In 2002, the Department of Health and Human Services estimated 5 to 9 percent of spending; in 2010, PricewaterhouseCoopers gave $210 billion. PricewaterhouseCoopers' Health Research Institute, *The Price of Excess: Identifying Waste in Healthcare Spending*, PricewaterhouseCoopers LLP, 2008; U.S. Department of Health and Human Services, *Confronting the New Health Care Crisis: Improving Health Care Quality and Lowering Costs by Fixing Our Medical Liability System* (Washington: U.S. Department of Health and Human Services, July 2002).

115. One is $650 billion; see "Physician Study: Quantifying the Cost of Defensive Medicine," Jackson Healthcare, February 2010, https://jacksonhealthcare.com/media-room/surveys/defensive-medicine-study-2010/.

116. Michelle M. Mello and Allen Kachalia, *Evaluation of Options for Medical Malpractice System Reform: A Report to the Medicare Payment Advisory Commission (MedPAC)* (Washington: MedPAC, April 2010), http://www.medpac.gov/docs/default-source/contractor-reports/Apr10_MedicalMalpractice_CONTRACTOR.pdf.

117. Allen Kachalia and Michelle M. Mello, "New Directions in Medical Liability Reform," *New England Journal of Medicine* 364, no. 16 (2011): 1564–72, https://doi.org/10.1056/nejmhpr1012821; Tara F. Bishop, Alex D. Federman, and Salomeh Keyhani, "Physicians' Views on Defensive Medicine: A National Survey," *Archives of Internal Medicine* 170, no. 12 (2010): 1081–83, https://doi.org/10.1001/archinternmed.2010.155; Brennan, Mello, and Studdert, "Liability, Patient Safety, Defensive Medicine"; and David M. Studdert et al., "Defensive Medicine among High-Risk Specialist Physicians in a Volatile Malpractice Environment," *Journal of the American Medical Association* 293, no. 21 (2005): 2609–17, https://doi.org/10.1001/jama.293.21.2609. See also Illinois State Medical Society and ISMIE Mutual Insurance Company, "Fear and Loathing in Illinois: Lawsuit Threat Leads to 'Defensive Medicine' in Health Care," 2011. In a 2010 survey of Illinois physicians, 89 percent reported that malpractice fears caused them to order "more tests than medically needed," 66 percent reported that they "reduced or eliminated high-risk services or procedures," and another 11 percent planned to do so.

118. Janet Currie and W. Bentley MacLeod, "First Do No Harm? Tort Reform and Birth Outcomes," *Quarterly Journal of Economics* 123, no. 2 (May 2008): 795–830, https://doi.org/10.1162/qjec.2008.123.2.795; and Daniel Montanera, "The Importance of Negative Defensive Medicine in the Effects of Malpractice Reform," *European Journal of Health Economics* 17, no. 3 (September 2015): 355–69, https://doi.org/10.1007/s10198-015-0687-8.

119. Daniel Matlock et al., "Geographic Variation in Cardiovascular Procedure Use among Medicare Fee-for-Service vs Medicare Advantage Beneficiaries," *Journal of the American Medical Association* 310, no. 2 (2013) 155–61, https://www.doi.org/10.1001/jama.2013.7837.

120. David Sclar and Michael Housman, "Medical Malpractice and Physician Liability: Examining Alternatives in Defensive Medicine," *Harvard Health Policy Review* 4, no. 1 (2003): 75–84, https://ssrn.com/abstract=924294.

121. Zenon Zabinski and Bernard S. Black, "The Deterrent Effect of Tort Law: Evidence from Medical Malpractice Reform," Northwestern Law & Econ Research Paper no. 13–09, 2015, http://dx.doi.org/10.2139/ssrn.2161362; and Darius N. Lakdawalla and Seth A. Seabury, "The Welfare Effects of Medical Malpractice Liability," *International Review of Law and Economics* 32, no. 4 (2011): 356–69, https://www.ncbi.nlm.nih.gov/pmc/articles/PMC3601788/; and Michelle M. Mello et al., "Malpractice Liability and Health Care Quality: A Review," *Journal of the American Medical Association* 324, no. 4 (January 2020): 352–66, https://www.doi.org/10.1001/jama.2019.21411.

122. Daniel P. Kessler and Mark McClellan, "Do Doctors Practice Defensive Medicine?," *Quarterly Journal of Economics* 111, no. 2 (May 1996): 353–90, https://www.jstor.org/stable/2946682?seq=1; and Daniel Kessler and Mark McClellan, "Malpractice Law and Health Care Reform: Optimal Liability Policy in an Era of Managed Care," *Journal of Public Economics* 84, no. 2 (2002): 175–97, https://doi.org/10.1016/s0047-2727(01)00124-4.

123. "Limiting Tort Liability for Medical Malpractice," Congressional Budget Office.

124. "Medical Malpractice Tort Limits and Health Care Spending," background paper, Congressional Budget Office, April 2006, https://www.cbo.gov/ftpdocs/49xx/doc4968/01-08-MedicalMalpractice.pdf or https://www.cbo.gov/publication/17748.

125. Frank A. Sloan and John H. Shadle, "Is There Empirical Evidence for 'Defensive Medicine'? A Reassessment," *Journal of Health Economics* 28, no. 2 (2009): 481–91, https://doi.org/10.1016/j.jhealeco.2008.12.006.

126. Lakdawalla and Seabury, "Welfare Effects."

127. Myungho Paik, Bernard S. Black, and David A. Hyman, "Damage Caps and Defensive Medicine, Revisited," *Journal of Health Economics* 51 (January 2017): 84–97, https://doi.org/10.1016/j.jhealeco.2016.11.001.

128. Ronen Avraham, Leemore Dafny, and Max Schanzenbach, "The Impact of Tort Reform on Employer-Sponsored Health Insurance Premiums," *Journal of Law, Economics, and Organization* 28, no. 4 (2009): 657–86, https://doi.org/10.1093/jleo/ewq017.

129. A number of studies focus on cesarean delivery rates and other childbirth outcomes, also with mixed results. See Currie and MacLeod, "First Do No Harm?"; David Dranove and Yasutora Watanabe, "Influence and Deterrence: How Obstetricians Respond to Litigation against Themselves and Their Colleagues," *American Law and Economics Review* 12, no. 1 (2010): 69–94, https://dx.doi.org/ahp016; Michael Frakes, "Defensive Medicine and Obstetric Practices," *Journal of Empirical Legal Studies* 9, no. 3 (2012): 457–81, https://doi.org/10.1111/j.1740-1461.2012.01259.x; Y. Tony Yang et al., "Relationship between Malpractice Litigation Pressure and Rates of Cesarean Section and Vaginal Birth after Cesarean Section," *Medical Care* 47, no. 2 (2009): 234–42, http://doi.org/10.1097/MLR.0b013e31818475de.

130. David Dranove and Anne Gron, "Effects of the Malpractice Crisis on Access to and Incidence of High-Risk Procedures: Evidence from Florida," *Health Affairs* 24, no. 3 (2005): 802–10, https://doi.org/10.1377/hlthaff.24.3.802.

131. Emily R. Carrier et al., "High Physician Concern about Malpractice Risk Predicts More Aggressive Diagnostic Testing in Office-Based Practice," *Health Affairs* 32, no. 8 (2013): 1383–91, https://doi.org/10.1377/hlthaff.2013.0233.

132. Emily R. Carrier et al., "Physicians' Fears of Malpractice Lawsuits Are Not Assuaged by Tort Reforms," *Health Affairs* 29, no. 9 (2010): 1585–92, https://doi.org/10.1377/hlthaff.2010.0135.

133. The 41 "other states" are all states (and the District of Columbia) other than the 9 states that adopted non-econ caps over 2003–2006 (Florida, Georgia, Illinois, Mississippi, Nevada, Ohio, Oklahoma, South Carolina, and Texas), plus Oregon, in which a cap was invalidated in 2000.

134. The 19 "no-cap states" are Alabama, Arizona, Arkansas, Connecticut, Delaware, District of Columbia, Iowa, Kentucky, Maine, Minnesota, New Hampshire, New York, North Carolina, Pennsylvania, Rhode Island, Tennessee, Vermont, Washington, and Wyoming. Obviously, these 19 no-cap states are a subset of the 41 other states that constitute the first control group. We obtain similar results if we exclude the 10 Northeast and Eastern no-cap states, so that the control group is limited to 9 no-cap states that are more geographically and culturally similar to Texas.

135. We include these controls because there is a tendency for urban counties and more heavily populated counties to have both higher spending and higher medical malpractice risk.

136. Katherine Baicker and Amitabh Chandra, "Defensive Medicine and Disappearing Doctors?," *Regulation* 28, no. 3 (2005): 25–31; and Katherine Baicker, Elliott S. Fisher, and Amitabh Chandra, "Malpractice Liability Costs and the Practice of Medicine in the Medicare Program," *Health Affairs* 26, no. 3 (May/June 2007): 841–52, https://www.doi.org/10.1377/hlthaff.26.3.841.

137. A difference-in-differences regression is a standard way to assess the causal effect of a legal shock, such as Texas's 2003 adoption of a non-econ cap.

138. For an introduction to difference-in-differences analysis, see Joshua David Angrist and Jörn-Steffen Pischke, *Mastering "Metrics": The Path from Cause to Effect* (Princeton, NJ: Princeton University Press, 2015). The regression models we use are specified in the academic articles on which this book is based.

139. We obtain a similar estimate—a 7 percent rise in spending—if we compare Texas to both the 19 states without damage caps and the 22 states that had damage caps in place throughout our sample period. If we do not weight counties by population, the regression estimates will be driven primarily by Texas's many small rural counties.

140. Atul Gawande, "The Cost Conundrum," *New Yorker*, June 1, 2009, http://www.newyorker.com/reporting/2009/06/01/090601fa_fact_gawande.

141. See Elliott Fisher et al., "The Implications of Regional Variation in Medicare Spending. Part 1," *Annals of Internal Medicine* 138, no. 4 (February 2003): 273–87, https://doi.org/10.7326/0003-4819-138-4-2003-2180-00006; Elliott Fisher et al., "The Implications of Regional Variation in Medicare Spending. Part 2," *Annals of Internal Medicine* 138, no. 4 (February 2003): 288–98, https://doi.org/10.7326/0003-4819-138-4-200302180-00007.

# CHAPTER 10

142. Kachalia and Mello, "New Directions."

143. Y. Tony Yang et al., "A Longitudinal Analysis of the Impact of Liability Pressure on the Supply of Obstetrician-Gynecologists," *Journal of Empirical Legal Studies* 5, no. 1 (2008): 21–53, https://doi.org/10.1111/j.1740-1461.2007.00117.x.

144. William Encinosa and Fred Hellinger, "Have State Caps on Malpractice Awards Increased the Supply of Physicians?," *Health Affairs* 24, no. 1 (2005): 250–58, https://doi.org/10.1377/hlthaff.w5.250.

145. Jonathan Klick and Thomas Stratmann, "Medical Malpractice Reform and Physicians in High-Risk Specialties," *Journal of Legal Studies* 36, no. S2 (2007): 121–42, https://doi.org/10.1086/520416.

146. Daniel P. Kessler, William M. Sage, and David J. Becker, "Impact of Malpractice Reforms on the Supply of Physician Services," *Journal of the American Medical Association* 293, no. 21 (June 2005): 2618–625, https://doi.org/10.1001/jama.293.21.2618.

147. David Matsa, "Does Malpractice Liability Keep the Doctor Away? Evidence from Tort Reform Damage Caps," *Journal of Legal Studies* 36, no. S2 (2007): 143–82, https://doi.org/10.1086/519466.

148. Eric Helland and Seth A. Seabury, "Tort Reform and Physician Labor Supply: A Review of the Evidence," *International Review of Law and Economics* 42 (June 2015): 192–202, https://doi.org/10.1016/j.irle.2015.01.005.

149. Myungho Paik, Bernard S. Black, and David A. Hyman, "Damage Caps and the Labor Supply of Physicians: Evidence from the Third Reform Wave," *American Law and Economics Review* 18, no. 2 (October 2016): 463–505, https://doi .org/10.1093/aler/ahw009.

150. Kessler, Sage, and Becker, "Impact of Malpractice Reforms."

151. Moving beyond difference-in-differences studies, Baicker and Chandra, in "Effect of Malpractice Liability," find no overall effect of insurance premiums on physician supply but a modest negative correlation in rural areas.

152. Ethan Lieber, "Medical Malpractice Reform, the Supply of Physicians, and Adverse Selection," *Journal of Law and Economics* 57, no. 2 (2014): 501–27, https://doi.org/10.1086/675236.

153. Ronald M. Stewart et al., "Tort Reform Is Associated with Significant Increases in Texas Physicians Relative to the Texas Population," *Journal of Gastrointestinal Surgery* 17, no. 1 (January 2013): 168–78, https://doi.org/10.1007/s11605 -012-2013-4.

154. Suzanne Batchelor, "Baby, I Lied: Rural Texas Is Still Waiting for the Doctors Tort Reform Was Supposed to Deliver," *Texas Observer*, October 19, 2007, https://www.texasobserver.org/2607-baby-i-lied-rural-texas-is-still-waiting-for -the-doctors-tort-reform-was-supposed-to-deliver/.

155. Howard Marcus and Bruce Malone, "2003 Reforms Helping Doctors Do Their Work," *Austin-American Statesman*, April 10, 2006.

156. A few examples: Joseph Nixon, "Why Doctors Are Heading for Texas," *Wall Street Journal*, May 17, 2008; Newt Gingrich and Rick Perry, "Let States Lead the Way: Washington's One-Size-Fits-All Reform Won't Work," *Washington Post*, November 6, 2009; and John Cornyn, "Health Care and Medical Malpractice Reform: The Necessity of Reform in the Current Debate," Heritage Foundation, January 28, 2010, https://www.heritage.org/health-care-reform /report/health-care-and-medical-malpractice-reform-the-necessity-reform-the.

157. Sarah Tung, "On Capitol Hill, Doctors Tout Texas' Brand of Tort Reform," *Houston Chronicle*, May 26, 2011, https://www.chron.com/news/houston-texas /article/On-Capitol-Hill-doctors-tout-Texas-brand-of-1686131.php.; "Brady's Bill Similar to State's Limits on Lawsuits," *Houston Chronicle*, May 27, 2011; "Burgess Reintroduces Legislation to End Unnecessary Health Care Lawsuits," Office of Rep. Michael C. Burgess (TX), March 3, 2011, https://burgess.house.gov/news/document single.aspx?DocumentID=227180.

158. See Rick Perry, "Tort Reform Has Done the Job It Was Designed to Do," Office of the Governor Rick Perry, July 2, 2012, https://web.archive.org /web/20121026215642/http://governor.state.tx.us/news/editorial/17549/.

159. With regard to Governor Perry's effort to question his objectivity, Professor Silver notes that he has "deep and extensive ties" to both the plaintiffs and the defense bar. His expertise on the professional responsibilities of insurance defense

lawyers has been recognized by the Republican-dominated Texas Supreme Court, which has cited his writings with approval. See *Unauthorized Practice of Law Committee v. American Home Assurance Company Inc.*, 261 S.W.3d 24 (Tex. 2008).

160. Texas Department of State Health Services (TDSHS), *Supply Trends among Licensed Health Professions, Texas, 1980–2011* (Austin: Texas Department of State Health Services, 2012).

161. For Figure 10.4, we rely on a national data series, the Area Health Resources Files (AHRF), which is based on annual surveys by the American Medical Association. The AHRF definition of active physicians is broader than the TDSHS definition of direct patient care physicians—in particular, AHRF includes interns and residents.

162. Matsa, "Keep the Doctor Away?"

163. TDSHS, "Supply Trends among Licensed Health Professions."

164. Eric Helland and Mark H. Showalter, "The Impact of Liability on the Physician Labor Market," *Journal of Law and Economics* 52, no. 4 (2009): 635–63, https://doi.org/10.1086/597427.

# CHAPTER 11

165. The 20 no-cap states are Alabama, Arizona, Arkansas, Connecticut, Delaware, Iowa, Kentucky, Maine, Minnesota, New Hampshire, New Jersey, New York, North Carolina, Pennsylvania, Rhode Island, Tennessee, Vermont, Washington, and Wyoming, plus the District of Columbia. For states where caps were overturned by the judiciary, we exercised judgment in choosing which category a state belonged in.

166. The 19 old-cap states are Alaska, California, Colorado, Hawaii, Idaho, Indiana, Kansas, Louisiana, Maryland, Massachusetts, Michigan, Missouri, Nebraska, New Mexico, Oregon, South Dakota, Utah, Virginia, and West Virginia.

167. The 12 new-cap states are Florida, Georgia, Illinois, Mississippi, Montana, Nevada, North Dakota, Ohio, Oklahoma, South Carolina, Texas, and Wisconsin. Three of these states adopted caps during the mid-1990s; the rest adopted caps during 2002–2005. Our analysis in this chapter covers 1992–2012, so we treat Montana (1996), North Dakota (1996), and Wisconsin (1995) as new-cap states. In Chapters 12 and 13, our study covers 1998–2011, so in those chapters, we treat Montana, North Dakota, and Wisconsin as old-cap states.

168. Brian Ostrom, Neal B. Kauder, and Robert C. LaFountain, *Examining the Work of State Courts, 1999–2000: A National Perspective from the Court Statistics Project* (Williamsburg, VA: National Center for State Courts, 2000), https://www.bjs.gov/content/pub/pdf/ewsc9900-npcsp.pdf.

169. Ryan K. Orosco et al., "Surgical Malpractice in the United States, 1990–2006," *Journal of the American College of Surgeons* 215, no. 4 (2012): 480–88, https://doi.org/10.1016/j.jamcollsurg.2012.04.028; and Tara Bishop, Andrew Ryan, and Lawrence Casalino, "Paid Malpractice Claims for Adverse Events in

Inpatient and Outpatient Settings," *Journal of the American Medical Association*, 305, no. 23 (2011): 2427–31, https://doi.org/10.1001/jama.2011.813.

170. Amitabh Chandra, Shantanu Nundy, and Seth A. Seabury, "The Growth of Physician Medical Malpractice Payments: Evidence from the National Practitioner Data Bank," *Health Affairs* 24, no. Suppl1 (2005): 240–49, https://doi.org/10.1377/hlthaff.w5.240.

171. Anupam B. Jena et al., "Malpractice Risk According to Physician Specialty," *New England Journal of Medicine* 365, no. 7 (2011): 629–36, https://doi.org/10.1056/nejmsa1012370.

172. The principal reforms include (a) punitive damage reforms: caps on punitive damages ("punitive caps"; 29 states), higher proof standards for punitive damages (35 states), and payment of punitive damages partly to the state (8 states); (b) limits on joint and several liability (39 states); (c) denying recovery of expenses paid by health insurance (34 states); (d) future damages paid over time rather than in a lump sum (31 states); (e) damages in some cases, or over a threshold amount, paid from a state compensation fund (13 states); and (f) limits on contingency fees (19 states). We treat punitive caps separate from caps on non-econ or total damages because punitive damages account for a small percentage of medical malpractice payouts.

173. See Carroll, Parikh, and Buddenbaum, "Impact of Defense Expenses."

174. Figure 11.3 presents mean payout for large paid claims, rather than all paid claims, because using all paid claims as the denominator would be misleading. As small paid claims disappear, the mean payout for the remaning claims will rise, even if nothing else is happening to payouts in the claims that are still brought. If we examine payout per claim for all paid claims, payout increases gradually in the first half of our sample period, from $284,000 in 1992 to $345,000 in 2001 (a total increase of 22 percent, or 2.2 percent per year).

175. States can enact reforms other than damage caps, which could affect paid claim rates. However, in regression analyses, we find that other reforms do not have a statistically significant effect on claim rates or payout per large claim.

176. Mello and Kachalia, in *Evaluation of Options*, estimate the sum of indemnity payments and insurance company administrative expenses at $9.9 billion in 2008; by comparison, physicians reported $3.5 billion in payouts to the National Practitioner Data Bank.

177. Michael J. Saks, "Do We Really Know Anything about the Behavior of the Tort Litigation System. And Why Not?," *University of Pennsylvania Law Review* 140, no. 4 (April 1992): 1147–1292, https://doi.org/10.2307/3312403.

178. Baker, *Medical Malpractice Myth*; Brennan, Mello, and Studdert, "Liability, Patient Safety, Defensive Medicine"; Michael D. Greenberg et al., *Is Better Patient Safety Associated with Less Malpractice Activity? Evidence from California* (Santa Monica, CA: RAND Corporation, 2010), https://www.rand.org/pubs/technical_reports/TR824.html; and Bernard S. Black, Amy Wagner, and Zenon Zabinski,

"The Association between Patient Safety Indicators and Medical Malpractice Risk: Evidence from Florida and Texas," *American Journal of Health Economics* 3, no. 1 (Spring 2017): 1–31, https://doi.org/10.1162/AJHE_a_00069.

179. David C. Classen et al., "'Global Trigger Tool' Shows That Adverse Events in Hospitals May Be Ten Times Greater Than Previously Measured," *Health Affairs* 30, no. 4 (2011): 581–89, https://doi.org/10.1377/hlthaff.2011.0190; Christopher P. Landrigan et al., "Temporal Trends in Rates of Patient Harm Resulting from Medical Care," *New England Journal of Medicine* 363, no. 22 (2010): 2124–34, https://doi.org/10.1056/nejmsa1004404; and Steven A. Farmer, Bernard S. Black, and Robert O. Bonow, "Tension between Quality Measurement, Public Quality Reporting, and Pay for Performance," *Journal of the American Medical Association* 309, no. 4 (2013): 349–50, https://doi.org/10.1001/jama.2012.191276.

180. Hyman, Black, and Silver, "Plaintiff-Side Personal Injury Practice"; and Joanna Shepherd, "Uncovering the Silent Victims of the American Medical Liability System," *Vanderbilt Law Review* 67, no. 1 (2014): 151–95.

181. Chandra, Nundy, and Seabury, "Growth of Malpractice Payments."

182. Myungho Paik et al., "Will Tort Reform Bend the Cost Curve? Evidence from Texas," *Journal of Empirical Legal Studies* 9, no. 2 (May 2012): 173–216, https//doi.org/10.1111/j.1740-1461.2012.01251.x.

183. Michael Frakes, "The Impact of Medical Liability Standards on Regional Variations in Physician Behavior: Evidence from the Adoption of National-Standard Rules," *American Economic Review* 103, no. 1 (February 2013): 257–76, https://doi.org/10.1257/aer.103.1.257; Michael Frakes and Anupam B. Jena, "Does Medical Malpractice Law Improve Health Care Quality?," *Journal of Public Economics* 143 (January 4, 2014): 1–49, http://dx.doi.org/10.2139/ssrn.2374599; Toshiaki Iizuka, "Does Higher Malpractice Pressure Deter Medical Errors?," *Journal of Law and Economics* 56, no. 1 (2013): 161–88, https://doi.org/10.1086/666977; and Zabinski and Black, "Deterrent Tort Law."

184. Zabinski and Black, "Deterrent Tort Law"; and Iizuka, "Higher Malpractice Pressure."

## CHAPTER 12

185. In Chapter 11, the sample period was 1992–2012, so we treated the three states that adopted caps in the 1990s as cap-adopting (new-cap) states. In this chapter, the sample period is 1998–2011, so we treat these states as states that already have damage caps in place (old-cap states). The nine states that adopted and their cap adoption years are: Florida (2003), Georgia (2005), Illinois (2005), Mississippi (2003), Nevada (2002), Ohio (2003), Oklahoma (2003), South Carolina (2005), and Texas (2003). The Georgia and Illinois caps were invalidated by state courts in early 2010; we treat them as in effect through 2009.

186. All percentage estimates in this chapter are based on converting coefficients from log-linear regressions, with the natural logarithm of spending as the dependent variable, to percentage equivalents: Percentage change $= 100 \star (e^x - 1)$. We do not study Medicare Part D spending, because Medicare Part D began only in 2006, after the third-wave reforms we study.

187. Bernard Black et al., "The Long-Term Effect of Health Insurance on Near-Elderly Health and Mortality," *American Journal of Health Economics* 3, no. 3 (Summer 2017): 281–311, https://doi.org/10.1162/ajhe_a_00076.

188. Moghtaderi, Black, and Farmer, "Damage Caps and Defensive Medicine."

189. Note that our data are for traditional Medicare.

190. We find evidence of a nonlinear relationship between managed care penetration and Medicare spending and therefore also control for (managed care penetration)$^2$.

191. See Vladimir Atanasov and Bernard S. Black, "Shock-Based Causal Inference in Corporate Finance and Accounting Research," *Critical Finance Review* 5, no. 2 (2016): 207–304, https://doi.org/10.1561/104.00000036.

192. Mello and Kachalia, in *Evaluation of Options*, survey prior studies and estimate savings at 2 percent of total spending.

193. Moghtaderi, Black, and Farmer, "Damage Caps and Defensive Medicine"; Ronen Avraham and Max Schanzenbach, "The Impact of Tort Reform on Intensity of Treatment: Evidence from Heart Patients," *Journal of Health Economics* 39 (January 2015): 273–88, https://doi.org/10.1016/j.jhealeco.2014.08.002; and Steven Farmer et al., "Association of Medical Liability Reform with Clinician Approach to Coronary Artery Disease Management," *Journal of the American Medical Association Cardiology* 3, no. 7 (July 2018): 609–18, https://doi.org/10.1001/jamacardio.2018.1360.

194. Kessler and McClellan, "Malpractice Law and Health Care Reform."

195. In the study that underlies this chapter, we re-analyze the 1980s caps and provide evidence that the estimated effect of those caps on aggregate Medicare spending is close to zero and statistically insignificant. Paik, Black, and Hyman, "Damage Caps and Defensive Medicine."

196. Andis Robeznieks, "Medical Malpractice: The Fear Factor," *Modern Healthcare*, September 13, 2010, https://www.modernhealthcare.com/article/20100913/MODERNPHYSICIAN/100919992/medical-malpractice-the-fear-factor.

## CHAPTER 13

197. Jena et al., "Malpractice According to Specialty."

198. Jena et al., "Malpractice According to Specialty."

199. For all patient care physicians, the point estimate for the impact of damage caps is close to zero at +.003 (0.3 percent). The 95 percent confidence interval

around this estimate is [−0.9 percent, +1.5 percent]. Thus, given our data, there is only a 2.5 percent chance that there is a true increase in supply of more than 1.5 percent, and a 2.5 percent chance of a true decrease of more than 0.9 percent.

200. Klick and Stratmann, "Medical Malpractice Reform"; Helland and Seabury, "Tort Reform and Physician Supply."

201. The point estimate for the effect of cap adoption on the eight high-risk specialties is −0.2 percent, which is not significantly distinguishable from zero. This is a precisely estimated zero; the 95 percent confidence interval is [−1.6 percent, +1.1 percent].

202. Matsa, "Keep the Doctor Away?"

203. Encinosa and Hellinger, "Caps on Malpractice Awards."

204. Helland and Showalter, "Physician Labor Market."

205. Lieber, "Medical Malpractice Reform."

## CHAPTER 14

206. Mohammad Rahmati et al., "Insurance Crisis or Liability Crisis? Medical Malpractice Claiming in Illinois, 1980–2010," *Journal of Empirical Legal Studies* 13, no. 2 (2016): 183–204, https://doi.org/10.1111/jels.12113.

207. James Griffith, "What It Will Take to Solve the Malpractice Crisis," *Med Econ* 59, no. 19 (September 1982): 192–96, https://pubmed.ncbi.nlm.nih.gov/10258371/.

208. Elly Yu, "'Largest Medical Malpractice Verdict in U.S. History' Awarded to Maryland Woman," WAMU (Washington, DC), September 26, 2019, https://wamu.org/story/19/09/26/largest-medical-malpractice-verdict-in-u-s-history-awarded-to-maryland-woman/.

209. Jermont Terry, "Jury Awards Family $101 Million in Verdict against West Suburban Medical Center over Boy's Brain Damage," CBS Chicago, November 5, 2019, https://chicago.cbslocal.com/2019/11/05/brain-damage-jury-award-west-suburban-medical-center/.

210. Associated Press, "Says Her Powers Vanished: 'Psychic' Awarded $988,000 in Hospital CAT-Scan Lawsuit," *LA Times*, March 30, 1986, https://www.latimes.com/archives/la-xpm-1986-03-30-mn-1672-story.html.

211. H. L. Mencken, "The Divine Afflatus," in *A Mencken Chrestomathy* (New York: Vintage Books, 1982), p. 443.

212. Laura Beil, "A Surgeon So Bad It Was Criminal," *ProPublica*, October 2, 2018, https://www.propublica.org/article/dr-death-christopher-duntsch-a-surgeon-so-bad-it-was-criminal.

213. Michele Gorman, "Yogi Berra's Most Memorable Sayings," *Newsweek*, September 23, 2015, https://www.newsweek.com/most-memorable-yogi-isms-375661.

214. Baker, *Medical Malpractice Myth*.

215. Baker, *Medical Malpractice Myth* describes this process for anesthesiologists.

216. Black, Wagner, and Zabinsi, "Patient Safety Indicators"; and Amos Grunebaum, Frank Chervenak, and Daniel Skupski, "Effect of a Comprehensive Obstetric Patient Safety Program on Compensation Payments and Sentinel Events," *American Journal of Obstetrics and Gynecology* 204, no. 2 (2011): 97–105, https://doi.org/10.1016/j.ajog.2010.11.009.

217. Martin A. Makary and Michael Daniel, "Medical Error—the Third Leading Cause of Death in the US," *BMJ: The British Medical Journal* (May 2016), https://doi.org/10.1136/bmj.i2139.

218. Peter Pronovost et al., "Fifteen Years after To Err is Human: A Success Story to Learn From," *BMJ Quality and Safety Online* 25, no. 6 (2016): 396–99, https://doi.org/10.1136/bmjqs-2015–004720.

219. Charles M. Balch et al., "Personal Consequences of Malpractice Lawsuits on American Surgeons," *Journal of American College of Surgeons* 213, no. 5 (November 2011): 657–67, https://doi.org/10.1016/j.jamcollsurg.2011.08.005.

## CHAPTER 15

220. James Q. Wilson, *Bureaucracy: What Government Agencies Do and Why They Do It* (New York: Basic Books, 1989).

221. Hyman and Silver, "Poor State of Health Care."

222. Paul Heaton provides evidence that the introduction of Medicare rules strengthening enforcement of subrogation rights in 2011 slowed down auto accident settlements. Paul Heaton, "The Effect of Mandatory Insurer Reporting on Settlement Delay," RAND Corporation Working Paper WR-1210-ICJ, August 2017, https://www.rand.org/pubs/working_papers/WR1210.html.

223. We study the screening process that a medical malpractice claim must undergo; see Mohammad Rahmati et al., "Screening Plaintiffs and Selecting Defendants in Medical Malpractice Litigation: Evidence from Illinois and Indiana," *Journal of Empirical Legal Studies* 15, no. 1 (2018): 41–79, https://doi.org/10.1111/jels.12173.

224. Hyman and Silver, "Poor State of Health Care"; Baker, *Medical Malpractice Myth*.

225. Erving Goffman, "On Cooling the Mark Out," *Psychiatry* 15, no. 4 (1952): 451–63, https://doi.org/10.1080/00332747.1952.11022896.

226. See Rahmati et al., "Screening Plaintiffs."

227. Medical Professional Liabliity Association, accessed February 17, 2021, https://www.mplassociation.org/Web/Membership__Member_Center/Membership/Web/Membership/Membership.aspx?hkey=744906bd-9021-49c5-bfaf-a7bf4f042b7e.

# SELECTED BIBLIOGRAPHY

## OUR OWN PRIOR MEDICAL MALPRACTICE RESEARCH AND RELATED RESEARCH

Black, Bernard, Jeanette W. Chung, Jeffrey Traczynski, Victoria Udalova, and Sonal Vats. "Medical Liability Insurance Premia: 1990–2015 Dataset, with Literature Review and Summary Information." *Journal of Empirical Legal Studies* 14, no. 1 (2017): 238–45. https://doi.org/ 10.1111/jels.12146.

Black, Bernard, David Hyman, and Charles Silver. "Settlement at Policy Limits and the Duty to Settle: Evidence from Texas." *Journal of Empirical Legal Studies* 8, no. 1 (2011): 48–84. https://doi.org/10.1111/j.1740-1461.2010.01207.x.

Black, Bernard, David A. Hyman, Charles Silver, and William M. Sage. "Defense Costs and Insurer Reserves in Medical Malpractice and Other Personal Injury Cases: Evidence from Texas." *American Law and Economics Review* 10, no. 2 (2008): 185–245. https://doi.org/10.1093/aler/ahn014.

Black, Bernard, David A. Hyman, Charles Silver, and William M. Sage. "Stability, Not Crisis: Medical Malpractice Claim Outcomes in Texas, 1988–2002." *Journal of Empirical Legal Studies* 2, no. 2 (2005): 207–59. https://doi.org/10.1111 /j.1740-1461.2005.00050.x.

Black, Bernard S., Amy R. Wagner, and Zenon Zabinski. "The Association between Patient Safety Indicators and Medical Malpractice Risk: Evidence from Florida and Texas." *American Journal of Health Economics* 3, no. 2 (2017): 109–39. https://doi.org/10.1162/AJHE_a_00069.

Farmer, Steven A., Bernard Black, and Robert O. Bonow. "Tension between Quality Measurement, Public Quality Reporting, and Pay for Performance." *Journal of the American Medical Association* 309, no. 4 (2013): 349–50. http://doi .org/10.1001/jama.2012.191276.

Farmer, Steven A., Ali Moghtaderi, Samantha Schilsky, David Magid, William Sage, Nori Allen, Frederick A. Masoudi, Avi Dor, and Bernard Black. "Association of Medical Liability Reform with Clinician Approach to Coronary Artery Disease Management." *JAMA Cardiology* 3, no. 7 (2018): 609–18. http://doi.org/10.1001/jamacardio.2018.1360.

Hyman, David A., Bernard Black, and Charles Silver. "The Economics of Plaintiff-Side Personal Injury Practice." *University of Illinois Law Review*, no. 4 (2015): 1564–603. http://dx.doi.org/10.2139/ssrn.1441487.

Hyman, David A., Bernard S. Black, Charles Silver, and William Sage. "Estimating the Effect of Damages Caps in Medical Malpractice Cases: Evidence from Texas." *Journal of Legal Analysis* 1, no. 1 (2009): 355–409. http://doi .org/10.4159/jla.v1i1.16.

Hyman, David A., Bernard Black, Kathryn Zeiler, Charles Silver, and William M. Sage. "Do Defendants Pay What Juries Award?: Post-Verdict Haircuts in Texas Medical Malpractice Cases, 1988–2003." *Journal of Empirical Legal Studies* 4 (2007): 3–68. https://doi.org/10.1111/j.1740-1461.2007.00081.x.

Hyman, David A., Mohammad Rahmati, Bernard S. Black, and Charles Silver. "Medical Malpractice Litigation and the Market for Plaintiff-Side Representation: Evidence from Illinois." *Journal of Empirical Legal Studies* 13, no. 4 (2016): 603–36. https://doi.org/10.1111/jels.12127.

Hyman, David A., Charles Silver, Bernard Black, and Myungho Paik. "Does Tort Reform Affect Physician Supply? Evidence from Texas." *International Review of Law and Economics* 42 (2015): 203–18. https://doi.org/10.1016/j.irle .2015.02.002.

Moghtaderi, Ali, Bernard Black, and Steven Farmer. "Damage Caps and Defensive Medicine: Reexamination with Patient-Level Data." *Journal of Empirical Legal Studies* 16, no. 1 (2019): 26–68. https://doi.org/10.1111/jels.12208.

Paik, Myungho, Bernard Black, and David A. Hyman. "Damage Caps and Defensive Medicine, Revisited." *Journal of Health Economics* 51 (2017): 84–97. http:// doi.org/10.1016/j.jhealeco.2016.11.001.

Paik, Myungho, Bernard Black, and David Hyman. "Damage Caps and the Labor Supply of Physicians: Evidence from the Third Reform Wave." *American Law and Economics Review* 18, no. 2 (2016): 463–505. https://doi.org/10.1093/aler/ahw009.

Paik, Myungho, Bernard Black, and David A. Hyman. "The Receding Tide of Medical Malpractice Litigation: Part 1—National Trends." *Journal of Empirical Legal Studies* 10, no. 4 (2013): 612–38. https://doi.org/10.1111/jels.12021.

Paik, Myungho, Bernard Black, and David Hyman. "The Receding Tide of Medical Malpractice Litigation: Part 2—Effect of Damage Caps." *Journal of Empirical Legal Studies* 10, no. 4 (2013): 639–69. https://doi.org/10.1111/jels.12022.

Paik, Myungho, Bernard S. Black, David A. Hyman, William M. Sage, and Charles Silver. "How Do the Elderly Fare in Medical Malpractice Litigation, before and after Tort Reform? Evidence from Texas." *American Law and Economics Review* 14, no. 2 (2012): 561–600. https://doi.org/10.1093/aler/ahs017.

Paik, Myungho, Bernard S. Black, David A. Hyman, and Charles Silver. "Will Tort Reform Bend the Cost Curve? Evidence from Texas." *Journal of Empirical Legal Studies* 9, no. 2 (2012): 173–216. https://doi.org/10.1111/j.1740-1461.2012.01251.x.

Rahmati, Mohammad, David A. Hyman, Bernard Black, Jing Liu, and Charles Silver. "Screening Plaintiffs and Selecting Defendants in Medical Malpractice Litigation: Evidence from Illinois and Indiana." *Journal of Empirical Legal Studies* 15, no.1 (2018): 41–79. https://doi.org/10.1111/jels.12173.

Rahmati, Mohammad, David A. Hyman, Bernard Black, and Charles Silver. "Insurance Crisis or Liability Crisis? Medical Malpractice Claiming in Illinois, 1980–2010." *Journal of Empirical Legal Studies* 13, no. 2 (2016): 183–204. https://doi.org/10.1111/jels.12113.

Silver, Charles, David A. Hyman, and Bernard S. Black. "The Impact of the 2003 Texas Medical Malpractice Damages Cap on Physician Supply and Insurer Payouts: Separating Facts from Rhetoric." *Texas Advocate* 44 (2008): 25–34. https://ssrn.com/abstract=1139190.

Silver, Charles, David A. Hyman, Bernard S. Black, and Myungho Paik. "Policy Limits, Payouts, and Blood Money: Medical Malpractice Settlements in the Shadow of Insurance." *Irvine Law Review* 5, no. 3 (2015): 559–86. https://scholarship.law.uci.edu/ucilr/vol5/iss3/5/.

Silver, Charles, Kathryn Zeiler, Bernard S. Black, David A. Hyman, and William M. Sage. "Malpractice Payouts and Malpractice Insurance: Evidence from Texas Closed Claims, 1990–2003." *The Geneva Papers on Risk and Insurance: Issues and Practice* 33, no. 2, (2018): 177–92. https://doi.org/10.1057/gpp.2008.3.

Zabinski, Zenon, and Bernard S. Black. "The Deterrent Effect of Tort Law: Evidence from Medical Malpractice Reform." Northwestern Law & Economics Research Paper 13-09, March 2020. http://dx.doi.org/10.2139/ssrn.2161362.

Zeiler, Kathryn, Charles Silver, Bernard Black, David A. Hyman, and William M. Sage. "Physicians' Insurance Limits and Malpractice Payments: Evidence from Texas Closed Claims, 1990–2003." *The Journal of Legal Studies* 36, no. S2 (2007): s9–s45. http://doi.org/10.1086/519467.

## OTHER RESEARCH

Abadie, Alberto, Alexis Diamond, and Jens Hainmueller. "Synthetic Control Methods for Comparative Case Studies: Estimating the Effect of California's Tobacco Control Program." *Journal of the American Statistical Association* 105, no. 490 (2010): 493–505. http://doi.org/10.1198/jasa.2009.ap08746.

American Medical Association. *Medical Liability Reform—Now!*, 2020 ed. https://www.ama-assn.org/practice-management/sustainability/state-medical-liability-reform.

Angrist, Joshua D., and Jörn-Steffen Pischke. *Mastering 'Metrics: The Path from Cause to Effect.* Princeton, NJ: Princeton University Press, 2015.

Atanasov, Vladimir, and Bernard Black. "Shock-Based Causal Inference in Corporate Finance and Accounting Research." *Critical Finance Review* 5, no. 2 (2016): 207–304. http://dx.doi.org/10.1561/104.00000036.

Avraham, Ronen. "An Empirical Study of the Impact of Tort Reforms on Medical Malpractice Settlement Payments." *The Journal of Legal Studies* 36, no. S2 (2007): S186–S229. https://doi.org/10.1086/527332.

Avraham, Ronen. "Database of State Tort Law Reforms (6.1)." University of Texas School of Law, Law and Economics Research Paper Series, no. e555 (2019). http://dx.doi.org/10.2139/ssrn.902711.

Avraham, Ronen, Leemore S. Dafny, and Max M. Schanzenbach. "The Impact of Tort Reform on Employer-Sponsored Health Insurance Premiums." *Journal of Law, Economics, and Organization* 28, no. 4 (October 2012): 657–86. https://doi.org/10.1093/jleo/ewq017.

Avraham, Ronen, and Max Schanzenbach. "The Impact of Tort Reform on Intensity of Treatment: Evidence from Heart Patients." *Journal of Health Economics* 39 (January 2015): 273–88. https://doi.org/10.1016/j.jhealeco.2014.08.002.

Baicker, Katherine, and Amitabh Chandra. "Defensive Medicine and Disappearing Doctors?" *Regulation* 28, no. 3 (Fall 2005): 24–31.

Baicker, Katherine, and Amitabh Chandra. "The Effect of Malpractice Liability on the Delivery of Health Care." *Forum for Health Economics & Policy* 8, no. 1 (2005). https://doi.org/10.2202/1558-9544.1010.

Baicker, Katherine, Elliott S. Fisher, and Amitabh Chandra. "Malpractice Liability Costs and the Practice of Medicine in the Medicare Program." *Health Affairs* 26, no. 3 (2007): 841–52. http://doi.org/10.1377/hlthaff.26.3.841.

Baker, Tom. "Blood Money, New Money, and the Moral Economy of Tort Law in Action." *Law and Society Review* 35, no. 2 (2001): 275–319. http://doi.org/10.2307/3185404.

Baker, Tom. "Medical Malpractice and the Insurance Underwriting Cycle." *DePaul Law Review* 54, no. 2 (Winter 2005): 393–438.

Baker, Tom. *The Medical Malpractice Myth*. Chicago: University of Chicago Press, 2005.

Berger, Lawrence A., J. David Cummins, and Sharon Tennyson. "Reinsurance and the Liability Insurance Crisis." *Journal of Risk and Uncertainty* 5, no. 5 (1992): 253–72. http://doi.org/10.1007/BF00057882.

Bishop, Tara F., Alex D. Federman, and Salomeh Keyhani. "Physicians' Views on Defensive Medicine: A National Survey." *Archives of Internal Medicine* 170, no. 12 (2010): 1081–83. http://doi.org/10.1001/archinternmed.2010.155.

Bishop, Tara F., Andrew M. Ryan, and Lawrence P. Casalino. "Paid Malpractice Claims for Adverse Events in Inpatient and Outpatient Settings." *Journal of the American Medical Association* 305, no. 23 (2011): 2427–31. http://doi.org/10.1001/jama.2011.813.

Black, Bernard, José-Antonio Espín-Sánchez, Eric French, and Kate Litvak. "The Long-Term Effect of Health Insurance on Near-Elderly Health and Mortality." *American Journal of Health Economics* 3, no. 3 (Summer 2017): 281–311. https://doi.org/10.1162/ajhe_a_00076.

Brennan, Troyen A., Michelle M. Mello, and David M. Studdert. "Liability, Patient Safety, and Defensive Medicine: What Does the Future Hold?" In *Medical Malpractice and the U.S. Health Care System*, edited by William M. Sage and Rogan Kersh, 93–114. Cambridge: Cambridge University Press, 2006. http://doi.org/10.1017/CBO9780511617836.007.

Brickman, Lester. "The Market for Contingent Fee-Financed Tort Litigation: Is It Price Competitive?" *Cardozo Law Review* 25, no. 1 (2003): 65–128. http://dx.doi.org/10.2139/ssrn.463226.

Broder, Ivy E. "Characteristics of Million Dollar Awards: Jury Verdicts and Final Disbursements." *Justice System Journal* 11, no. 3 (Winter 1986): 349–59, 382–87.

Carrier, Emily R., James D. Reschovsky, David A. Katz, and Michelle M. Mello. "High Physician Concern about Malpractice Risk Predicts More Aggressive Diagnostic Testing in Office-Based Practice." *Health Affairs* 32, no. 8 (August 2013): 1383–91. https://doi.org/10.1377/hlthaff.2013.0233.

Carrier, Emily R., James D. Reschovsky, Michelle M. Mello, Ralph C. Mayrell, and David Katz. "Physicians' Fears of Malpractice Lawsuits Are Not Assuaged by Tort Reforms." *Health Affairs* 29, no. 9 (September 2010): 1585–92. https://doi.org/10.1377/hlthaff.2010.0135.

Carroll, Aaron E., Parul Divya Parikh, and Jennifer L. Buddenbaum. "The Impact of Defense Expenses in Medical Malpractice Claims." *Journal of Law, Medicine and Ethics* 40, no. 1 (Spring 2012): 135–42. http://doi.org/10.1111/j.1748-720X.2012.00651.x.

Carter, Terry. "Tort Reform Texas Style: New Laws and Med-Mal Damage Caps Devastate Plaintiff and Defense Firms Alike." *ABA Journal* 93, no. 10 (October 2006): 30–36.

Chandra, Amitabh, Shantanu Nundy, and Seth A. Seabury. "The Growth of Physician Medical Malpractice Payments: Evidence from the National Practitioner Data Bank." *Health Affairs* 24, no. 1 (2005): 240–49. https://doi.org/10.1377/hlthaff.w5.240.

Classen, David C., Roger Resar, Frances Griffin, Frank Federico, Terri Frankel, Nancy Kimmel, John C. Whittington, Allan Frankel, Andrew Seger, and Brent C. James. "'Global Trigger Tool' Shows that Adverse Events in Hospitals May Be Ten Times Greater than Previously Measured." *Health Affairs* 30, no. 4 (2011): 581–89. https://doi.org/10.1377/hlthaff.2011.0190.

Cohen, Thomas H. *Medical Malpractice Trials and Verdicts in Large Counties, 2001.* Washington: U.S. Department of Justice, Bureau of Justice Statistics, 2004.

Cohen, Thomas H., and Kristen A. Hughes. *Medical Malpractice Insurance Claims in Seven States.* Washington: U.S. Department of Justice, Bureau of Justice Statistics, 2007.

Congressional Budget Office. "Limiting Tort Liability for Medical Malpractice." Economic and Budget Issue Brief, January 8, 2004. https://www.cbo.gov/sites/default/files/108th-congress-2003-2004/reports/01-08-medicalmalpractice.pdf.

Congressional Budget Office. *Medical Malpractice Tort Limits and Health Care Spending.* Washington: Congressional Budget Office, April 2006.

Connecticut Insurance Department. *Connecticut Medical Malpractice Closed Claims Report.* Hartford, CT: Connecticut Insurance Department, April 2007.

Cross, Frank, and Charles Silver. "In Texas, Life Is Cheap." *Vanderbilt Law Review* 59 (2006): 1875–923.

Currie, Janet, and W. Bentley MacLeod. "First Do No Harm? Tort Reform and Birth Outcomes." *The Quarterly Journal of Economics* 123, no. 2 (2008): 795–830. https://doi.org/10.1162/qjec.2008.123.2.795.

Daniels, Stephen, and Joanne Martin. "It Is No Longer Viable from a Practical and Business Standpoint: Damage Caps, 'Hidden Victims,' and the Declining Interest in Medical Malpractice Cases." *International Journal of the Legal Profession* 17, no. 1 (2010): 59–82. https://doi.org/10.1080/09695951003588923.

Diederich Healthcare. *2012 Medical Malpractice Payout Analysis Infographic Released.* Marion, IL: Diederich Healthcare, March 2012.

Donohue III, John, and Daniel E. Ho. "The Impact of Damage Caps on Malpractice Claims: Randomization Inference with Difference-in-Differences." *Journal of Empirical Legal Studies* 4, no. 1 (2007): 69–102. https://doi.org/10.1111/j.1740-1461.2007.00082.x.

Dranove, David, and Anne Gron. "Effects of the Medical Malpractice Crisis on Access to and Incidence of High-Risk Procedures: Evidence from Florida." *Health Affairs* 24, no. 3 (2005): 802–10. https://doi.org/10.1377/hlthaff.24.3.802.

Dranove, David, and Yasutora Watanabe. "Influence and Deterrence: How Obstetricians Respond to Litigation against Themselves and Their Colleagues." *American Law and Economics Review* 12, no. 1 (2010): 69–94. http://doi.org/10.1093/aler/ahp016.

Edwards, Amanda. "Medical Malpractice Non-Economic Damages Caps." *Harvard Journal on Legislation* 43 (2006): 213–30.

Eisenberg, Theodore, and Martin T. Wells. "The Significant Association between Punitive and Compensatory Damages in Blockbuster Cases: A Methodological Primer." *Journal of Empirical Legal Studies* 3, no. 1 (2006): 175–95. https://doi.org/10.1111/j.1740-1461.2006.00067.x.

Encinosa, William, and Fred Hellinger. "Have State Caps on Malpractice Awards Increased the Supply of Physicians?" *Health Affairs* 24, no. 1 (2005): 250–58. https://doi.org/10.1377/hlthaff.w5.250.

Finley, Lucinda. "The Hidden Victims of Tort Reform: Women, Children, and the Elderly." *Emory Law Journal* 53, no. 1263 (2004): 1253–314.

Fisher, Elliott S., David E. Wennberg, Thérèse A. Stukel, Daniel J. Gottlieb, F. L. Lucas, and Etoile L. Pinder. "The Implications of Regional Variations in Medicare Spending. Part 1: The Content, Quality, and Accessibility of Care." *Annals of Internal Medicine* 138, no. 4 (2003): 273–88. http://doi.org/10.7326/0003-4819-138-4-200302180-00006.

Fisher, Elliott S., David E. Wennberg, Thérèse A. Stukel, Daniel J. Gottlieb, F. L. Lucas, and Etoile L. Pinder. "The Implications of Regional Variations in Medicare Spending. Part 2: Health Outcomes and Satisfaction with Care." *Annals of Internal Medicine* 138, no. 4 (2003): 288–98. http://doi.org/10.7326/0003-4819-138-4-200302180-00007.

Frakes, Michael. "Defensive Medicine and Obstetric Practices." *Journal of Empirical Legal Studies* 9, no. 3 (2012): 457–81. https://doi.org/10.1111/j.1740-1461.2012.01259.x.

Frakes, Michael. "The Impact of Medical Liability Standards on Regional Variations in Physician Behavior: Evidence from the Adoption of National-Standard Rules." *American Economic Review* 103, no. 1 (2012): 257–76. http://doi.org/10.2139/ssrn.1432559.

Frakes, Michael, and Anupam B. Jena. "Tort Liability and Health Care Quality: The Divergent Impacts of Remedy-Focused and Substantive Tort Reforms." National Bureau of Economic Research Working Paper no. w19841, January 2014. https://ssrn.com/abstract=2384298.

Frech III, H. E., William G. Hamm, and C. Paul Wazzan. "An Economic Assessment of Damage Caps in Medical Malpractice Litigation Imposed by State Law and the Implications for Federal Policy and Law." *Health Matrix: Journal of Law-Medicine* 16, no. 2 (2006): 693–722.

Gawande, Atul. "The Cost Conundrum." *New Yorker*, June 1, 2009.

General Accounting Office, *Medical Malpractice: Medicare/Medicaid Beneficiaries Account for a Relatively Small Percentage of Malpractice Losses.* Washington: U.S. General Accounting Office, August 1993.

Goffman, Erving. "On Cooling the Mark Out: Some Aspects of Adaptation to Failure." *Psychiatry* 15, no. 4 (1952): 451–63. https://doi.org/10.1080/00332747.1952.11022896.

Graham, John. "Saving Lives through Administrative Law and Economics." *University of Pennsylvania Law Review* 157, no. 2 (2008): 395–540.

Greenberg, Michael, Amelia Haviland, J. Scott Ashwood, and Regan Main. "Is Better Patient Safety Associated with Less Malpractice Activity? Evidence from California." RAND Corporation working paper, 2010.

Gron, Anne. "Capacity Constraints and Cycles in Property-Casualty Insurance Markets." *RAND Journal of Economics* 25, no. 1 (1994): 110–27.

Gron, Anne. "Evidence of Capacity Constraints in Insurance Markets." *Journal of Law and Economics* 37, no. 2 (1994): 349–77. https://doi.org/0.1086/467317.

Gron, Anne. "Price and Profit Cycles in the Property-Casualty Insurance Industry." Mimeo, Department of Economics, Massachusetts Institute of Technology (1989).

Gron, Anne. "Property-Casualty Insurance Cycles, Capacity Constraints, and Empirical Results." PhD diss., Department of Economics, Massachusetts Institute of Technology, 1990.

Guirguis-Blake, Janelle, George E. Fryer, Robert L. Phillips Jr., Ronald Szabat, and Larry A. Green. "The U.S. Medical Liability System: Evidence for Legislative Reform." *Annals of Family Medicine* 4, no. 3 (2006): 240–46. http://doi.org/10.1370/afm.535.

Harrington, Scott. "Tort Liability, Insurance Rates, and the Insurance Cycle." *Brookings-Wharton Papers on Financial Services* (2004): 97–138. http://doi.org/10.1353/pfs.2004.0010.

Hartwig, Robert P. *Special Report: Earlybird Forecast 2003.* New York: Insurance Information Institute, 2003.

Heaton, Paul. "The Effect of Mandatory Insurer Reporting on Settlement Delay." RAND Corporation Working Paper no. WR-1210-ICJ, 2017.

Helland, Eric, and Seth Seabury. "Tort Reform and Physician Supply: A Review of the Evidence." *International Review of Law and Economics* 42 (2015): 192–202. https://doi.org/10.1016/j.irle.2015.01.005.

Helland, Eric, and Mark H. Showalter. "The Impact of Liability on the Physician Labor Market." *Journal of Law and Economics* 52, no. 4 (2009): 635–63. http://doi.org/10.1086/597427.

Hellinger, Fred, and William E. Encinosa. "The Impact of State Laws Limiting Malpractice Damage Awards on Health Care Expenditures." *American Journal of Public Health* 96, no. 8 (2006): 1375–81.

Hyman, David A. "Convicts and Convictions: Lessons from Transportation for Health Reform." *Pennsylvania Law Review* 159 (2011): 1999–2042.

Hyman, David A. "Regulating Managed Care: What's Wrong with a Patient Bill of Rights." *Southern California Law Review* 73, no. 2 (2000): 221–75.

Hyman, David A., and Charles Silver. "Medical Malpractice Litigation and Tort Reform: It's the Incentives, Stupid." *Vanderbilt Law Review* 59, no. 4 (2006): 1085–136.

Hyman, David A., and Charles Silver. "The Poor State of Health Care Quality in the U.S.: Is Malpractice Liability Part of the Problem or Part of the Solution?" *Cornell Law Review* 90, no. 4 (2005): 893–994.

Iizuka, Toshiaki. "Does Higher Malpractice Pressure Deter Medical Errors?" *Journal of Law and Economics* 56, no. 1 (2013): 161–88. http://doi.org/10.1086/666977.

Institute of Medicine. *To Err Is Human: Building a Safer Health System.* Washington: National Academies Press, 2000.

Jackson Healthcare. *Physician Study: Quantifying the Cost of Defensive Medicine.* Atlanta, GA: Jackson Healthcare, February 2010.

Jena, Anupam B., Seth Seabury, Darius Lakdawalla, and Amitabh Chandra. "Malpractice Risk According to Physician Specialty." *New England Journal of Medicine* 365 (2011): 629–36. http://doi.org/10.1056/NEJMsa1012370.

Kachalia, Allen, and Michelle M. Mello. "New Directions in Medical Liability Reform." *New England Journal of Medicine* 364, no. 16 (2011): 1564–72. http://doi.org/10.1056/NEJMhpr1012821.

Kessler, Daniel. "The Determinants of the Cost of Medical Liability Insurance." Prepared for Physicians Insurance Association of America. Unpublished paper, 2006.

Kessler, Daniel, and Mark B. McClellan. "Do Doctors Practice Defensive Medicine?" *Quarterly Journal of Economics* 111, no. 2 (1996): 353–90. http://doi.org/10.2307/2946682.

Kessler, Daniel, and Mark B. McClellan. "Malpractice Law and Health Care Reform: Optimal Liability Policy in an Era of Managed Care." *Journal of Public Economics* 84, no. 2 (2002): 175–97. https://doi.org/10.1016/S0047-2727(01)00124-4.

Kessler, Daniel, William M. Sage, and David J. Becker. "Impact of Malpractice Reforms on the Supply of Physician Services." *Journal of the American Medical Association* 293, no. 21 (2005): 2618–25. http://doi.org/10.1001/jama.293.21.2618.

Klick, Jonathan, and Thomas Stratmann. "Medical Malpractice Reform and Physicians in High-Risk Specialties." *Journal of Legal Studies* 36 (2007): s121–42. http://doi.org/ 10.1086/520416.

Lakdawalla, Darius, and Seth Seabury. "The Welfare Effects of Medical Malpractice Liability." *International Review of Law and Economics* 32, no. 4 (2012): 356–69. https://doi.org/10.1016/j.irle.2012.07.003.

Landrigan, Christopher P., Gareth J. Parry, Catherine B. Bones, Andrew D. Hackbarth, Donald A. Goldmann, and Paul J. Sharek. "Temporal Trends in Rates of Patient Harm Resulting from Medical Care." *New England Journal of Medicine* 363 (2010): 2124–34. http://doi.org/10.1056/NEJMsa1004404.

Lee, Cynthia, and Robert C. LaFountain. "Medical Malpractice Litigation in State Courts." *Court Statistics Project Caseload Highlights* 18, no. 1 (2011): 1–6.

Lei, Yu, and Mark J. Browne. "Medical Malpractice Insurance Market Entry and Exit: 1994–2006." *Journal of Insurance Regulation* 27, no. 1 (January 2008): 47–71.

Lei, Yu, and Joan Schmit. "Entry and Exit in the Malpractice Insurance Market from 1994 to 2003—Part I." *Professional Liability Underwriting Society Journal* XIX, no. 12 (2006): 2–3.

Lei, Yu, and Joan Schmit. "Entry and Exit in the Malpractice Insurance Market from 1994 to 2003—Part II." *Professional Liability Underwriting Society Journal* XX, no. 1 (2007): 6–8.

Lieber, Ethan. "Medical Malpractice Reform, the Supply of Physicians, and Adverse Selection." *Journal of Law and Economics* 57, no. 2 (2014): 501–27. http://doi.org/10.1086/675236.

Mackay, Charles. *Memoirs of Extraordinary Popular Delusions and the Madness of Crowds.* London: Richard Bentley, 1841.

Matlock, David, Peter W. Groeneveld, Steve Sidney, Susan Shetterly, Glenn Goodrich, Karen Gleen, Stan Xu, Lin Yang, Steven A. Farmer, Kristi Reynolds, Andrea E. Cassidy-Bushrow, Tracy Lieu, Denise M. Boudreau, Robert T. Greenlee, Jeffrey Tom, Suma Vupputuri, Kenneth F. Adams, David H. Smith, Margaret J. Gunter, Alan S. Go, and David J. Magid. "Geographic Variation in Cardiovascular Procedure Use among Medicare Fee-for-Service vs Medicare Advantage Beneficiaries." *Journal of the American Medical Association* 310, no. 2 (2013): 155–62. http://doi.org/10.1001/jama.2013.7837.

Matsa, David. "Does Malpractice Liability Keep the Doctor Away? Evidence from Tort Reform Damage Caps." *Journal of Legal Studies* 36, no. S2 (2007): s143–82. http://doi.org/10.1086/519466.

Mello, Michelle M., Amitabh Chandra, Atul A. Gawande, and David M. Studdert. "National Costs of the Medical Liability System." *Health Affairs* 29, no. 9 (2010): 1569–77. http://doi.org/10.1377/hlthaff.2009.0807.

Mello, Michelle M., and Allen Kachalia. *Evaluation of Options for Medical Malpractice System Reform: A Report to the Medicare Payment Advisory Commission.* Washington: MedPAC, February 2010.

Montanera, David. "The Importance of Negative Defensive Medicine in the Effects of Malpractice Reform." *European Journal of Health Economics* 17, no. 3 (2016): 355–69. http://doi.org/10.1007/s10198-015-0687-8.

Morreim, Haavi. "Malpractice, Mediation, and Moral Hazard: The Virtues of Dodging the Data Bank." *Ohio State Journal on Dispute Resolution* 27, no. 1 (2012): 109–77.

Obama, Barack. "Obama's Heath Care Speech to Congress." Speech (prepared text), Washington, DC, September 9, 2009. *New York Times.*

Orosco, Ryan, Jonathan Talamini, David C. Chang, and Mark A. Talamini. "Surgical Malpractice in the United States, 1990–2006." *Journal of the American College of Surgeons* 215, no. 4 (2012): 480–88. http://doi.org/10.1016/j.jamcollsurg .2012.04.028.

Ostrom, Brian, Roger Hanson, and Henry Daley. "So the Verdict Is In—What Happens Next? The Continuing Story of Tort Awards in the State Courts." *Justice System Journal* 16, no. 2 (1993): 97–115. http://doi.org/10.1080/23277556 .1993.10871173.

Ostrom, Brian, Neal B. Kauder, and Robert C. LaFountain, eds. *Examining the Work of State Courts, 1999–2000: A National Perspective from the Court Statistics Project.* Washington: National Center for State Courts, 2001.

Pace, Nicholas, Daniela Golinelli, and Laura Zakaras. *Capping Non-Economic Awards in Medical Malpractice Trials: California Jury Verdicts under MICRA.* Santa Monica, CA: RAND Institute for Civil Justice, 2004.

Peck, Robert S. "Tort Reform's Threat to an Independent Judiciary." *Rutgers Law Journal* 33 (2002): 851–56.

Prescott, J. J., Kathryn Spier, and Albert Yoon. "Trial and Settlement: A Study of High-Low Agreements." *Journal of Law and Economics* 57, no. 3 (2014): 699–746. http://doi.org/10.2139/ssrn.1676404.

PricewaterhouseCoopers' Health Research Institute. *The Price of Excess: Identifying Waste in Healthcare Spending.* PricewaterhouseCoopers LLP, 2008.

Pronovost, Peter, James I. Cleeman, Donald Wright, and Arjun Srinivasan. "Fifteen Years after *To Err Is Human*: A Success Story to Learn From." *BMJ Quality and Safety* 25, no. 6 (2016): 396–99. http://doi.org/10.1136/bmjqs-2015-004720.

Public Citizen. *Medical Malpractice Payments Sunk to Record Low in 2011.* Washington: Public Citizen, July 2012.

Quinn, Robert. "Medical Malpractice Insurance: The Reputation Effect and Defensive Medicine." *Journal of Risk and Insurance* 65, no. 3 (1998): 467–84. http://doi.org/ 10.2307/253660.

Robeznieks, Andis. "Medical Malpractice: The Fear Factor." Modern Healthcare (website), September 13, 2010.

Ruggles, Steven, Sarah Flood, Sophia Foster, Ronald Goeken, Jose Pacas, Megan Schouweiler, and Matthew Sobek. *Integrated Public Use Microdata Series (IPUMS USA): Version 10.0 [dataset].* Minneapolis: University of Minnesota, 2020. https://doi.org/10.18128/D010.V11.0.

Rustad, Michael L. "Neglecting the Neglected: The Impact of Noneconomic Damage Caps on Meritorious Nursing Home Lawsuits." *Elder Law Journal* 14 (2006): 331–91.

Sager, Mark, Susan Voeks, Paul Drinka, Elizabeth Langer, and Paul Grimstad. "Do the Elderly Sue Physicians?" *Archives of Internal Medicine* 150, no. 5 (1990): 1091–93. http://doi.org/10.1001/archinte.1990.00390170119026.

Saks, Michael. "Do We Really Know Anything about the Behavior of the Tort Litigation System—and Why Not?" *University of Pennsylvania Law Review* 140, no. 4 (1992): 1147–292.

Sclar, David I., and Michael Gene Housman. "Medical Malpractice and Physician Liability: Examining Alternatives in Defensive Medicine." *Harvard Health Policy Review* 4, no. 1 (2003): 75–84.

Seabury, Seth, Amitabh Chandra, Darius N. Lakdawalla, and Anupam B. Jena. "On Average, Physicians Spend Nearly 11 Percent of Their 40-Year Careers with an Open, Unresolved Malpractice Claim." *Health Affairs* 32, no. 1 (2013): 111–19. https://doi.org/10.1377/hlthaff.2012.0967.

Seabury, Seth A., Nicholas M. Pace, and Robert T. Reville. "Forty Years of Civil Jury Verdicts." *Journal of Empirical Legal Studies* 1, no. 1 (2004): 1–25. https://doi.org/10.1111/j.1740-1461.2004.00001.x.

Shanley, Michael, and Mark A. Peterson. *Comparative Justice: Civil Jury Verdicts in San Francisco and Cook Counties, 1959–1980.* Santa Monica, CA: RAND Institute for Civil Justice, 1983.

Sharkey, Catherine. "Unintended Consequences of Medical Malpractice Damages Caps." *NYU Law Review* 80, no. 2 (2005): 391–512.

Shepherd, Joanna. "Uncovering the Silent Victims of the American Medical Liability System." *Vanderbilt Law Review* 67, no.1 (2014): 151–95. http://doi.org/10.2139/ssrn.2147915.

Silver, Charles. "Does Civil Justice Cost Too Much?" *Texas Law Review* 80, no. 7 (June 2002).

Sloan, Frank, and Lindsey M. Chepke. *Medical Malpractice.* Boston: Massachusetts Institute of Technology, 2008.

Sloan, Frank A., and John H. Shadle. "Is There Empirical Evidence for 'Defensive Medicine'? A Reassessment." *Journal of Health Economics* 28, no. 2 (2009): 481–91. http://doi.org/10.1016/j.jhealeco.2008.12.006.

Spier, Kathryn E. "Litigation." In *Handbook of Law and Economics*, vol. 1, edited by A. Mitchell Polinsky and Steven Shavell, 259–342. Amsterdam: Elsevier, 2007.

Stewart, Ronald M., Kathy Geoghegan, John G. Myers, Kenneth R. Sirinek, Michael G. Corneille, Deborah Mueller, Daniel L. Dent, Steven E. Wolf, and Basil A. Pruitt Jr. "Malpractice Risk and Cost Are Significantly Reduced after Tort Reform." *Journal of the American College of Surgeons* 212, no. 4 (2011): 463–67. http://doi.org/10.1016/j.jamcollsurg.2010.12.025.

Stewart, Ronald M., Molly West, Richard Schirmer, and Kenneth R. Sirinek. "Tort Reform Is Associated with Significant Increases in Texas Physicians Relative to the Texas Population." *Journal of Gastrointestinal Surgery* 17, no. 1 (2013): 168–78. http://doi.org/10.1007/s11605-012-2013-4.

Studdert, David M., Michelle M. Mello, William M. Sage, Catherine M. DesRoches, Jordon Peugh, Kinga Zapert, and Troyen A. Brennan. "Defensive Medicine among High-Risk Specialist Physicians in a Volatile Malpractice Environment." *Journal of the American Medical Association* 293, no. 21 (2005): 2609–17. http://doi.org/10.1001/jama.293.21.2609.

Studdert, David M., Michelle M. Mello, Atul A. Gawande, Tejal K Gandhi, Allen Kachalia, Catherine Yoon, Ann Louise Puopolo, and Troyen A. Brennan. "Claims, Errors, and Compensation Payments in Medical Malpractice Litigation." *New England Journal of Medicine* 354 (2006): 2024–33. http://doi.org/10.1056/NEJMsa054479.

Studdert, David M., Eric J. Thomas, Helen R. Burstin, Brett I. W. Zbar, E. John Orav, and Troyen A. Brennan. "Negligent Care and Malpractice Claiming Behavior in Utah and Colorado." *Medical Care* 38, no. 3 (2000): 250–60. http://doi.org/10.1097/00005650-200003000-00002.

Studdert, David M., Y. Tony Yang, and Michelle M. Mello. "Are Damages Caps Regressive? A Study of Malpractice Jury Verdicts in California." *Health Affairs* 23, no. 4 (2004): 54–67. https://doi.org/10.1377/hlthaff.23.4.54.

Sunstein, Cass R. "Lives, Life-Years, and Willingness to Pay." *Columbia Law Review* 104, no. 1 (2004): 205–52. http://doi.org/10.2307/4099352.

Svorny, Shirley. "Could Mandatory Caps on Medical Malpractice Damages Harm Consumers?" Cato Institute Policy Analysis no. 685, October 20, 2011.

Texas Department of State Health Services, *Supply Trends among Licensed Health Professions, Texas, 1980–2011.* Austin: Texas Department of State Health Services, 2012.

U.S. Department of Health and Human Services. *Confronting the New Health Care Crisis: Improving Health Care Quality and Lowering Costs by Fixing Our Medical Liability System.* Washington: U.S. Department of Health and Human Services, July 2002.

Vidmar, Neil. "Juries and Jury Verdicts in Medical Malpractice Cases: Implications for Tort Reform in Pennsylvania." Unpublished report, 2002.

Vidmar, Neil, Paul Lee, Kara MacKillop, Kieran McCarthy, and Gerald McGwin. "Uncovering the 'Invisible' Profile of Medical Malpractice Litigation: Insights from Florida." *DePaul Law Review* 54 (2005): 315–56.

Vidmar, Neil, Kara MacKillop, and Paul Lee. "Million Dollar Medical Malpractice Cases in Florida: Post-Verdict and Pre-Suit Settlements." *Vanderbilt Law Review* 59, no. 4 (2006): 1343–81.

Viscuci, W. Kip. "The Devaluation of Life." *Regulation and Governance* 3, no. 2 (2009): 103–27. https://doi.org/10.1111/j.1748-5991.2009.01052.x.

Washington State, Office of Insurance Commissioner. *Medical Malpractice Closed Claim Study: Claims Closed from July 1, 1994 through June 30, 2004.* Olympia, WA: Office of the Insurance Commissioner, 2005.

Waters, Teresa M., Peter P. Budetti, Gary Claxton, and Janet P. Lundy. "Impact of State Tort Reforms on Physician Malpractice Payments." *Health Affairs* 26, no. 2 (2007): 500–9. https://doi.org/10.1377/hlthaff.26.2.500.

Waters, Teresa M., David M. Studdert, Troyen A. Brennan, Eric J. Thomas, Orit Almagor, Martha Mancewicz, and Peter P. Budetti. "Impact of the National Practitioner Data Bank on Resolution of Malpractice Claims." *Inquiry* 40, no. 3 (2003): 283–94. http://doi.org/10.5034/inquiryjrnl_40.3.283.

Winter, Ralph A. "The Dynamics of Competitive Insurance Markets." *Journal of Financial Intermediation* 3, no. 4 (1994): 379–415. https://doi.org/10.1006/jfin.1994.1011.

Winter, Ralph A. "The Liability Crisis and the Dynamics of Competitive Insurance Markets." *Yale Journal on Regulation* 5, no. 2 (1988): 455–500.

Winter, Ralph A. "The Liability Insurance Market." *Journal of Economics Perspectives* 5, no. 3 (1991): 115–36. http://doi.org/10.1257/jep.5.3.115.

Winter, Ralph A. "Solvency Regulation and the Property-Liability 'Insurance Cycle.'" *Economic Inquiry* 29, no. 3 (1991): 458–72. https://doi.org/10.1111/j.1465-7295.1991.tb00839.x.

Yang, Y. Tony, Michelle M. Mello, S. V. Subramanian, and David M. Studdert. "Relationship between Malpractice Litigation Pressure and Rates of Cesarean Section and Vaginal Birth after Cesarean Section." *Medical Care* 47, no. 2 (2009): 234–42. http://doi.org/10.1097/MLR.0b013e31818475de.

Yang, Y. Tony, David M. Studdert, S. V. Subramanian, and Michelle M. Mello. "A Longitudinal Analysis of the Impact of Liability Pressure on the Supply of Obstetrician-Gynecologists." *Journal of Empirical Legal Studies* 5, no. 1 (2008): 21–53. http://doi.org/10.1111/j.1740-1461.2007.00117.x.

Yeazell, Stephen C. "Refinancing Civil Litigation." *DePaul Law Review* 5, no. 1 (2001): 183–217. http://doi.org/10.2139/ssrn.315759.

Yoon, Albert. "Damage Caps and Civil Litigation: An Empirical Study of Medical Malpractice Litigation in the South." *American Law and Economics Review* 3, no. 2 (2001): 199–227. https://doi.org/10.1093/aler/3.2.199.

Zuckerman, Stephen, Randall R. Bovbjerg, and Frank Sloan. "Effects of Tort Reforms and Other Factors on Medical Malpractice Insurance Premiums." *Inquiry* 27, no. 2 (1990): 167–82.

## OTHER BOOK-LENGTH SOURCES, NOT CITED IN PARTICULAR CHAPTERS

Although we did not have reason to cite them in particular chapters, we would be remiss in not noting the important early work by Patricia Danzon, some of which is collected and summarized in Patricia M. Danzon, *Medical Malpractice: Theory, Evidence, and Public Policy* (Cambridge, MA: Harvard University Press, 1985).

We have largely adopted a "just the facts, ma'am" approach, but we should also note the more policy-oriented work by Paul Weiler, *Medical Malpractice on Trial* (Cambridge, MA: Harvard University Press, 1991).

# INDEX

Note: Page numbers with "n" indicate endnotes; page numbers with "f" indicate figures; page numbers with "t" indicate tables.

# About the Authors

BERNARD S. BLACK, JD, is the Nicholas D. Chabraja Professor at Northwestern University, with positions in the Pritzker School of Law, the Institute for Policy Research, and the Kellogg School of Management Department of Finance. His research areas include health policy and medical malpractice, applied empirical methods for causal inference, law and finance, and international corporate governance. From 2006 to 2016, he was the founding chairman of the annual Conference on Empirical Legal Studies (CELS, a major annual conference on empirical legal research). Since 2010, Black has run an annual summer workshop at Northwestern on Research Design for Causal Inference, including both a weeklong main workshop and a three-day advanced workshop. He is among the leading empirical legal scholars in the United States, with more than 150 published articles and more than 29,000 citations to his research on Google Scholar.

DAVID A. HYMAN, MD, JD, is an adjunct scholar at the Cato Institute and a professor at Georgetown University Law Center. He teaches or has taught health care regulation, civil procedure, insurance, medical malpractice, law and economics, professional responsibility, consumer protection, and tax policy. While serving as special counsel to the Federal Trade Commission, Hyman was the principal author and project leader for the first joint report ever issued by the Federal Trade Commission and the U.S. Department of Justice, "Improving Health Care: A Dose of Competition" (2004). He is the coauthor of *Overcharged: Why Americans Pay Too Much for Health Care* (2018) and the author of *Medicare Meets Mephistopheles*, which was selected by the U.S. Chamber of Commerce/National Chamber Foundation as one of the top 10 books of 2007.

MYUNGHO PAIK, PhD, is an associate professor in the Department of Policy Studies at Hanyang University. Before joining Hanyang University in 2015, he worked as a postdoctoral fellow at the University of Texas School of Law and as a research associate at Northwestern University School of Law, where he collaborated on multiple research projects on medical malpractice litigations and health policy in the United States. He received his BA and MA degrees from Yonsei University and his PhD degree from the University of Texas at Austin, where he majored in labor economics and applied econometrics. His research works have appeared in well-known academic journals, including the *Journal of Health Economics, Demography*, the *Journal of Empirical Legal Studies*, the *American Law and Economics Review*, and the *Canadian Journal of Economics*. Paik resides in Seoul, South Korea.

WILLIAM M. SAGE, MD, JD, is the James R. Dougherty Chair for Faculty Excellence in the School of Law at the University of Texas at Austin and professor of surgery and perioperative care in the Dell Medical School. From 2006 to 2013, he served as UT-Austin's first vice provost for health affairs. Sage is a member of the National Academy of Medicine, where he serves on the Board on Health Care Services and the Committee on the Future of Nursing 2020–2030. He has written more than 200 articles and has edited three books, including the *Oxford Handbook of U.S. Health Law* (2016). He was a tenured professor of law at Columbia until 2006 and has been a visiting law professor at Yale, Harvard, NYU, Duke, and Emory. He holds an undergraduate degree from Harvard College, medical and law degrees from Stanford University, and an honorary doctorate from Université Paris Descartes.

CHARLES SILVER, MA, JD, is an adjunct scholar at the Cato Institute and holds the Roy W. and Eugenia C. McDonald Endowed Chair in Civil Procedure at the University of Texas School of Law, where he teaches about civil litigation, health care policy, legal ethics, and insurance. His writings on class actions and other aggregate proceedings, litigation finance, medical malpractice, and legal and medical ethics have appeared in leading peer-reviewed journals and law reviews. In 2009, the Tort Trial & Insurance Practice Section of the American Bar Association awarded him the Robert B. McKay Law Professor Award for outstanding scholarship on tort and insurance law. He is the coauthor of *Overcharged: Why Americans Pay Too Much for Health Care* (2018).